Your Gateway to Packet Radio

By Stan Horzepa, WA1LOU

American Radio Relay League
Newington, CT 06111 USA

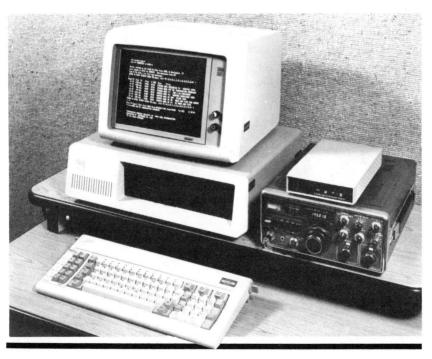

Foreword

Ten years ago, packet radio was a new mode of Amateur Radio communications that was in its infancy. Experimenters north and south of the 49th parallel were tweaking hardware and software of that new mode to make it work, and to make it work better.. Today, it *is* working...working so well that packet radio has become one of the most popular modes of communications in the Amateur Radio world.

Packet radio is not a self-contained mode of communications. Rather, it is making an impact in all areas of Amateur Radio. It is a tool for the public-service minded and has become an intricate part of the National Traffic System (NTS) and the Amateur Radio Emergency Service (ARES). DXers use packet radio to spot DX and contesters use packet radio to spot multipliers. Since packet radio is able to transfer data faster and more accurately than any other Amateur Radio mode, it is being used to move and distribute vast quantities of information to a degree never before seen in Amateur Radio.

The packet-radio bulletin-board systems throughout the Amateur Radio world are the conduit and warehouse of this information, which includes bulletins, newsletters, computer programs, directories, hardware tips and any other type of information that is of interest to hams. Of course, packet radio is providing a feast of opportunities for experimenters, both hardware designers and software writers.

Two years ago, the ARRL published a new book that presented the soup-to-nuts story of amateur packet radio. A lot can happen in two years in a technology that is still evolving, so the ARRL is pleased to present the Second Edition of *Your Gateway to Packet Radio*. This edition updates the first and reveals the new components that are available in the packet-radio world today.

Let me reiterate the closing statement of the Foreword of the first edition: "We...hope that you will be inspired by this book to build on the work that has already been done, for the history of the development of packet radio is still being made." That statement is just as true today as it was two years ago. Witness the changes that have occurred in two years. Use your imagination to discover what will happen in the next two.

David Sumner, K1ZZ
Executive Vice President
October 1989

About the Author

Stan Horzepa, WA1LOU, first licensed in 1969, is an Amateur Extra Class licensee and a life member of the ARRL. As former Communications Assistant of the Public Service branch of the ARRL's old Communications Department, Stan edited two editions of the *Repeater Directory* and, in June 1979, began writing the "FM/RPT" column in *QST*. In August 1981, Stan started the "On Line" column in *QST*, and began editing *Gateway: The ARRL Packet-Radio Newsletter* in July 1987. Stan has also contributed to *The ARRL Operating Manual*, *The ARRL Handbook for the Radio Amateur* and *Operating an Amateur Radio Station*. Besides his Amateur Radio writing achievements, Stan has held a number of ARRL appointments (ASCM, NM, OBS, ORS, OVS) and is the former Section Communications Manager of Connecticut. He also has numerous operating awards, including A-1 Operator, BPL, DXCC, Public Service, PSHR, WAC, WAS, The Polska Award and a Central Radio Club Cosmos silver medal.

WA1LOU lives in downtown Wolcott, Connecticut (near *the* traffic light) with his wife, Laurie, and daughter, Hayley. He has a BA from the University of Connecticut and a JD from Western New England College, and is supervisor of technical writing for General DataComm, Inc. Needless to say, Stan is very active on packet radio and monitors 145.010 MHz whenever he is home. If you connect with Stan (via W1AW-5), he will gladly explain to you, whether you ask or not, why the Boston Red Sox will win it all next year (or any year). If you are not within earshot of WA1LOU or W1AW-5, packet-radio mail can be sent to WA1LOU @ W1AW-4.

Acknowledgments

I would like to ACKnowledge the people who made the Second Edition of *Your Gateway to Packet Radio* a reality: my editor, Jeff Kilgore, KC1MK; his boss, Joel Kleinman, N1BKE; and my former editor, Bruce Hale, KB1MW, who got the Second Edition rolling.

I would also like to thank the following people who answered my questions, provided information and made suggestions that were used in this book: Phil Anderson, WØXI, of Kantronics; Jeff Bauer, WA1MBK, the SYSOP of W1AW-4; Deb Davis, N7IHY, of AEA; Andy Demartini, KC2FF, of DRSI; Bob Farrell, WB2COY; Lyle Johnson, WA7GXD; Fred Jones, WA4SWF; Greg Jones, WD5IVD; Ron Raikes, WA8DED; Gwyn Reedy, W1BEL, of PacComm; Deborah Sanders of GLB; and John Wiehn, General DataComm's librarian.

Finally, thanks to my family and friends for their encouragement and support, especially my wife, Laurie, and daughter, Hayley, who put up with my crabgrass all summer long.

Stan Horzepa, WA1LOU
September 1, 1989

*The Second Edition is dedicated
to Pop, a loving father
and a real gentle man.*

Trademark Notices

Table of Contents

CHAPTER ONE

The Radio Hacker

C all me Radio Hacker.
   In the past, I was called Radio Ham, but that was before the
dawning of the Computer Age in Amateur Radio.

Before the Computer Age, every Radio Ham who communicated with Morse code used his fist to send it and his ears to receive it.

Back then, the shack of the Radio Ham who used radioteletype (RTTY) contained an obtrusive mechanical teleprinter that served a dual purpose. It originated and received RTTY messages, and it anchored the shack whenever a tornado or hurricane passed through the neighborhood.

During contests, the shack of the contesting Radio Ham looked like a CPA's office on April 15th. Log sheets and complicated dupe sheets overflowed the operating desk and threatened to relocate the radio equipment to the floor.

Weeks and months after the contest, when the mailman started delivering sacks of QSL cards, the Radio Ham spent hours completing his response QSL cards with pen, ink and elbow grease.

The Radio Ham, who spent each weekend tweaking antennas, used pencil, paper, long division and an eraser to calculate how much wire he had to cut or splice to get his newest aerial's SWR down to a healthy level.

Back then, Amateur Radio was hard work!

Home-Built Computers

The computer hobby got off the ground in the 1970s. In the beginning, computer hobbyists had to build their own computers, just as the first Radio Hams had to build their own radios. In some cases, the pioneers in the computer hobby were used to building their own equipment because some of them were also Radio Hams, and as a result, *The Radio Amateur's Handbook* was an important reference book for the computer hobby pioneers.

Later, a few enterprising computer hobbyists started gathering parts in plastic sandwich bags and began selling computer kits. One such kit, the Altair 8800, achieved notoriety when it was featured on the cover of the January 1975 issue of *Popular Electronics*. When the kits appeared, anyone with a little soldering talent was able to build his own computer without scrounging high and low for parts.

Figure 1.1—As the Computer Age dawned in Amateur Radio, radio hackers had to be very resourceful. Here, a young radio hacker built a wall of aluminum and steel cylinders to contain the RF generated by his TRS-80 Model I computer. (*WA1LOU photo*)

The hobby really took off in 1977, when three new computers were unveiled that could be purchased off-the-shelf with no assembly required: Commodore Business Machines' PET, Apple Computer's Apple II and Radio Shack's TRS-80 Model I. You no longer had to own a soldering iron in order to own a computer!

The Dawn Of The Amateur Radio Computer Age

About the time the first preassembled home computers appeared, the first Radio Hackers showed up on the air.

One of the sample programs in the back of the TRS-80 Model I manual was called "Design Program For Cubical Quad Antenna." Blink! That program turned on light bulbs in the minds of many hams who were tinkering with the Model I and other computers. "Hey! I could use a computer for Amateur Radio applications!"

Hams across the land wrote programs that printed QSL cards, calculated antenna bearings, generated Morse code practice, tracked ham radio awards, calculated MUF, and logged and duped contests.

Although these programs made Amateur Radio a little easier, none of them used the computer as a communications device; the computer was not on the air. Finally, some talented programmers wrote programs that allowed the computer to transmit and receive CW and RTTY. With this new software, computers were on the air and most of the hams using them were happy with their new communication tools.

Yet some hams were discontented. There was a lot of power packed into these computers, but this power was not being used to its fullest. Why spend thousands of dollars for a computer to transmit and receive 60-WPM Baudot when the same task could be performed as well with a $50 surplus teleprinter? The computer was being wasted performing trivial chores.

The Birth Of Packet Radio

Just in time, Canada's Department of Communications (DOC) authorized a new mode of Amateur Radio communications called *packet radio*. Here was a mode that had computers written all over it; a mode that would utilize the full power of the computer; a mode that would revolutionize Amateur Radio.

The discontented radio hackers had something they could sink their teeth into, and it was not long before the first amateur packet-radio transmission was on the air. That first amateur packet-radio transmission was followed by a second and a third, and soon packet radio became the fastest growing mode in Amateur Radio since FM repeaters.

What Is Packet Radio?

Packet radio is a product of the computer age, and as a result, packet radio has computer-age features that provide a very efficient means of communication.

Packet radio provides error-free communications. With packet radio, no time is wasted trying to decipher communications that contain "hits" or "misses" caused by electrical interference or changes in propagation. The receiving station receives information exactly as it is sent by the transmitting station. When a packet-radio station transmits "Send a surgeon," that station can be sure that the receiving station will not send him a fish.

Packet radio uses the radio spectrum efficiently. One radio frequency may be used for multiple communications at the same time. Station A can be in contact with station B on frequency C, while station D is in contact with station E, also on frequency C.

Packet radio uses other stations efficiently. Any packet-radio station can command other packet-radio stations to create a network for the transfer of information. If station A cannot communicate with station C, it can command an intermediate station to act as a conduit to station C.

Packet uses time efficiently. Packet-radio bulletin-board systems shift time by permitting packet-radio operators to store messages for retrieval by other amateurs at a later time. If station A has information for station B, but station B is not on the air at that time, station A can address a message to station B and store it on a bulletin-board system for retrieval by station B at its convenience.

Since you are reading this book, you must be interested in finding out more about packet radio. So, let's buckle our seat belts and unleash the power of the computer as we explore this revolutionary (and evolutionary) mode of Amateur Radio communications.

CHAPTER TWO

History

Store-and-forward packet-switching techniques date back to a 1964 study by the RAND Corporation. The term *packet* was coined in 1965 by D. W. Davies of the British National Physical Laboratory. In that year, the United States Advanced Research Projects Agency (DARPA) started working on time-sharing concepts that would lead to the activation of its packet-based, hard-wired *ARPANET* in 1969. Since then, a whole new science of packet communications technology has matured, and numerous government and commercial packet-switched networks have emerged.

In 1970, the University of Hawaii put its *ALOHA* packet-based radio system on the air to provide communications between its central computer and the university community that was dispersed throughout the Hawaiian Islands. *ALOHANET* operated in the UHF radio spectrum (at 407.350 and 413.475 MHz), and may be considered the direct forerunner of amateur packet radio.

Canada's Pioneers

Amateur packet-radio experimentation began in Canada. Dr John deMercado, the Director General of Telecommunications Regulations in Canada, was responsible for combining Amateur Radio and packet. It was Dr deMercado and the Canadian Department of Communications (DOC) who encouraged Canadian hams to experiment with packet radio even before the DOC officially permitted it as an amateur communications mode. As a result, amateur packet-radio experiments began in 1978, with the first actual amateur packets being transmitted and received without error at a meeting of the Montreal Amateur Radio Club in May 1978. The group responsible for this historic first packet transfer consisted of Montreal-area hams, who had banded together to build the Montreal Packet Net (MP-Net).

During this era of Canadian experimentation, MP-Net operated on a single 220-MHz channel using start-stop *ASCII* with the Ethernet Carrier Sense, Multiple Access with Collision Detection (*CSMA/CD*) *protocol*. The protocol was modified for amateur application by Robert Rouleau, VE2PY, and implemented by Fred Basserman, VE2BQF, using a Southwest Technical Products 6800 (SWTPC 6800) computer. MP-Net operated at 2400 *bit/s* using home-built *modems* based on the XR2206-XR2211 modem IC set. The modems were designed by Jacques Orsali, VE2EHP, and Ted Baleshta, VE3CAF. The *network* included a store-and-forward Z80-microprocessor-based repeater located on Mount Rigaud, which could be specifically addressed whenever its services were required for the relay of a packet. Bram Frank, VE2BFH, was responsible for the Mount Rigaud repeater, while Norm Pearl, VE2BQS, was responsible for the rest of the network's hardware design.

On September 15, 1978, the DOC announced that "all Canadian amateurs will be permitted to use 'packet radio'..." In Vancouver, Doug Lockhart, VE7APU, began packet-radio experiments using the *High-level Data Link Control (HDLC)* protocol of the *International Organization for Standardization (ISO)*. His experiments resulted in the creation of an 8085-microprocessor-based device that performed the task of assembling and disassembling packets. He called the device a *terminal-node controller (TNC)*, and he connected it to a *Bell-202*-compatible modem to modulate and demodulate the TNC's packets at 1200 bauds on 144 MHz. In the midst of this experimentation, Doug also founded the *Vancouver Amateur Digital Communications Group (VADCG)* in January 1979. As a result, his TNC became known as the *VADCG board* or *VADCG TNC* (Figure 2.1). Hundreds of VADCG board kits were sold to amateurs in North America.

Figure 2.1—The first amateur packet-radio terminal node controller (TNC), the VADCG board. This TNC was the creation of Doug Lockhart, VE7APU.

In addition to that first TNC, VADCG developed a Station Node Controller (SNC) that was used with a CSMA/CD protocol to establish a *virtual circuit* between the *source* and *destination* TNCs. (A virtual circuit looks like a direct connection to the TNCs.) The first public demonstration of the complete VADCG packet-radio system occurred on April 26, 1980, at the Canadian Amateur Radio Federation (CARF) Symposium in New Westminster, British Columbia. Meanwhile, amateurs using VADCG TNCs in Hamilton, Ontario wanted to communicate directly from TNC to TNC rather than through station nodes, so VE7APU accommodated them by writing a protocol that was based on the IBM *Synchronous Data Link Control* (*SDLC*) protocol. It became known as the *Vancouver protocol* or *VADCG protocol* (later called *V-1* to differentiate it from later VADCG protocols).

In addition to these hardware and protocol developments, VADCG was responsible for transmitting a packet-radio *beacon* on 14.0765 MHz every five minutes to assist others who were getting their TNCs on the air for the first time. VADCG members also successfully transferred packets to amateur packet-radio operators in Ontario via the Canadian ANIK B satellite.

In other Canadian developments, packet-radio experimenters in Ottawa, Ontario, developed a *polling protocol* that used multiple virtual circuits through a station *node* at 9600 bauds on 220-MHz *FSK*. (In a polling environment, each station in the system is checked regularly and in an orderly manner to see if it is ready to send data. If a polled station has data to send, it transmits its data after being polled. The controller then checks the next station in the system.)

1980-1982: United States Plays Catch Up

On March 17, 1980, one and one-half years after Canadian amateur packet radio was permitted, new FCC rules took effect that allowed US Amateur Radio operators to use ASCII for radio teleprinter communications, remote-control operations, the operation of data networks (including packet-switching systems) and other uses consistent with the Amateur Radio Service.

The US amateurs did not let grass grow under their feet. Once the FCC gave the go-ahead, packet-radio experimentation south of the Canadian border forged ahead. The first US packet-radio demonstration was conducted at the 1980 ARRL National Convention in Seattle, Washington. Most of the initial experimentation involved building and tinkering with the VADCG TNC, but on December 10, 1980, the first "made in the USA" amateur packet-radio development hit the airwaves: Hank Magnuski, KA6M, put a simplex *digipeater* (KA6M/R) on 2 meters in San Francisco. Hank's system used a home-built TNC based on the Z80 microprocessor and a Western Digital 1933 HDLC IC. Like packet radio north of the border, Hank used a Bell-202-compatible modem on his TNC because the modems were readily available as surplus equipment. As a result of Hank's operations, a group of interested amateurs joined him in the founding of the Pacific Packet Radio Society (PPRS).

The *Amateur Radio Research and Development Corporation* (*AMRAD*) in the Washington, DC area was the hotbed of packet-radio activity on the East Coast of the United States. AMRAD published information about packet radio in their newsletter. The "Protocol" column, conducted by Dave Borden, K8MMO, was a sounding board for developing packet-radio ideas.

Bill Moran, W4MIB, put the first East Coast packet-radio station on the air on May 4, 1981. To relay packets, AMRAD members used a standard

2-meter *duplex* voice repeater. The visibility of packet-radio experimentation was increased considerably when the article "The Making of an Amateur Packet-Radio Network," by K8MMO and Paul Rinaldo, W4RI, appeared in the October 1981 issue of *QST*.

In October 1981, AMRAD joined forces with *The Radio Amateur Satellite Corporation* (*AMSAT*) to sponsor the first ARRL Amateur Radio Computer Networking Conference. The attendees at that first conference included most of the people who had already made amateur packet-radio history or who were on the verge of making history. A number of presentations were made at the conference, including VE7APU's presentation on "Network Architecture and Protocols for a Widespread Amateur Digital Communications Network," and KA6M's presentation "On the Care and Feeding of Your Packet Repeater." The proceedings of that first conference (and all subsequent conferences) were published by the ARRL (see Figure 2.2) and are still available today for interesting reading and study.

Figure 2.2—The presentations made at each ARRL Amateur Radio Computer Networking Conference have been published by the ARRL.

Late in 1981, the *Tucson (Arizona) Amateur Packet Radio Corporation* (*TAPR*) was founded by Den Connors, KD2S. TAPR immediately embarked on a project to build a TNC; their first effort, the *TAPR* (pronounced "tapper") *alpha board* was introduced early the following year. The alpha board was based on the 6502 microprocessor. It was short-lived however, as the *TAPR beta board* premiered in the autumn of 1982. The beta board was based on the 6809 microprocessor and was the forerunner of the TAPR *TNC 1*, which was introduced one year later.

While TAPR developed packet-radio hardware, AMRAD and the *Radio Amateur Telecommunications Society* (*RATS*) began work on a new packet-radio protocol. In early 1982, AMRAD began investigating the various commercial protocols in use at the time and recommended adapting *CCITT* Recommendation X.25 for amateur packet radio. (CCITT is the *International Telegraph and Telephone Consultative Committee.*) In June 1982, AMRAD and RATS members met to hammer out the new protocol. After working out some problems, the prototype *amateur X.25*, or simply *AX.25*, protocol was formulated. The primary movers of this development were Gordon Beattie, N2DSY; Jon Bloom, KE3Z; Dave Borden, K8MMO; Terry Fox, WB4JFI; Paul Rinaldo, W4RI; and Eric Scace, K3NA, who was one of the authors of CCITT X.25 and, as a result, was invaluable during the development of AX.25.

In October 1982, AMSAT president Tom Clark, W3IWI, called a meeting of the active US packet-radio groups, including AMRAD, AMSAT, the ARRL Ad Hoc Committee on Amateur Radio Digital Communications, PPRS, St Louis Amateur Packet Radio (SLAPR) and TAPR to come to an agreement concerning AX.25. The result was a modification of AX.25 that added an optional third *address* for a digipeater. Another result of that meeting was a proposal to begin the packet-radio satellite (*PACSAT*) project, with the intention of launching a low-orbit amateur satellite with an onboard packet-radio *mailbox*.

1983: The March Of The TNCs Begins

In July, Bob Richardson, W4UCH, published his *Synchronous Packet Radio Using the Software Approach, Volume I* software for the Radio Shack TRS-80 Models I, III and 4 computers. W4UCH's *software approach* performed the TNC hardware functions in software and only required an external modem. *Volume I* provided VADCG V-1 protocol capability, while *Volume II*, published in March 1984, provided AX.25 Version 1 protocol capability.

· Also in July, a proposal to link northern and southern California via packet radio was formulated. This network became known as *WESTNET*, and in response to its creation, *EASTNET* was proposed to link the Washington, DC and Boston areas, and *SOUTHNET* was proposed to interlink the southeastern United States. To facilitate these packet-radio networks, a modification of AX.25 that expanded the optional third address to include as many as eight digipeater call signs was approved by the ARRL Ad Hoc Committee on Amateur Radio Digital Communications in November.

New packet-radio hardware became available in late 1983. Gil Boelke, W2EUP, of GLB Electronics, took W4UCH's software approach one step further by making it available for all computers. This was accomplished via GLB's PK-1, a Z80-based TNC that performed TNC hardware tasks, primarily the HDLC function, in the software that was programmed into the PK-1's EPROM (see Figure 2.3). The philosophy of this approach was that it would make the final product smaller and less expensive. This philosophy continued in other commercial TNCs that became available later, most notably some Kantronics TNCs and later GLB offerings. The PK-1 was one of the first TNCs to include a Bell-202-compatible modem. Initially, the PK-1 provided VADCG V-1 protocol capability only, but AX.25 protocol capability was added shortly after the unit's introduction. Since the PK-1 was the least expensive preassembled TNC available in ham radio for a number of years, it was very popular among those who wanted to get their feet wet in packet radio without committing a lot of dollars to a new mode with an uncertain future.

TAPR also made a hardware offering in November with the introduction of their TNC kit. The new TNC included packet assembly and disassembly circuitry and a Bell-202-compatible modem (Figure 2.4). The 6809-microprocessor-based TAPR TNC used the current VADCG V-1 protocol, as well as the new AX.25 protocol. Dave Henderson, KD4NL, Margaret Morrison, KV7D, and Harold Price, NK6K, were responsible for programming the new protocol into the TNC's firmware. Initially, this TNC became known as the *TAPR board* to differentiate it from the VADCG

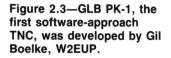

Figure 2.3—GLB PK-1, the first software-approach TNC, was developed by Gil Boelke, W2EUP.

Figure 2.4—TAPR's TNC 1 was the first TNC to provide AX.25 protocol capability, as well as the VADCG V-1 protocol.

board. Later, it was also called the *TNC 1* to differentiate it from TAPR's second TNC, the *TNC 2*.

To keep pace with these new TNC developments that included AX.25 capability, KA6M modified the software in the VADCG TNC to also run the AX.25 protocol.

1984: Historic Firsts

On February 18, digipeater W1AW-5 came on the air in central Connecticut and was soon joined by *PBBS* W1AW-4. W1AW-5 was located at the home of ARRL Executive Vice President Dave Sumner, K1ZZ, while W1AW-4 was located at ARRL Headquarters. The PBBS ran on a *Xerox 820-1* computer, using software written by KE3Z.

In March, Bob Bruninga, WB4APR, activated one of the first packet-radio gateways. Using the WB4APR operation, 2-meter packet-radio operators were able to make HF connections on 30 meters.

Amateur satellite OSCAR 10 was used as a repeater on March 11 for connections between packet-radio stations on the East and West Coasts of the United States. Ron McMurday, WA0OJS, in California, and W3IWI, in Maryland, made the first packet-radio contact via the satellite.

A personal historic note: on May 20, this author used a GLB PK-1 TNC to complete his first packet-radio contact (with KE3Z via W1AW-5).

In midyear, Hank Oredson, W0RLI, activated a packet-radio mailbox in Westford, Massachusetts using the software that he developed for the Xerox 820-1 computer.

On August 5, 50 MHz provided Ralph Wallio, W0RPK, in Iowa, and Bob Carpenter, W3OTC, in Maryland, with the first completed amateur packet-radio *meteor-scatter* contact. After that initial contact, the two operators continued to make 50-MHz meteor-scatter contacts on a routine basis.

The first issue of *Gateway: The ARRL Packet-Radio Newsletter* premiered on August 14. Edited by Jeff Ward, K8KA, *Gateway* promised to be a "news" newsletter.

Curtis Spangler, N6ECT, and Mike Flynn, W2FRT, exchanged packets at 9600 bauds on August 23, using quadrature amplitude modulation (QAM) techniques. Over a five-mile path, there were no errors using 10 watts, and 60% to 70% throughput using 1 watt.

On September 15, the ARRL Ad Hoc Committee on Amateur Radio Digital Communications approved the AX.25 Version 2.0 Level Two (*link layer*) packet-radio protocol. This protocol included the capability of using as many as eight digipeaters to complete a connection. It was adopted by the ARRL Board of Directors on October 26.

In the autumn of 1984, the new VADCG V-2 protocol's implementation of CCITT Recommendations X.3 and X.28 had been completed by VE7APU. Also, that autumn, Lynn Taylor, WB6UUT, completed a PBBS program for the Apple II computer and the Washington, DC and Philadelphia areas were linked via EASTNET.

Beginning on October 18, a 180-day special temporary authorization (STA) permitting the operation of automatic digital earth-to-space teleport stations took effect. This jointly sponsored ARRL-AMSAT STA allowed unattended digital *gateway* stations to store and forward messages for amateur satellite relay and to provide a real-time gateway for satellite communications. On October 28, W3IWI's automatic PBBS was placed in operation on OSCAR 10 and was successfully used by several amateur stations in the United States and Canada.

The ARRL Ad Hoc Committee on Amateur Radio Digital Communications met on November 11, and agreed to encourage TNC developers to cooperate in standardizing the user *interface* to be similar to that presented in CCITT Recommendations X.3 and X.28 (a standard interface makes life easier for users who operate TNCs made by different manufacturers). The committee also discussed how to best present digipeater information in *The ARRL Repeater Directory*.

The ARRL filed a petition for rule making on November 14, asking the FCC to allow automatic control of digital communications above 30 MHz. On April 5, 1985, the FCC issued a Notice of Proposed Rule Making in response to this petition.

Late in 1984, WØRLI added automatic message-forwarding capabilities to his mailbox software for the Xerox 820-1 computer.

1985: The Boom Begins

Steve Goode, K9NG, demonstrated a 9600 bit/s FSK modem on January 12. Steve designed the modem to provide high-speed, intercity, packet-radio message forwarding on 220 MHz. The modem was built around Hamtronics 220-MHz transmitter and receiver strips.

On January 16, the Digital Communications Experiment (DCE) was activated on *UoSAT-OSCAR 11* to prove that satellites could be used to store and forward packet-radio messages. Using the DCE, messages were stored and forwarded from the UoSAT-OSCAR command station in Surrey, England, a joint operation by Rick Dittmer, WH6AMX, Larry Kayser, WA3ZIA, and Hugh Pett, VE3FLL, in Hawaii, and Harold Price, NK6K, in California. WA3ZIA and NK6K developed the basic store-and-forward software for the DCE, and the software was uploaded to the satellite by NK6K.

The first reliable WESTNET link between northern and southern California was completed on February 3.

In April, TAPR announced the availability of their new TNC kit (Figure 2.5). Dubbed the TNC 2, the new TAPR unit was nearly half the size of the TNC 1 and used CMOS technology for reduced power consumption. The software no longer provided the VADCG protocol capability, but new features were added that surpassed the capabilities of the TNC 1 software.

The TNC 2 became the most popular TNC design in amateur packet-radio history (so far). Its offspring from various developers populated amateur packet-radio shacks throughout the world. To the delight of amateur programmers, TAPR used a Z80 microprocessor in the TNC 2. Software-development tools for the 6809 used in the TNC 1 were virtually nonexistent,

Figure 2.5—TAPR's TNC 2, the most popular TNC in amateur packet-radio history, used CMOS technology to reduce power consumption. The TNC 2 provided an advanced implementation of the AX.25 protocol.

and anyone trying to write new software for the TNC 1 had a very difficult task. Z80 software-development tools were plentiful and as a result, upgrades and replacements for the TNC 2 software continue to be developed even today. Where there is a will, there is a way, as Ron Raikes, WA8DED, developed new firmware for the TNC 1 in 1985 that provided some of the capabilities available with the new TNC 2, including the ability to simultaneously *connect* with multiple stations.

A 100-point bonus for completing a packet-radio contact was added to Field Day in 1985. Thomas Clements III, W1ICH, suggested the packet-radio bonus, and it was approved by the ARRL Contest Advisory Committee for the 1985 installment of the event.

During the summer, packet radio played an important role in aiding firefighters involved with the fires that raged in the California forests and grasslands. WESTNET relayed much of the emergency traffic generated during the calamities.

In October, AMSAT and the ARRL began the groundwork for development of a second Shuttle Amateur Radio Experiment (SAREX II) to be conducted by astronaut Ron Parise, WA4SIR, aboard space shuttle flight STS-61E, which was scheduled for launch on March 6, 1986. SAREX II would provide packet-radio robot operation aboard the shuttle. Preparation for the experiment came to a grinding halt in the wake of the *Challenger* disaster in January 1986.

In November, Jeff Jacobsen, WA7MBL, announced that he had rewritten the *WØRLI Mailbox/Gateway* software in Turbo Pascal for the IBM PC/XT/AT computers; he called it the *WA7MBL Packet Bulletin Board System (PBBS)*.

1986: The Year Of Applications

Early in 1986, Utah became part of WESTNET and western Pennsylvania joined EASTNET.

Three pieces of traffic in standard ARRL NTS format were relayed from S. Voron, VK2BVS, to Don Stiver, N6EEG, on January 10 and then forwarded to Jim Johnston, K6APW, for direct input into the Pacific Area Net.

February flooding in northern California left tens of thousands homeless and isolated, with amateur packet radio providing the only communication links into many of the devastated areas. Packet-radio stations were set up at various emergency agency headquarters throughout the stricken area.

In a Report and Order, the FCC documented its opinion that the control operator of any amateur station must be present at the control point whenever the station relays third-party traffic. This Report and Order dealt a blow to the operation of any PBBS that handled third-party traffic, either in mailbox fashion or in the automatic-forwarding mode. In response to the FCC's Report and Order, the ARRL filed a petition for extraordinary relief;

the FCC granted a waiver in March. That waiver became a permanent amendment of the FCC rules in October and allowed packet-radio stations on 50 MHz and above to retransmit third-party traffic while under automatic control (without a control operator present). The Commission said that the nature of packet radio was such that control operators of intermediate retransmitting stations were unable to screen retransmitted messages, so it would be up to other amateur stations who were monitoring the traffic to detect the introduction of messages from nonamateur stations.

In the spring, Arizona joined WESTNET and WØRLI compiled a list of 113 active automatic-forwarding PBBSs.

The ARRL Ad Hoc Committee on Amateur Radio Digital Communications met in Newington in June to discuss progress on networking using *datagram* and *virtual circuit protocols*. Other topics of discussion included the need for high-speed RF modems, a study of packet-radio frequencies, an STA for automatic control of HF packet-radio stations and amendments to the FCC rules to accommodate packet radio (and other new communication techniques).

On June 29, W3IWI and Rich Strand, KL7RA, used an 85-foot dish antenna in Fairbanks, Alaska, to transmit a 700-kW EIRP packet-radio signal at the moon on 432 MHz. After the 2.2-second round trip, they successfully copied their own packet-radio beacon.

During the running of the 1986 New York City marathon, Amateur Radio stations relayed reports of those runners dropping out of the race, with the 21 participating voice stations reporting 685 dropouts and the two participating packet-radio stations reporting 303 dropouts. That works out to 32.6 reports per voice station, and 151.5 reports per packet-radio station.

On November 4, packet radio was used to transmit digital color pictures from Barry Robinson, VE3CJC, in Belleville, Ontario, to Syd Horne, VE3EGO, in Kingston, Ontario, via a two-digipeater path. TELIPAK, a system that provides the capability to exchange high-resolution, errorless, digital color images (as well as text and speech) was used in this successful application.

Effective November 22, digipeater operation was permitted in Great Britain.

Late in the year, WØRLI and Dave Toth, VE3GYQ, released a version of the WØRLI Mailbox/Gateway software written in C for the IBM PC line of computers. In addition, WESTNET was linked to New Mexico and Texas.

1987: The Beginnings of a Network

A major train wreck occurred in the Baltimore area on January 4, and amateur packet radio provided emergency communications from the site of the disaster with a portable packet-radio station operated by Bob Bruninga, WB4APR. Most of the outgoing traffic from the train wreck was passed through the W3IWI PBBS; this enabled WB4APR to pass a large volume of traffic in a very short time. W3IWI handled distribution of the survivor lists, coordinated traffic on the 75-meter Maryland Emergency Phone Net and even delivered a few messages personally by phone.

An experimental satellite link between packet-radio network nodes located in California and Maryland was established early in the year to provide a temporary one-hop connection between packet-radio stations on the US East and West Coasts. Mike Bach, WB6FFC, co-founder of the Vitalink Communications Corporation, provided the *wormhole* link via Vitalink's commercial geosynchronous satellite. In essence, the satellite provided the interconnection between the *serial ports* of the TNCs on each coast. The call sign of the operation was WA3YMH-1.

Effective March 21, FCC regulations were revised to grant packet-radio privileges to Novice operators in the 28-MHz, 220-MHz and 1270-MHz amateur bands.

In the spring, the *Fuji-OSCAR 12* (*FO-12*) satellite, developed by Japan AMSAT and launched on August 12, 1986, began providing limited PBBS capabilities on Mode JD; its call sign was 8J1JAS. Meanwhile, the number of PBBSs capable of automatic mail forwarding using the WØRLI mail-forwarding system stood at 420, according to a compilation by Dave Zeph, W9ZRX.

A 56-kbaud packet-radio contact was conducted between WA4DSY and KD4NC over a 17-mile path on 430 MHz on April 11. The 56-kbaud modem used for this contact was designed and built by Dale Heatherington, WA4DSY, using bandwidth-limited *minimum-shift keying* (*MSK*) with a 70-kHz bandwidth.

The ARRL Ad Hoc Committee on Amateur Radio Digital Communications met in Newington in May. Discussions at the meeting included recommended HF, VHF and UHF packet-radio operating frequencies, the ARRL's request for an STA for unattended HF packet-radio operations, message-format protocols, developments in the implementation of Network- and Transport-level protocols, proposed changes in the AX.25 link-layer protocol, and the need for an improved HF packet-radio link-layer protocol to include broadcast (bulletin) capability. Also discussed were the AMSAT Phase-4 satellite design and current trends and needs in packet-radio modem design. The ARRL Board of Directors, meeting in July, approved the Committee's recommendations with regard to packet-radio band plans for the frequencies below 225 MHz.

By midyear, a number of networking implementations were available, and each was vying for preeminence in the packet-radio community. In Texas, a number of towns and cities were linked via *TexNet*, a packet-radio network composed of dual-port network control processors that provided AX.25-compatible user access on 2 meters and node-to-node linking at 9600 bit/s on 70 cm. TexNet was developed by the Texas Packet Radio Society. Meanwhile, *NET/ROM*, a firmware substitute for the TNC 2 that provided networking capabilities, was being installed in various locations throughout the packet-radio world. NET/ROM was developed by WA8DED and Mike Busch, W6IXU. Finally, Phil Karn, KA9Q, had his *TCP/IP* implementation for the IBM PC (called *NET.EXE*) running successfully in various locations. At this early stage in the networking contest, NET/ROM had the greatest number of actual installations.

In July, the FCC granted the ARRL's request for an STA for unattended HF packet-radio operations. This STA was granted for 180 days and laid the groundwork for the development of SKIPNET, the HF packet-radio network dedicated to automatically forwarding packet-radio messages over the long distances that HF propagation affords.

The Sixth ARRL Amateur Radio Computer Networking Conference was held in Redondo Beach, California on August 29. The main thrust of the papers presented at the conference was how to improve the developing packet-radio network by means of hardware and software innovations. The next day, the ARRL Ad Hoc Committee on Amateur Radio Digital Communications met to formulate packet-radio band-plan recommendations for the frequencies above 420 MHz. The committee's recommended band plans for 70, 33 and 23 cm were subsequently adopted by the ARRL Board of Directors in January 1988.

In the fall, PacComm introduced a miniature TNC 2 *clone* that was approximately half the size of the TAPR TNC 2. Harold Price, NK6K, announced that packet-radio DXCC was now possible, as he counted 100 different countries that were active on the mode. At year's end, approximately 700 PBBSs were in operation around the world.

1988: The Network Grows

The big story during the winter of 1988 was the successful skiing expedition from the Soviet Union to Canada, by way of the North Pole, by Canadian and Soviet scientists. SKITREK kept in contact with civilization via packet radio.

During the year, new and improved versions of the NET/ROM, KA9Q TCP/IP and TexNet networking software and hardware were released and installed throughout the United States and Canada. By year's end, the network was starting to shape up as almost every populated nook and cranny was covered by some kind of packet-radio network. Network nodes were replacing digipeaters everywhere, and it seemed that NET/ROM nodes were springing up on every corner. In support of KA9Q's TCP/IP software, the *KISS* mode was added to the firmware of most of the current crop of TNCs. The KISS (for keep it simple, stupid) mode is required to allow a standard TNC to be used with KA9Q's networking software.

Out of the blue, NORD > < LINK, a West German packet-radio group, presented the world with a free NET/ROM clone called TheNet. The popularity of TheNet was immediate because it was free (in comparison to

NET/ROM, which was not free) and offered new features not found in NET/ROM. The new wave of TheNet installations was dampened by the claim of NET/ROM developer Ron Raikes, WA8DED, that TheNet was a rip-off of NET/ROM. According to WA8DED, NORD > <LINK simply disassembled the NET/ROM firmware, made some minor changes, recompiled it and offered it as an original product. NORD > <LINK denied WA8DED's charges and claimed that they wrote TheNet code from scratch based on the NET/ROM specifications published by Amatech International (formerly Software 2000) the distributors of NET/ROM. After these claims were exchanged, a controversy raged throughout the packet-radio world; as of this writing, the controversy continues.

In January, the FCC granted a one-year extension of the STA for unattended HF packet-radio operations. The extension was granted again in January 1989.

The Dayton HamVention in April proffered some new packet-radio hardware, including AEA's 9600-baud, 220-MHz RF modem, DRSI's TNC on a plug-in card for IBM PC computers and clones and Heathkit's pocket-sized TNC. Later in the spring, James Miller, G3RUH, announced the development of a 9600-baud packet-radio modem for use with amateur voice-band NBFM radios.

On June 15, OSCAR 13 was successfully launched from the Guiana Space Center in French Guiana, but the *RUDAK* packet-radio digipeater aboard the satellite failed and disappointed packet-radio satellite enthusiasts throughout the world. Just a few months later, however, AMSAT and UoSAT announced plans to simultaneously launch four microsatellites, or "MicroSats," and two UoSATs (UoSATs D and E) in 1989. Two of the MicroSats and both UoSATs will have store-and-forward packet-radio capabilities.

Mid-year, interesting things were occurring on the international packet-radio front. Packet-radio activity was reported as originating from Taiwan, the South Pole and the Soviet Union. John Wiseman, G8BPQ, introduced the G8BPQ AX.25 Packet Switching System, a multiple-link networking software system that runs on an IBM PC or clone computer. The first RSGB Data Symposium was held at the University of Surrey in the United Kingdom and the first AsiaNet PBBS SYSOP Conference was held in Brisbane, Australia. The Japanese Packet Radio User's Group (PRUG) developed a 9600-bit/s modem for the TNC 2 and its clones. A new satellite wormhole was activated between Ottawa, Ontario and Calgary, Alberta. (The Canadian wormhole was joined by another wormhole in the US between Maryland and Minnesota.)

In August, the FCC devastated 220-MHz packet-radio development by reallocating the 220-222 MHz Amateur Radio subband to the Land Mobile Service. (As of this writing, the ARRL is fighting this reallocation and the development of a 220-MHz packet-radio network continues, albeit at a slower, more cautious pace.)

The Seventh ARRL Amateur Radio Computer Networking Conference was held at Johns Hopkins University in Maryland on October 1. As always, the emphasis of the conference was on bigger and better things for packet radio. This time, however, there was a lot of talk concerning proposed modifications of the AX.25 protocol that were initiated and continued by the renamed ARRL Ad Hoc Committee on Amateur Radio Digital Communications (its new name is simply the ARRL Digital Committee).

On the public-service front, TexNet performed admirably under alert conditions. As Hurricane Gilbert lurched through the Lone Star State, health-and-welfare traffic was handled throughout the US via the packet-radio network. After a major earthquake devastated the Soviet state of Armenia, Soviet officials accepted the ARRL's offer of assistance. Seemingly overnight, portable packet-radio stations were assembled from equipment donated by various manufacturers and shipped to the USSR to provide communications during the relief efforts.

At year's end, Doug Bennett, K4NGC, counted 1622 PBBSs and 1943 digipeaters in operation around the world.

1989: The Network Expands Into Outer Space?

In January, the 18-MHz band was opened to amateurs in the United States, and packet radio was one of the modes authorized on the new band.

A new addition to the growing networking software family was introduced as the long-awaited *ROSE* (*RATS Open Systems Environment*) *X.25 Packet Switch* software was formally released by The Radio Amateur Telecommunications Society (RATS). Another TNC-2 firmware replacement, the ROSE Switch was free to all takers.

In April, the ARRL announced the creation of a new project to develop the next generation of HF packet-radio modems and protocols. The project was intended to coordinate the efforts of designers whose proposals were adopted by the ARRL.

The Dayton HamVention again offered many new packet-radio products, including 9600-baud RF modems from TAPR and PacComm. TAPR also introduced an upgrade kit for the TNC 1 that turned it into a TNC with all of the capabilities of the TNC 1 and TNC 2.

The NET/ROM-TheNet controversy continued in 1989. In May, TAPR asked NORD><LINK, the purveyors of TheNet, to return the Network Node Controller software development system that TAPR had provided to NORD><LINK, after NORD><LINK failed to answer to TAPR's satisfaction questions that had been raised concerning TheNet. According to TAPR president Andy Freeborn, NØCCZ, "The principal question raised... states '...that TheNet is not an original development but rather

a direct copy of NET/ROM.' It was the response to this allegation that the TAPR board sought. It was the reply to this allegation that did not satisfy the board.''

Conclusion

The history of amateur packet radio encompasses approximately one decade, but during that short time, hams have taken the idea of combining packet switching and Amateur Radio and have made great strides in its implementation. If we can equal in the next 10 years what we have accomplished in the last 10, we will truly revolutionize our communications hobby and prepare it for a healthy future in the 21st century.

CHAPTER THREE

Theory of Operation
(Do You Believe in Magic?)

How does it work? Although amateur packet radio may seem like magic, it actually involves logic (and lots of it). There are specific rules (or protocols) for packet-radio data communications. What seems like magic to you now will make sense after you read this chapter.

ISO Begot OSI

Have you ever tried to replace one component in a stereo hi-fi system and discovered that the connectors on the new component did not match the connectors on the old component? As a result, you had to replace the interconnecting cables or solder new connectors onto the old cables. Worse yet, you may have also discovered that there were some electrical signal incompatibilities. The new component required a signal not available in your system, or the new component did not provide a signal that your system needed. Wouldn't it be nice if the signals and connectors were standardized? Then, components could be swapped at will.

In the computer industry, the *International Standards Organization* (*ISO*) has attempted to standardize the communications between computer systems. As a result of their efforts, they have formulated a model, the ISO *Open Systems Interconnection Reference Model* (*OSI-RM*), that permits different computer systems to communicate with each other as long as the communication protocols used by the computer systems adhere to the model.

The model consists of a seven-layer hierarchy. The first layer represents the lowest level and the seventh layer represents the highest level. Each layer is able to communicate only with the layers directly above and below it, and the interface between each layer is clearly defined (this is shown in Figure 3.1). This means that one implementation of a particular layer can be directly interchanged with another implementation of the same layer.

OSI-RM is similar to an idealized stereo hi-fi component system consisting of a stylus, cartridge, turntable, preamplifier, equalizer, amplifier and speaker system. In the hierarchy of this system, the stylus is the lowest level and the speaker system is the highest level. Each component can only be connected to the component above it and below it in the hierarchy. If the interface (the connections) between each component are standardized,

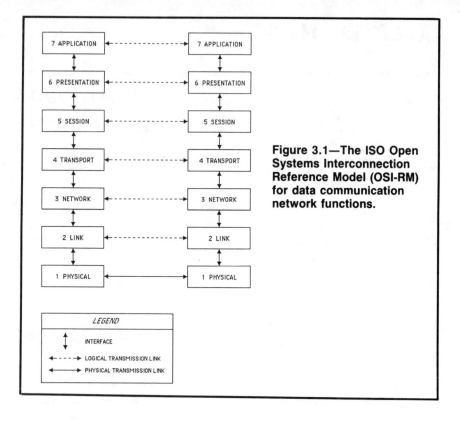

Figure 3.1—The ISO Open Systems Interconnection Reference Model (OSI-RM) for data communication network functions.

similar components can be swapped at will (see Figure 3.2).

Packet-radio operators have an interest in OSI-RM because it provides a model for the development of amateur packet-radio protocols. If all amateurs who are developing packet-radio protocols adhere to the model, they can be sure that their protocols will be compatible with the other protocol developments. Portions of OSI-RM have already been used for the standardization of the interface to public packet-switching networks. This standard or protocol is called CCITT Recommendation X.25, and it is the basis of the amateur packet-radio protocol AX.25 (for amateur X.25).

The Seven Levels Of OSI-RM

Starting with the lowest level, the seven layers of OSI-RM are:
1) the *Physical layer*
2) the *Link layer*
3) the *Network layer*
4) the *Transport layer*
5) the *Session layer*
6) the *Presentation layer* and

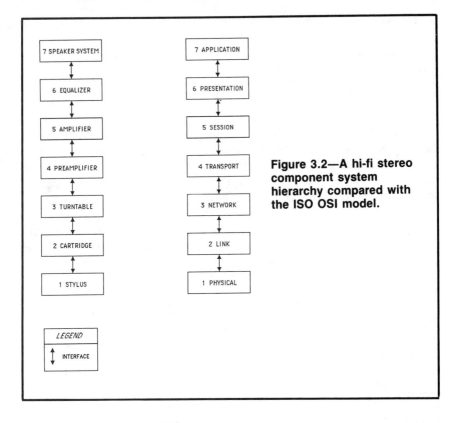

Figure 3.2—A hi-fi stereo component system hierarchy compared with the ISO OSI model.

7) the *Application layer* (the highest level)

At this point in the development of amateur packet-radio protocols, the lower four levels are most significant. Protocols for the Physical and Link layers are already in place, while some protocols for the Network and Transport layers are being tried and tested and others are being developed.

The Physical layer is concerned with physically (mechanically and electrically) moving data from one device to another via the chosen medium of communications. For example, the *Electronic Industries Association* (*EIA*) has formulated a standard for the Physical layer that defines the electrical and mechanical interface for the transfer of *serial*, *binary* data between *data terminal equipment* (*DTE*) and *data circuit-terminating equipment* (*DCE*). The current version of this standard is *EIA-232-D*; its predecessor was the omnipresent EIA *RS-232-C*.

The second level, the Link layer, has the tasks of arranging data *bits* into *frames* and providing for the error-free transfer of the frames over a communications link. Address information is added to each frame to facilitate the transfer from source to destination. A code is calculated for each frame at the destination station, and this code is checked with the code sent by the source station. If there is a discrepancy between the code contained in a received frame and the recalculated code, the frame contains an error and is rejected. ISO's High-level Data Link Control procedure (HDLC) is one standard that has been defined for the Link layer. Another is IBM's Synchronous Data Link Control (SDLC).

The third level (the Network layer) is concerned with routing frames through a network of links. This is accomplished by adding networking information to each frame. Two basic Network layer approaches exist. A connection or virtual-circuit protocol sets up and maintains a clearly defined path (the path appears as a direct connection) for all of the packets transferred between the source and destination during a single data-communication session. Once the virtual circuit is established, each subsequent packet does not need to contain all the addressing information about the circuit.

A connectionless or datagram protocol transfers each packet independently along the best available route. Since the best available route may change periodically, packets transferred between the same source and destination during a single data-communication session may travel different routes. This means that each packet must include complete addressing information.

The task of the fourth level of OSI-RM, the Transport layer, is to maintain a connection that is transparent to the source and destination by assuring that the data received at the destination is complete and in the same sequence as the data that was sent from the source.

The fifth level, the Session layer, provides data-flow synchronization. The sixth level, the Presentation layer, provides standards for the translation or interpretation of the data exchanged between the source and destination (for example, when the source and destination use different ways to represent the data).

The seventh, and highest, level of OSI-RM, the Application layer, provides an interface between the OSI-RM layers and the user application program (or programs) running on the computer.

AX.25: The Amateur Link-Layer Protocol

The *AX.25 Amateur Packet-Radio Link-Layer Protocol, Version 2.0*, commonly known as AX.25, was approved by the ARRL Board of Directors in October 1984. AX.25 is recognized by most packet-radio operators as the *de facto* standard packet-radio protocol. AX.25 specifies the content and format of an amateur packet-radio frame and how that frame is handled at the Link layer by packet-radio stations.

As defined, AX.25 works equally well in either *half-duplex* or *full-duplex* radio environments. It is designed to work with connections between individual packet-radio stations or between an individual packet-radio station and a *multiport controller*. AX.25 allows for *multiple connections* (if the packet-radio device is capable of multiple connections), and the protocol does not prohibit a packet-radio device from connecting with itself. The *Balanced*

Link Access Procedure (LAPB) of CCITT Recommendation X.25 was used as the model for AX.25, so the two protocols are similar. The primary differences are that AX.25 accommodates Amateur Radio call signs for the addressing of each transmitted packet, and it provides the ability for an unconnected station to send packets (to permit packet-radio operators to send CQs, beacons and round-table transmissions, and to support datagrams at the Link layer.)

AX.25 Frames and Fields

AX.25 transmissions consist of small blocks of information called frames. There are three basic types of frames, the *Information frame* (or *I frame*), the *Supervisory frame* (or *S frame*) and the *Unnumbered frame* (or *U frame*). An I frame contains the user data that is being transferred from one station to the other. An S frame provides control of the communications link. For example, S frames acknowledge the receipt of I frames or request the retransmission of I frames. U frames provide additional control of the communications link and also make it possible to send unconnected frames (*UI frames*).

A frame is subdivided into smaller blocks of information called *fields*. Each field is an integral length which is measured in *octets* (an octet is the equivalent of a *byte*, or eight bits). Each frame contains a *flag field*, an *address field*, a *control field*, a *frame-check sequence field* and a final flag field. I frames and UI frames also include a *protocol identifier field* and an *information field*. (Figure 3.3 shows the formats of the three basic frame types).

The flag field indicates the beginning and end of a frame. One flag field may be shared by two frames; in such a situation, the single flag field indicates the end of the first frame and the beginning of the second frame. The flag field is one octet long and its contents are unique [01111110 (7E hexadecimal)], so that no other octet will be interpreted as a flag field.

A process called *zero bit insertion* or *bit stuffing* prevents the other octets between flag octets from having the same unique contents of the flag field. Whenever five consecutive one bits occur in the other octets (not flag octets) of a frame that is intended for transmission, the transmitting packet-radio station inserts (or stuffs) a zero bit after the fifth one bit. Whenever five consecutive bits occur in a received frame, the receiving packet-radio station discards the zero bit after the fifth one bit (to restore intelligence to the contents of the frame).

The address field contains the call signs of the source and destination of the frame. Optionally, it may also contain the call signs of one to eight digipeaters. The length of the address field varies from a minimum of 112 bits (14 octets) to a maximum of 560 bits (70 octets), depending on whether or not digipeaters are contained in the field, and if so, how many.

The first 7 octets of the address field contain the call sign and the

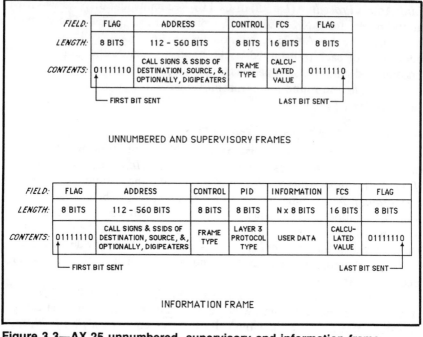

FIELD:	FLAG	ADDRESS	CONTROL	FCS	FLAG
LENGTH:	8 BITS	112 - 560 BITS	8 BITS	16 BITS	8 BITS
CONTENTS:	01111110	CALL SIGNS & SSIDS OF DESTINATION, SOURCE, &, OPTIONALLY, DIGIPEATERS	FRAME TYPE	CALCU- LATED VALUE	01111110

FIRST BIT SENT   LAST BIT SENT

UNNUMBERED AND SUPERVISORY FRAMES

FIELD:	FLAG	ADDRESS	CONTROL	PID	INFORMATION	FCS	FLAG
LENGTH:	8 BITS	112 - 560 BITS	8 BITS	8 BITS	N x 8 BITS	16 BITS	8 BITS
CONTENTS:	01111110	CALL SIGNS & SSIDS OF DESTINATION, SOURCE, &, OPTIONALLY, DIGIPEATERS	FRAME TYPE	LAYER 3 PROTOCOL TYPE	USER DATA	CALCU- LATED VALUE	01111110

FIRST BIT SENT   LAST BIT SENT

INFORMATION FRAME

Figure 3.3—AX.25 unnumbered, supervisory and information frame formats.

Secondary Station Identifier (*SSID*) of the destination station. (The SSID permits one call sign to be used by more than one packet-radio station. For example, the same call sign may be used by a digipeater station and the call-sign-holder's home station. The SSID may be a number from 0 to 15; in most TNCs, if no SSID is specified, it is set to 0.) Octets 8 through 14 of the address field contain the call sign and SSID of the packet-radio station that has originated the frame (the source station).

If one or more digipeaters are specified for routing the frame, each digipeater's call sign and SSID is contained in the address field octets following the call sign and SSID of the source station (octets 16 through 70 maximum). Like the destination and source stations, the digipeater call sign and SSID are 7 octets in length. If more than one digipeater is contained in the address field, the first digipeater in the address field is the first digipeater in the specified route (the first one to retransmit the frame) and the last digipeater in the address field is the last digipeater in the specified route (the one that finally transmits the frame to the destination station).

The control field indicates the frame type. It is one octet long.

The protocol identifier field (or *PID field*) is only present in an I or UI frame and it indicates the type of network layer protocol that is in use, if any. The PID field is one octet long.

The information field contains the actual user data or intelligence that is transferred in an I, UI or *frame reject* (*FRMR*) frame. The maximum length of an information field is 256 octets (prior to bit stuffing).

The *frame check sequence* (*FCS*) field is used for frame error checking. It contains a 16-bit number that is calculated from the transmitted data by the transmitting station according to *ISO 3309* (*HDLC*) *Recommendations*. When the frame is received, the receiving station recalculates the FCS from the received data; if the contents of the FCS field are equal to the FCS calculated by the receiving station, the frame has been received without error. If the two are not equal, then the frame was received with an error (and the receiving station discards the frame).

Supervisory Frames

Supervisory frames are used to control the communications link. The *Receive Not Ready* (*RNR*) frame indicates that the destination station is not able to accept any more I frames because of a temporary "busy" condition. The *Receive Ready* (*RR*) supervisory frame indicates that the destination station is able to receive more I frames (an RR clears an RNR condition). The RR and RNR frames may also acknowledge properly received I frames (frames where the received and recalculated FCSs are equal and the frames are in sequence). The *Reject* (*REJ*) supervisory frame is used by the destination station to request a retransmission when an out-of-sequence frame is received.

Unnumbered Frames

There are six types of Unnumbered frames. Five perform supervisory functions and the sixth permits stations to make unconnected transmissions.

The *Set Asynchronous Balanced Mode* (*SABM*) unnumbered frame initiates a connection between two packet-radio stations, while the *Disconnect* (*DISC*) frame terminates a connection between two packet-radio stations. The receipt and acceptance of an SABM or DISC frame is acknowledged by the *Unnumbered Acknowledge* (*UA*) frame. If the packet-radio station is busy and unable to accept a connection at the moment, it rejects the SABM frame by transmitting a *Disconnected Mode* (*DM*) frame.

The Frame Reject (FRMR) frame indicates that the source station is unable to process a frame and that the error is such that resending the frame will not correct the problem. An FRMR is only sent when something abnormal occurs; it is rare and has only been seen by this author once in six years of packet-radio operating.

The *Unnumbered Information* (*UI*) frame allows data to be transmitted from a source station without a connection to the destination station. Because there is no connection between a source station and destination station when a UI frame is sent, there is no end-to-end error-checking. This means that there is no guarantee that a UI frame will be received without error. UI frames are used for calling CQ, sending general announcements (beacons), in round-table discussions or any time error-free link-layer communication is not a requirement.

How AX.25 Works

WA1LOU wishes to connect with N1ID, so WA1LOU commands his packet-radio device to initiate the connection. (In TAPR TNC 2 parlance, typing CONNECT N1ID <CR> at the command prompt does the trick.) In response, the WA1LOU terminal node controller (TNC) constructs a frame with "N1ID0" in the destination address field and "WA1LOU0" in the source address field. The control field is set as an SABM frame. The SABM frame is transmitted to N1ID-0 and the *acknowledgment timer (T1)* is started at WA1LOU. T1 is equal to at least twice the amount of time it takes to transmit the longest possible frame plus the amount of time it takes for the destination station to transmit the proper response frame. If one or more digipeaters are included in the route, T1 must be increased accordingly.

If N1ID-0 is monitoring the channel and is able to accept WA1LOU's request for a connection, the N1ID TNC will respond to the SABM frame with a UA frame (TNC 2s display ***** CONNECTED to N1ID-0**). If N1ID is busy and unable to accept the connect request, the TNC will respond with a DM frame (TNC 2s display ***** N1ID-0 busy** followed by ***** DISCONNECTED**).

When WA1LOU receives N1ID's response, the TNC cancels the T1 timer. If a UA frame was received, WA1LOU enters the data-transfer mode. If no response is received before T1 times out, WA1LOU continues to transmit SABM frames until a response is received or until the maximum number of retries permitted by WA1LOU's TNC is reached. (TNC 2s display ***** retry count exceeded** followed by ***** DISCONNECTED.**)

In the data-transfer mode, WA1LOU transmits data to N1ID. This data is transmitted by the TNC in the form of I frames. As each new I frame is transmitted, the T1 timer is started (or restarted, if it is already running) by the transmitting station. A maximum of seven I frames can be outstanding (unacknowledged) at one time.

If the destination station receives the I frame in the proper sequence and without error (the FCS checks out), the destination station sends an acknowledgment of reception. If the station has no I frames to send, it sends an RR frame (or RNR frame if it doesn't want to receive further I frames for the time being). If it has I frames to send, it can use the I frame to indicate the acknowledgment, or it can send an RR frame followed by the I frame.

If the destination station receives an I frame out of sequence, the frame is discarded and an REJ frame is transmitted. Out of sequence means that an I frame was received at the destination station in a different sequence than it was transmitted by the source station (as indicated by a difference between the received I frame's *send sequence number* and the destination station's *receive state variable*). When the sending station receives an REJ frame, it retransmits the rejected frame.

The destination station also discards an I frame if the frame's FCS does not match the calculated FCS. In this case, the destination station does not send an REJ, RR or RNR, so the source station's T1 timer runs out and the source station retransmits the frame and restarts T1.

When the exchange of data between WA1LOU and N1ID is completed, either station may initiate a disconnection. (With a TNC 2, this is done by entering the *command mode* and typing DISCONNECT at the command prompt.) In response, the TNC transmits a DISC frame to the other station and starts its T1 timer. The receiving station responds by sending a UA frame and entering the disconnected mode. When the UA frame is received by the station initiating the disconnection, it cancels the T1 timer and enters the disconnected mode (TNC 2s display ***** DISCONNECTED**). If no response is received before T1 times out, the station retransmits the DISC frame until a response is received, or until the maximum number of retries is reached (TNC 2s display ***** retry count exceeded** followed by ***** DISCONNECTED**).

That's basically how AX.25 works! For full details concerning this protocol, *AX.25 Amateur Packet-Radio Link-Layer Protocol, Version 2.0, October 1984* is available from ARRL Headquarters.

The Protocol From Vancouver

Before AX.25, Doug Lockhart, VE7APU, wrote amateur packet-radio protocols for the packet-radio equipment that he designed and developed. His most influential protocol was based on IBM's Synchronous Data Link Control (SDLC) link-layer protocol and was called the Vancouver protocol, the VADCG protocol and, later, the V-1 protocol. V-1 was the first amateur packet-radio protocol to be widely used and accepted, and it is still in use today.

V-1 and AX.25 are very similar. The primary differences between the two protocols are the address and protocol identifier fields. In V-1, numbers are used to identify packet-radio stations, rather than call signs and SSIDs. The V-1 address field may contain a number from 0 to 255. V-1 address numbers 1 through 254 are assigned to packet-radio stations in a given area. Number 255 is used to address all stations (for general announcements), while number 0 is used to address no stations. In V-1, there is no equivalent to the protocol identifier field found in AX.25 I and UI frames.

PADs, Modems, And TNCs

A *packet assembler-disassembler* (*PAD*) is a computer circuit that assembles packets. The circuit accepts data from a terminal and formats it into packet frames for transmission via a communications medium. The PAD also disassembles packets; it accepts packet frames received via a communications medium, extracts data from the packet frames and transfers the data to a terminal. Figure 3.4 is the functional block diagram of the Amateur Radio PAD designed by Doug Lockhart, VE7APU.

In amateur packet radio, a PAD is connected to a modem to convert (modulate) the PAD's digital signals into analog signals for transmission by an Amateur Radio transmitter and to accept analog signals from an Amateur Radio receiver and translate (demodulate) them into digital signals for transfer to the PAD. (Modem is a contraction of modulator-demodulator.) Figure 3.5 is the functional block diagram of a typical modem.

TNCs (PADs Plus)

Originally, a terminal node controller (TNC) was a PAD designed specifically for amateur packet-radio operations. A modern TNC does more than simply assemble and disassemble packets, however. In most cases, today's TNCs include both the PAD and modem functions, thus eliminating the requirement of adding an external modem to a PAD-function-only TNC. Figure 3.6 is the functional block diagram of the TAPR TNC 1; this TNC has an internal modem.

The primary components in a typical amateur packet-radio PAD or TNC, such as the VADCG and TAPR TNCs, are the microprocessor and HDLC controller. The microprocessor is the brain of the TNC. It supervises all of the other components according to the packet-radio protocol software stored in the TNC's *read-only memory* (*ROM*).

The HDLC controller is the heart of the TNC. It formats data from the microprocessor into the frames that are transmitted over the air and it extracts data from each received frame for transfer to the microprocessor.

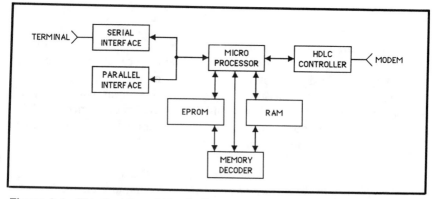

Figure 3.4—The functional block diagram of VE7APU's PAD, also known as the VADCG TNC.

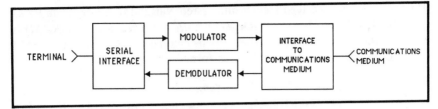

Figure 3.5—The functional block diagram of a typical modem.

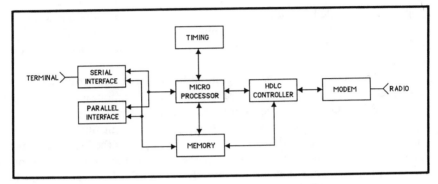

Figure 3.6—The functional block diagram of the TAPR TNC 1.

In addition, the HDLC chip calculates the FCS when a frame is assembled in preparation for transmission and recalculates the FCS for each frame received over the air to check its integrity. Some TNC designs have been successful in performing the function of the HDLC controller in software, most notably some GLB and Kantronics offerings, but most TNCs still rely on the hardware approach of implementing HDLC operation.

In addition to the brain and heart of the TNC, there is an interface for the connection of a terminal for the transfer of data and commands between the TNC and the terminal. Typically, this interface is a *serial interface* that is compatible with RS-232-C specifications. Some TNCs provide a *parallel interface* or *TTL interface* in addition to or instead of the serial interface. (A serial interface transfers characters one bit at a time, while a parallel interface transfers characters one character after another by simultaneously transferring all the bits that make up each character.)

Various forms of memory are also included in a TNC. ROM, typically in the form of *erasable programmable ROM* (*EPROM*), is used to permanently store the packet-radio protocol software. *Random access memory* (*RAM*) is used to store information temporarily (frames in queue for transmission, received frames and system variables). *Nonvolatile RAM* (*NVRAM, NV-RAM* or *NOVRAM*) or *battery-backed RAM* (*bbRAM*) is used to store TNC parameters that may be changed by the user. Such RAM will store data even after the TNC is turned off.

Modems

When the amateur packet-radio pioneers looked for a modem to connect to their first TNCs, Bell 202 modems were readily available as surplus equipment. As a result, Bell 202 modems were used in early packet-radio applications and continue to be used today, primarily in VHF 1200-baud applications. (Most TNCs that have internal modems for 1200-baud applications use Bell 202 devices.) Bell 202 modems are *asynchronous*, half-duplex devices that operate at a maximum of 1200 bit/s using *frequency-shift keying* (*FSK*) with a *mark* frequency of 1200 Hz and a *space* frequency of 2200 Hz.

Bell refers to modems that are compatible with the standards that were developed by the US telephone company, American Telephone and Telegraph Co (AT&T). Different Bell standards were developed for different applications; each standard is designated by a three-digit number and an optional letter. *Bell 103* and *Bell 212A* are two examples of the Bell standards. (Bell modems are not compatible with the modem recommendations or standards that were developed by the CCITT. Different CCITT recommendations are designated with the letter V, followed by a period and a two-digit number; for example, *CCITT Recommendation V.21.*)

In FSK, the transmitted carrier is modulated between two frequencies (the mark and space frequencies). In HDLC, the mark and space designations do not directly relate to the state (0 or 1) of a data bit. Rather, a 0 bit is indicated by a change between mark and space (or space and mark), while a 1 bit causes no change in the transmitted frequency. This encoding system is called *non-return to zero, inverted* (*NRZI*) encoding, and it is an integral part of the AX.25 link-layer specification.

Half duplex is the ability to transmit and receive at different times; that is, not simultaneously or full duplex. A Bell 202 modem cannot transmit and receive simultaneously on one channel.

Asynchronous refers to the fact that there is no direct relationship between the timing of the modulated signals of the modem and the timing of the transmitted data. The beginning and end of each received bit must be determined by the digital device connected to the modem. *Synchronous* is another form of data transmission which uses the internal clock in the modem to synchronize data.

Bell 103 modems are often used in HF 300-baud applications. Bell 103s are asynchronous, full-duplex modems that operate at a maximum of 300 bit/s using FSK. Full-duplex telephone line operation is achieved by using different mark and space frequency pairs at each end of the data communications circuit. At one end, the modem transmits on frequency pair F1 and receives on frequency pair F2, while at the other end, the modem transmits on frequency pair F2 and receives on frequency pair F1. (F1 marks are 1270 Hz, F1 spaces are 1070 Hz; F2 marks are 2225 Hz, F2 spaces are 2025 Hz.) HF packet-radio applications are half-duplex and do not take advantage of the Bell 103 full-duplex capability. The narrow 200-Hz shift between mark and space (as compared with the Bell 202 1000-Hz shift) provides a smaller signal bandwidth for HF transmissions.

The majority of packet-radio modems used today are either Bell 202s or Bell 103s. Some work has been done using other types of modems to achieve better performance, however. A number of 1200-baud modems using *phase-shift keying* (PSK) have been developed for satellite operation and have proven to be good performers in weak-signal terrestrial applications as well. A packet adaptive modem (PAM) was developed by Bob Watson and Paul Rinaldo, W4RI, that provided 75, 150, 300, 600 and 1200-baud data rates that could be adjusted higher or lower depending on operating conditions, while switched-capacitor filtering maintained a minimum bandwidth at all speeds. In addition, 1200-baud modems under development today will provide minimum-shift keyed (MSK) signals, occupying very small bandwidths.

On the high-speed front, Kantronics' KPC-2400 TNC includes a PSK modem that operates at 2400 bit/s [the 2400 bit/s *data rate* is derived from a *dibit* (a group of two bits) data stream operating at 1200 bauds]. Hamilton (Ontario) and Area Packet Network (HAPN) has developed a 4800-baud modem. Steve Goode, K9NG, designed a 9600 bit/s FSK RF modem around a Hamtronics FM-5 220-MHz transmitter, while James Miller, G3RUH, developed a 9600-baud modem that could be used with off-the-shelf NBFM radios. (An RF modem is a device that includes a modem and a radio transmitter and receiver.) Commercial RF modems have also appeared, with 9600-baud units from AEA, GLB, PacComm and TAPR leading the way. Meanwhile, Dale Heatherington, WA4DSY, has attained the highest data rate (so far) with his 56-kbit/s modem that uses bandwidth-limited MSK.

And so it goes, upwards!

Digipeaters

A digipeater (contraction for "digital repeater") is a device that receives, temporarily stores and then retransmits (repeats) packet-radio transmissions. Digipeaters only repeat transmissions that are specifically addressed for routing through that digipeater (as opposed to typical voice repeaters, which retransmit everything they receive).

The AX.25 frame address field may optionally include one to eight call signs (and SSIDs) for routing frames through digipeaters. When this option is used, the first call sign in the extended address field represents the first packet-radio station asked to repeat the frame. If a second call sign is included in the extended address field, it represents the packet-radio station that will repeat the frame after it has been repeated by the first station. A maximum of eight packet-radio stations may be used to repeat a frame. (The last call sign in the extended address field hands the frame off to the destination station listed in the unextended portion of the address field.)

To assure that the frames are digipeated in the right order, one bit (the *H bit*) in the SSID octet of each digipeater addressed in a frame is set to zero until the frame is repeated. When the frame is repeated, the H bit is set to one. A frame will not be digipeated by the second through eighth addressed digipeaters until the first addressed digipeater's H bit is set to one; after that, the frame will not be digipeated by the third through eighth addressed digipeater until the second addressed digipeater's H bit is set to one, and so on.

As a digipeater receives a frame, it recalculates the FCS. If the content of the received FCS field is equal to the recalculated FCS, the frame was received without error and the digipeater retransmits the frame. If the two FCSs are not equal, the frame was received with an error and the digipeater discards it.

AX.25 digipeaters do not acknowledge correctly received frames. Only the destination station acknowledges frames, by sending an acknowledging frame back through the same chain of digipeaters that the received frame was originally routed through. As a result, no matter where a frame or acknowledgment is lost, the source TNC must wait the same amount of time (the setting of T1) before it retransmits the lost frame. In other words, a frame may be lost within a time period that is substantially shorter than the setting of T1, yet no retransmission will occur until the setting of T1 is completely expired. When digipeaters are used, the source packet-radio station's T1 timer is lengthened to compensate for the extra time it takes to send frames and receive acknowledgments through the addressed number of digipeaters.

Any AX.25 TNC is capable of functioning as a digipeater without modification. (A VADCG TNC must be reprogrammed to function as a digipeater.) The digipeater function may be disabled on command, but as long as it is enabled, any AX.25 packet-radio station may include the call sign of any other AX.25 packet-radio station in its extended address field to use the other packet-radio station as a digipeater.

Multiport Digipeaters

The standard AX.25 digipeater receives and transmits on the same frequency. A *multiport digipeater* may receive and transmit on different frequencies, with different parameters on each frequency. For example, one *port* may operate at 300 bauds on 20 meters, while another port may operate at 1200 bauds on 2 meters; or one port may operate on 145.01 MHz, while the other port operates on 145.09 MHz, with both ports operating at 1200 bauds. This multiport operation permits packet-radio stations on one frequency to communicate through the multiport digipeater with packet-radio stations on another frequency.

The standard TNC cannot function as a multiport digipeater, but a number of options are available for multiport digipeater operation. Commercial multiport digipeaters are available (such as PacComm's DR-200 dual-port digipeater and several Kantronics TNCs), or commercial software (such as Amatech International's NET/ROM networking software) may be used to replace the software contained in two TNC 2s; the two modified TNCs may be cabled together to function as a multiport digipeater. Jon Bloom, KE3Z, has written multiport digipeater software for the ubiquitous Xerox 820-1 computer. In addition to the multiport digipeater hardware, modems and radio equipment for each port are required (Figure 3.7 shows a functional block diagram of a multiport digipeater).

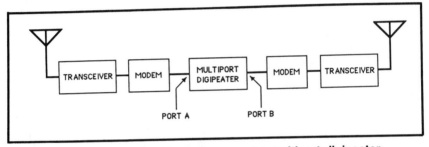

Figure 3.7—The functional block diagram of a multiport digipeater system.

Network

By the late 1980s, networking software, hardware and firmware have replaced digipeaters in many areas of the packet-radio world. KA9Q TCP/IP, NET/ROM, TexNet and ROSE are the four major players in the packet-radio networking today. A full description of their workings can be found in Chapter 11—Network Communications.

Conclusion

Packet radio really isn't magic—the protocol and the logic behind it make it all work as if it were magic.

CHAPTER FOUR

TNCs (I Love A Parade)

In the beginning, you either built a VADCG TNC or rolled your own. As packet radio caught on, however, other TNCs became available. When packet radio became the hottest thing since the FM repeater craze, the trickle of new TNCs became a flood.

Today, the march of TNCs continues as new products become available every month. With all of the choices, someone starting out in packet radio may find that the TNC marketplace is a real jungle. The goal of this chapter is to sort out what is available and ease the process of selecting a TNC.

The following compilation of TNCs is as complete as possible. At the rate that new TNCs are appearing on the market, this list should almost be updated on a daily basis! This means that some new products may be missing. If a particular TNC has been reviewed in *QST*, it is so noted; the addresses of the TNC manufacturers are listed in Appendix F—Sources.

The Beginning Of The TNC Parade

Doug Lockhart, VE7APU, designed the first amateur TNC. It was a kit that initially used the packet-radio protocol that was developed by Doug and the Vancouver Amateur Digital Communications Group (VADCG). As a result, Doug's TNC became known as the VADCG board or VADCG TNC, and the protocol became known as the Vancouver protocol and later as V-1 (to differentiate it from later versions of the VADCG protocol).

The VADCG TNC functioned only as a packet assembler and disassembler (PAD). The user had to connect an external modem between the TNC and his radio equipment. For VHF 1200-baud packet-radio applications, VADCG chose to use modems that were compatible with the Bell-202 standard because they were readily available. These modems are still being used today for VHF applications, to the near exclusion of all others.

Today, the term TNC indicates a device that performs more than the PAD function. Many TNCs sold today include the modem function as well as the PAD function. These TNCs do not need an external modem. The Tucson Amateur Packet Radio Corporation (TAPR) was the first to design a TNC that included a modem (Bell-202-compatible) and a PAD. This effort became known as the TAPR board or TNC 1 and it supported VADCG V-1, as well as a new protocol known as AX.25 (for amateur X.25). Later, TAPR introduced a new TNC dubbed the TNC 2. It implemented only AX.25, but provided a more advanced implementation of that protocol (Version 2). As a result, the TNC 2 offered the user more AX.25 features and capabilities than the TNC 1.

The VADCG and the two TAPR TNC designs became very popular; most of the TNCs available today are clones or near duplicates of the VADCG or TAPR TNC designs, or are based on their designs.

TNC Innovations

Modem requirements for HF and VHF packet radio are different. While the 1200-bit/s, Bell-202-compatible modem is the modem of choice on 2 meters, FCC regulations do not permit 1200-baud operation below 28 MHz. HF packet-radio operators are presently using 300-bit/s modems below 28 MHz. The TAPR TNCs and the initial TAPR-compatible TNCs provided only a 1200-bit/s modem. If you wanted to use those TNCs on HF, you had to modify the built-in modem or add an external modem. Today, some TNCs include built-in switchable or separate modems for HF and VHF applications. On command or at the push of a button, these TNCs can operate on 300-bit/s HF or 1200-bit/s VHF.

The original TNCs functioned with any terminal or computer that had a *serial interface* that was compatible with the EIA standard (EIA RS-232-C/EIA-232-D). The user interface (the set of TNC commands and status messages that were available to a user) did not differ from one terminal or computer system to another. Whether you used an IBM PC or a Radio Shack TRS-80 Model I computer, *** **CONNECTED to WA1LOU** was the message you received after successfully connecting with this station using a TAPR TNC. Today, a handful of TNCs are computer specific. They are designed for operation with one computer, so computer-specific firmware or software may be included that makes the user interface more "friendly." Such features as command menus and split-screen displays of received and transmitted text are possible when a user interface is created for a specific computer.

Other TNC innovations are units that operate in other modes and at higher speeds. Some TNCs provide packet-radio functions that go beyond the basic connection with another station. All of these innovations and variations will be explored in the remainder of this chapter.

The Original VADCG TNC and a Compatible

The original VADCG TNC required an external modem connected to its serial port. Originally, the TNC only supported VADCG V-1; this was the only protocol in existence. The current VADCG board, known as the *TNC+*, supports AX.25 and VADCG V-1, V-2 and V-3. Four LEDs provide status indication. The unit requires 12 V dc and an external modem.

Bill Ashby & Son PAC/NET System

The PAC/NET system (see Figure 4.1) is a smaller version (4.5 × 6.0 × 1.0 inches) of the original VADCG TNC. An EIA-compatible serial port provides the external modem connection. It is available as a bare PC board or assembled and tested with AX.25 in EPROM. A kit of all required ICs (except two EPROMs) is available separately.

Figure 4.1—Bill Ashby & Son PAC/NET System, a VADCG-board compatible.

The First AX.25 Implementation: TAPR TNC 1 and Compatibles

The TAPR TNC 1 was the first TNC to include a modem (Bell-202-compatible, 1200 bit/s) and to use AX.25 Version 1 (as well as VADCG V-1). An EIA-compatible serial port provided the connection between the TNC and a terminal or computer and supported standard data rates between 50 and 19,200 bauds. The *radio port* on the TNC 1 supported data rates between 50 and 4800 bauds, but an external modem was required above 1200 bauds. The data rates of both ports could be selected from software. The unit used a 6809 microprocessor and provided eight status indicators. It operated from 117 V ac and included a *watchdog timer* for protection during unattended operation. The TNC 1 was a kit that included all necessary parts and extensive documentation. The TNC 1 is no longer available new, but it was the precursor of the following TNCs and some of them are still available.

AEA PKT-1

The PKT-1 (see Figure 4.2) was one of the first commercial TNCs. It was functionally the same as the TNC 1, but it used a 12 V dc power supply and it could be purchased preassembled. The PKT-1 was covered in Product Review, November 1985 *QST*.

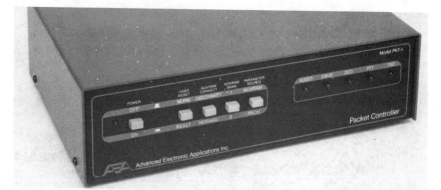

Figure 4.2—AEA PKT-1 TNC, the first TAPR TNC-1 compatible.

Heath HD-4040

The Heath TNC (see Figure 4.3) was a duplicate of the TNC 1 in a different enclosure. Naturally, Heath's duplication of the TNC 1 was a kit, and it included the HD-4040-1 status indicators/connect-alarm kit and the HCD-4040-2 HF modem filter (also available separately). The HD-4040 was covered in Product Review in November 1985 *QST*.

Kantronics Packet Communicator KPC-1

This TNC was the first to provide modems for both HF and VHF. It used a 6803 microprocessor and a modified version of the TNC-1 firmware. The Kantronics firmware modification allowed the TNC to perform certain hardware tasks in software, so Kantronics eliminated the components that perform these same tasks in a TNC 1 (most significantly, the HDLC controller IC). As a result, the KPC-1 was smaller than a TNC 1 (5.9 × 8.0 × 1.9 inches). The user interface was the same as that of the TNC 1, but the maximum data rate of the radio port was 1200 bit/s and the unit did not have a watchdog timer. In all other respects, the first Kantronics entry in the TNC field was functionally the same as the TNC 1.

Figure 4.3—Heath HD-4040 TNC, the first commercial TNC-1 kit.

Packeterm IPT

This portable packet-radio terminal includes a 9-inch video display, 74-key keyboard and a TNC (TNC-1 compatible) with modems for HF and VHF operation. A serial printer port is provided and the whole terminal may be powered by 13.8 V dc.

A Different Approach

GLB tried something different. It was called the software approach and, in essence, was an attempt to perform certain TNC hardware tasks (primarily the HDLC function) in software. GLB's effort predated Kantronics by two years. The philosophy of this approach was that it would eliminate expensive components and make the final product smaller and less expensive. GLB's first TNC was smaller and less expensive than others and, in general, it performed like a TNC should. There were some differences between it and the other TNCs, however. Once you begin typing a message, the GLB TNC cannot send or receive packets until you finish entering the message. In addition, the radio port operates at a maximum data rate of 1200 bit/s. Its user interface is unique, a complete departure from the TAPR and VADCG user interfaces, but the TNC does support AX.25 and VADCG V-1. This Z80A microprocessor-controlled TNC is also able to save received packets in RAM for later retrieval and it may be remotely controlled over the air. An optional teleprinter interface allows it to use a TTY machine as a terminal.

GLB's software-approach TNCs came in two preassembled versions. The PK-1 (see Figure 4.4), without an enclosure, is the older and larger (4.5 × 9.5 × 2.0 inches) and requires 12 V dc at 200 mA. It has 4 kbytes of RAM, which may be expanded by the user to 14 kbytes or at the factory to 56 kbytes.

Figure 4.4—GLB PK-1 TNC, the first software-approach TNC.

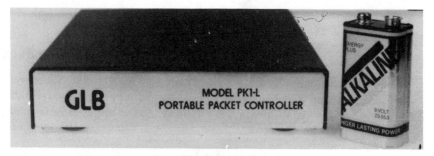

Figure 4.5—GLB PK1-L TNC, a 25-mA version of the GLB PK-1.

A watchdog timer for unattended operation is included. The PK1-L (see Figure 4.5), enclosure included, is smaller (4.6 × 5.9 × 1.0 inches) and requires 9 to 15 V dc at a miniscule 25 mA. Its low power consumption makes it attractive for remote digipeater applications. It includes a watchdog timer, 8 kbytes of RAM and a lithium battery for RAM backup. The latest version of the PK1-L firmware includes a selective call-sign filtering function.

The Ongoing AX.25 Implementation: TAPR TNC 2 And Compatibles

The TAPR TNC 2 was the next logical step after the TNC 1. It differed from the TNC 1 in that it was physically smaller, used a more fully developed AX.25 (Version 2) and did not support the VADCG protocol. The maximum data rate of the radio port was now 9600 bit/s, and the data rates of the radio port and serial port were selected by hardware (using a DIP switch) rather than selected in software. The new TAPR offering was a well-documented kit using a Z80A microprocessor, lithium battery backup for retention of operating parameters and a 12 V dc power supply. After the initial limited production run of TAPR TNC 2s, TAPR licensed manufacturers to build TNC 2 clones and returned to the research and development business. The following TNCs are direct descendants of the TNC 2.

AEA PK-80

This preassembled version of the TNC 2 has beefed-up circuitry to suppress RFI. Because it does not use CMOS parts, its power requirements are 12 to 15 V dc at 400 mA.

AEA PK-87

The PK-87 might be called the *TNC 2 Plus*. In addition to TAPR TNC-2 compatibility, this AEA offering includes a number of software and hardware enhancements. Among the enhancements are eight front-panel status indicators, a mailbox monitor command, restricted usage commands, the capability to remotely configure the TNC, and *autobaud* between 300 and 9600 bauds. (Autobaud is the ability of a data-communications device to automatically adapt to whatever data rate is being used by the terminal connected to it.) The PK-87 may be used for HF as well as VHF operation.

AEA PK-88

If we can call the PK-87 the *TNC 2 Plus*, then we can call the PK-88 the *PK-87 Plus* (see Figure 4.6). The PK-88 is smaller than the PK-87, but packs more features than its predecessor, including a small personal mailbox using a subset of the WØRLI/WA7MBL PBBS commands. Like its predecessor, the PK-88 is operational on both HF and VHF.

California Packet Concepts TNC II

Four versions of this TAPR TNC-2 compatible are available. The TNC

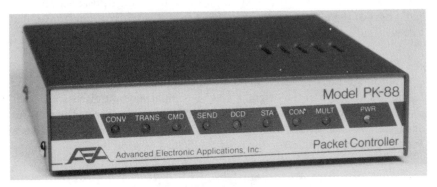

Figure 4.6—AEA PK-88 TNC, a preassembled TAPR TNC-2 compatible.

is available preassembled or as a kit, both with or without CMOS components. A bare PC board (with documentation) is also available. There are some cosmetic differences, but otherwise the TNC II and its TAPR forefather are identical.

GLB Electronics TNC2A

GLB's kit (see Figure 4.7) is available in two versions: a CMOS version rated at 10 to 15 V dc at 110 mA and an NMOS version rated at 10 to 15 V dc at 260 mA. Other than cosmetic differences, the GLB TNC2A and the TAPR TNC 2 are the same.

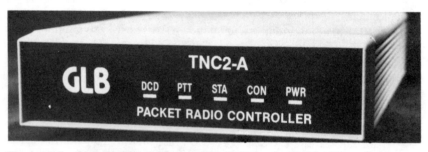

Figure 4.7—GLB TNC2A TNC, a TAPR TNC-2-compatible kit available in CMOS and NMOS versions.

Heath HK-21

The HK-21 is the smallest TNC of all (2.5 × 4.3 × 1.0 inches) and requires only 9 to 13.8 V dc at 40 mA. Yet inside this non-kit Heath TNC are all of the functions of a TNC 2 plus a miniature PBBS function. The radio port of the HK-21 is unique in that it uses a modular connector similar to that used in telephone jacks.

Kantronics KPC-1

Although the KPC-1 is only available as a used item today, it may be found in two flavors: the original TNC-1-compatible unit discussed earlier in this chapter or an upgraded TNC-2 compatible that supports the features of AX.25 Version 2. The two versions exist because Kantronics provides a TNC-2 factory upgrade for the original TNC-1 version.

Kantronics KPC-2

The KPC-2 (see Figure 4.8) is similar to the original KPC-1 in that it has the same internal HF and VHF modems, the same 6803 microprocessor

Figure 4.8—Kantronics KPC-2 TNC, a preassembled TAPR TNC-2 compatible with internal HF and VHF modems.

and modified firmware with a maximum radio data rate of 1200 bit/s. The KPC-2 is not a TNC-2 clone, but it is compatible with AX.25 Version 2. In addition to a normal EIA-compatible serial port, the KPC 2 also has a TTL interface (for computers such as the Commodore C-64). Serial port and radio port data rates are *software selectable*. The KPC-2 also supports the Kantronics *KA-Node* of operation, which allows the TNC to act as a network node that provides local acknowledgment of packets rather than the standard digipeater type of end-to-end acknowledgment.

Kantronics KPC-4

The KPC-4 (see Figure 4.9) is a unique TNC. It has two 1200-baud VHF ports that allow you to connect to stations simultaneously on each port, while other stations use the KPC-4 for digipeating or as a gateway between ports. The unit also includes an internal mailbox function that allows you and other stations to leave and retrieve messages. A 63B03X microprocessor controls the unit and 32 kbytes of RAM are available. The serial port supports TTL

Figure 4.9—The Kantronics KPC-4 TNC permits digipeating and gateway operation between its two VHF ports. In addition, the KPC-4 includes a mailbox function.

or EIA. Over 100 software commands control the AX.25-compatible KPC-4. It also supports the Kantronics KA-Node.

MFJ MFJ-1270

This unit (see Figure 4.10) is preassembled and it provides a TTL interface (for Commodore C-64 compatibility) as well as the standard EIA serial port. Cosmetically, it is very different than the other TNC-2 clones, but it is functionally the same. The MFJ-1270 appeared in a September 1986 *QST* Product Review.

Figure 4.10—MFJ-1270 TNC, an inexpensive, preassembled TAPR TNC-2 compatibile.

MFJ MFJ-1270B

The MFJ-1270B is essentially an MFJ-1270 with a rear-panel switch that allows the user to select HF or VHF modem tones.

MFJ MFJ-1274

Like the MFJ-1270B, the MFJ-1274 is an MFJ-1270 with added features: a front-panel 20-segment LED HF tuning indicator and a rear-panel switch that allows the user to select HF or VHF modem tones.

PacComm TNC-200

The TNC-200 (see Figure 4.11) is available in a variety of flavors: assembled and tested CMOS and NMOS versions, kit versions (CMOS or NMOS), kit versions less cabinet (CMOS or NMOS), PC board and hard-to-find parts (CMOS or NMOS) and bare PC board. Again, other than cosmetic differences, PacComm's versions of the TNC 2 are the same as the original. The TNC-200 was covered in a June 1987 *QST* Product Review.

PacComm TNC 220

Another TNC-2 work-alike, the TNC-220 (kit or assembled), includes two radio ports. Each port may be configured for 300-baud (HF) or 1200-

Figure 4.11—PacComm TNC-200, a TNC-2 compatible that was available in nine flavors.

baud (VHF) operation. Switching between ports is software controlled and an active band-pass filter is included for the HF-configured port. The TNC has both TTL and EIA serial ports. Front-panel status indicators are color coded and there are provisions for an optional tuning indicator.

PacComm Tiny-2

As its name implies, the Tiny-2 is a compact TNC 2 compatible (5.0 × 7.0 × 1.3 inches) that sacrifices none of the features of its full-size TNC-2-compatible brethren. In addition to its small size, the Tiny-2 differs from the TNC 2 by using a low-power TI TCM3105J modem.

PacComm Micropower2

The Micropower2 is essentially a PacComm Tiny-2 with low power consumption (9 to 13.8 V dc at 40 mA, in comparison to the Tiny-2's 230-mA requirement). In most respects, the Micropower2 and Tiny-2 are identical.

PacComm TNC-320

The TNC-320 provides VHF and HF modems on separate software-selectable radio ports that may be connected simultaneously. The TNC-2-compatible firmware in the TNC-320 has been modified to provide additional features, including a personal mailbox function that is WØRLI-PBBS compatible.

TAPR TNC 1

The AX.25 Version 1 protocol in the TNC 1 does not support some of the features that the AX.25 Version 2 protocol in the TNC 2 provides, such as multiple connections and full-function monitoring. To solve this problem, TAPR has an upgrade kit that results in a TNC 1 that has all of the features of a TNC 2, plus software-selectable serial and radio ports, two sets of *default* parameters in battery-backed RAM, two sets of EPROM-based software, complete TNC-2 firmware capability, two modem disconnect headers, a front-panel reset switch and a complete TNC 1.

Another solution to the lack of AX.25 Version 2 features in a TNC 1 has been provided by Ron Raikes, WA8DED, who has written new firmware for the TNC 1 and its compatibles (the AEA PKT-1 and Heath HD-4040) that provides the AX.25 Version 2 features that are missing in the TNC 1. The user interface to the WA8DED firmware is different from the standard TNC-1 or TNC-2 user interface, but it is easy to learn and use. His code is available on various landline and packet-radio bulletin-board systems and must be downloaded and burned into two 2764 EPROMs that replace the original TNC-1 EPROMs. WA8DED's firmware is also available for the TAPR TNC 2, TNC-2 clones and the AEA PK-87.

For Your I/Os Only: Computer-Specific TNCs

Certain computers are found in ham shacks more often than others; this makes it economically feasible to design packet-radio products specifically for the more popular computers. Packet-radio ware has been specifically designed for use with the Commodore VIC-20, C-64 and C-128, for the IBM PC, and for the Radio Shack TRS-80 Model I, III and 4 computers.

AAPRA

The Australian Amateur Packet Radio Association (AAPRA) has developed a packet-radio hardware and software package for the Commodore C-64 and C-128 computers. The hardware portion of the package consists of a bare 1200/300 bit/s modem PC board that plugs into the cartridge port of the Commodore. The modem board contains provisions for a watchdog timer and a PTT relay. The computer powers the PTT circuit to ensure that a transmitter is not activated if the computer is turned off. The software portion of the package is on disk, and it emulates the function of a TNC. The software was written by Chris Mills, VK4BCM, and is compatible with AX.25 Version 2. The user interface is similar to that written for the TNC 1 by Ron Raikes, WA8DED. For Commodore owners who do not own a disk drive, an EPROM plug-in cartridge version of the AAPRA package is also available.

AEA PK-64

The PAKRATT Model PK-64 (see Figure 4.12) provides packet-radio

Figure 4.12—AEA PK-64 provides all-digital-mode capability for the Commodore C-64 and C-128 computers.

capability for the Commodore C-64 and C-128 computers. In addition, Morse, *RTTY* (Baudot and ASCII) and AMTOR operation are possible. This unit is compatible with the TNC 2 and AX.25 Version 2. The PK-64's user interface is menu driven, so you do not have to remember all of the various TNC commands. All the commands are shown on the computer's display. Split-screen operation provides separate windows for received text, transmitted text and status indications.

This unit is preassembled and it plugs into the cartridge port of the Commodore computer. The PK-64 has an internal VHF modem, but HF operation is also possible. An optional HFM-64 modem provides improved HF operation. The unit is equipped with an audible alarm that sounds if a connection is made. The PK-64 unit requires 13 V dc for power. For a Product Review of the PK-64, see June 1986 *QST*.

DIGICOM > 64

DIGICOM > 64 is a public-domain program for the Commodore C-64 computer that causes the computer to perform the packet assembly and disassembly functions of a TNC. A simple two-chip modem is the only hardware that is needed (the modem can be built for approximately $20). Written by German amateurs, DIGICOM > 64 is available from a number of sources (A & A Engineering; Barry Kutner, W2UP; N3EFN; and Craig Rader, N4PLK). Send a self-addressed stamped envelope to one of the sources (listed in Appendix F—Sources) to obtain further information.

DRSI PC*Packet Adapter

The DRSI PC*Packet Adapter, or *PC*PA*, is a "half-length" expansion card for an IBM PC or compatible computer. It contains TNC-2-compatible hardware that is run by a variety of DRSI-provided software, including a terminal emulator with five separate split-screen windows, one for monitoring channel activity and four for separate connections; a multiple-connection

PBBS; KA9Q's TCP/IP package; and G8BPQ's NET/ROM-compatible networking system.

The PC*PA is available in three versions and each version has two ports that are active simultaneously. Type 1 provides a 1200-baud modem on one port and a serial interface on a second port that may be connected to an external modem, Type 2 provides 1200-baud modems on each port, and Type 3 provides serial interfaces on each port that may be connected to external modems. (Optional 2400-baud DPSK VHF modems and 300-baud HF modems are available from DRSI.)

HAPN HAPN-1

The Hamilton (Ontario) and Area Packet Network (HAPN) HAPN-1 packet-radio adapter (Figure 4.13) hardware and software package, available preassembled with software or bare PC board with software, is designed for the IBM PC and compatibles. The hardware consists of an 8.5-inch card that plugs into an expansion slot of the PC. In addition to the TNC hardware, the card also includes a watchdog timer circuit, a prototyping area and a modem for VHF operation.

The board supports data rates up to 9600 bauds using an external modem (HAPN has a 4800-baud modem available). The card is powered by the computer, and HAPN-1's software provides AX.25 Version 2 compatibility. Optional VADCG V-1, V-2, packet-radio bulletin-board and file-transfer software packages are also available. The user interface is function-key driven with pop-up menus and dialog boxes.

Figure 4.13—Hamilton and Area Packet Network HAPN-1, a TNC that plugs into an expansion slot in an IBM PC or compatible. The prototype area at the left side of the card contains HAPN's 4800-baud modem.

KA9Q NET

Phil Karn, KA9Q, has written software for IBM PC and compatible computers that, among other things, performs all of the PAD functions of a TNC (a TNC that supports the KISS mode is still required to provide the modem function). The software has been *ported* to other computers, including the Apple Macintosh and Commodore Amiga, and provides a sophisticated packet-radio networking system that is based on the *Defense Advanced Research Projects Agency* (*DARPA*) *Internet Protocol* (*IP*) and *Transmission Control Protocol* (*TCP*), which is commonly known as TCP/IP. (Refer to Chapter 11—Network Communications for a full description of KA9Q's software and how to obtain a copy.)

Newsome Electronics PACKMON

Not quite a TNC, PACKMON is a receive-only device that permits a Commodore VIC-20, C-64 or C-128 computer to display packets received on a VHF or UHF receiver or transceiver. The unit consists of a program cartridge that plugs into the computer and is available as a kit or preassembled.

PacComm PC-110

The PC-110 is a half-height expansion card for IBM PC and compatible computers that contains a TNC 2 with software-selectable HF or VHF operation through a single radio port. A second port provides a serial interface for connection to an external modem. The PC-110 is available in NMOS and CMOS versions.

PacComm PC-120

The PC-120 is essentially a PC-110 with two simultaneously active radio ports. One port is equipped with an AM7910 modem that provides software-selectable HF and VHF operation. The second port uses the TCM3105 modem for low-power-consumption VHF operation.

PacComm PC-320

The PC-320 is a ¾-length expansion card for IBM PC and compatible computers that provides VHF and HF modems on separate software-selectable radio ports that may be active simultaneously. The PC-320 firmware is a modification of the TNC 2 firmware that provides additional features, including a personal mailbox function that is WØRLI-PBBS compatible. HF-tuning and status indicators are simulated on the computer screen.

Richcraft Engineering's Synchronous Packet Radio Using The Software Approach, Volumes 1 and 2

Bob Richardson, W4UCH, wrote two TNC-emulation software packages for the Radio Shack TRS-80 Model I, III and 4 computers. Running this software on a TRS-80 causes it to perform all TNC hardware functions (an appropriate external modem is required). The user interface is menu driven. Volume 1 is based on VADCG V-1, while Volume 2 is based on AX.25 Version 1 (Volume 1 or 2 documentation including program listings or Volume 1 or 2 programs on disk without documentation are available).

All Digital Wonders: Multi-Mode Products

If you are interested in other Amateur Radio modes in addition to packet radio, you might seriously consider one of the following multi-mode products. Because this book is concerned with packet radio, only the packet-radio capabilities of these units will be described here.

AEA PK-64

This Commodore C-64- and C-128-specific product was covered under the discussion of computer-specific TNCs.

AEA PK-232

The PAKRATT Model PK-232 (see Figure 4.14) provides Morse, RTTY (Baudot and ASCII), AMTOR, FAX, Navtex and packet-radio operation for any computer that has an EIA serial port. This unit is preassembled and includes internal modems for HF (200-Hz frequency shift) and VHF (1000-Hz shift) operation. Provisions are included for using external modems operating from 2400 to 9600 bauds. A Z80A microprocessor runs the show. The unit operates from 13 V dc at 700 mA. In addition to normal packet-radio operation, the PK-232 has a KISS mode for compatibility with the TCP/IP networking protocol (refer to Chapter 11—Network Communications). The PK-232 was reviewed in the January 1988 issue of *QST*.

Figure 4.14—AEA PK-232 is capable of operating all digital modes, including the KISS TNC mode for TCP/IP network operation.

Heath HK-232

This Heath kit (see Figure 4.15) permits any computer with an EIA serial port to operate Morse, RTTY (Baudot and ASCII), AMTOR, FAX, Navtex

Figure 4.15—Heath HK-232 is an all-digital-mode kit that is capable of Morse, Baudot, ASCII, AMTOR and packet-radio operation. Weather facsimile picture reception is also provided.

and packet radio (both HF and VHF) modes. The unit provides connectors for simultaneous connection to an HF and a VHF transceiver. It was reviewed in January 1988 *QST*.

Kantronics KAM

The *Kantronics All Mode* (see Figure 4.16) does just that—Morse, RTTY (Baudot and ASCII), AMTOR and packet radio (see Figure 4.15). The KAM may be connected to any computer or terminal with an EIA standard serial port or a TTL interface. Two radio ports are provided for HF and VHF operation; the two ports may be used simultaneously for connections and digipeating plus HF-VHF gateway operation. On HF, the mark and space tone frequencies are programmable and a front-panel tuning indicator is provided. One-hundred software commands control the operation of this unit. The KAM was reviewed in the June 1989 issue of *QST*.

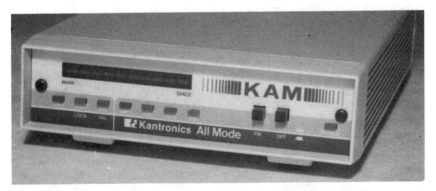

Figure 4.16—Kantronics All Mode (KAM), an all-digital-mode controller, provides gateway operation between its HF and VHF ports.

Kantronics UTU-XT/P

The UTU-XT/P supports HF packet radio as well as Morse, RTTY (Baudot and ASCII) and AMTOR Amateur Radio modes. In the packet-radio mode, it also supports the Kantronics KA-Node mode. The unit may be connected to any computer or terminal with a standard EIA serial port or a TTL interface.

MFJ MFJ-1278

The MFJ-1278 (see Figure 4.17) offers Morse (with a contest memory keyer submode), RTTY (Baudot and ASCII), AMTOR, FAX, Navtex and SSTV modes, as well as packet radio (with KISS and mailbox sub-modes). The unit provides software-selectable HF and VHF modem operation via two software-selectable radio ports. A standard EIA serial port and a TTL interface are provided for connection to a computer or terminal and a parallel port is provided for connection of a printer. The MFJ-1278 was reviewed in the July and September 1989 issues of *QST*.

Figure 4.17—MFJ MFJ-1278, a multi-mode controller that offers a variety of modes, including SSTV.

Breaking The 1200 Bit/s Barrier: Kantronics KPC-2400

The KPC-2400 Packet Communicator (see Figure 4.18) includes a modem that operates at 2400 bit/s. Using phase-shift keying (PSK), the 2400-bit/s signal rate is derived from a dibit (a group of two bits) data stream operating at 1200 bauds. In addition to the 2400-bit/s modem, the unit also includes the 300- and 1200-bit/s modems used in the TNC-2-compatible Kantronics KPC-2. The three modems are software selectable. The 2400 bit/s modem is available separately for use with TNC 1 and TNC 2 compatibles. Like the KPC-2, the KPC-2400 uses AX.25 Version 2, provides both a TTL

Figure 4.18—Kantronics KPC-2400 TNC, the first TNC with a modem operating above 1200 bit/s.

port and an EIA serial port, emulates HDLC in software, supports the Kantronics KA-Node and operates from 12 V dc. It was reviewed in November 1987 *QST*.

What Can We Look For Next?

New TNCs are appearing all the time. There are a number of well-designed units being developed and used in other countries. Japan has over 5000 active packet-radio stations, and there are several Japanese-designed TNCs and modems available. No doubt many of them will make their way to the United States in the near future.

Conclusion

There is a good selection out there in TNC land, with something to suit everyone's needs. The guidance provided in this chapter should help you determine which TNC is right for you.

TNC Comparison Chart

The pages that follow contain a feature comparison chart of the TNCs that are available today on the new and used market. The TNCs in the chart are divided into two categories: general-purpose TNCs, that is, those that may be used with any terminal or computer; and computer-specific TNCs, that is, those that are designed for use with a specific computer. Not charted for comparison are software-intensive items like the DIGICOM>64, receive-only items like the Newsome Electronics PACKMON, and DTE-TNC combos like the Packeterm IPT. The first two uncharted categories were avoided because their features are unique; therefore, there would be no useful comparison between them and the other TNCs. The third uncharted category was avoided because the typical DTE-TNC combo uses a brand-name TNC that has already been charted.

An explanation of each charted feature follows:

Brand and Model—Typically, the manufacturer's name and the TNC's model number.

Type—The type of TNC: TAPR TNC 1 compatible, TAPR TNC 2 compatible or VADCG compatible. A plus sign (+) after the type indicates that the TNC had additional firmware features not found in its TNC forefather. For example, a TNC of the "TNC 2 +" type is a TNC that is compatible with the TAPR TNC 2, but has additional firmware features not found in the TAPR TNC 2. A multiplication sign (×) after the TNC type indicates that the TNC is a multi-mode unit.

Command Set—The command set used by the TNC: GLB PK-1, TAPR TNC 1, TAPR TNC 2 or VADCG. A plus sign (+) after the command set indicates that the TNC supports other commands in addition to those provided in the original command set.

Power Requirements—The voltage and current needed by the TNC.

Size (W × D × H in)—The physical dimensions (width by depth by height) of the TNC in inches.

Computer Ports—The type of interface provided by the TNC for connection to a terminal or computer: EIA RS-232-C/EIA-232-D compatible, TTL-compatible or other type.

Modems—The type(s) of modem(s) (VHF 1200 baud and/or HF 300 baud) provided by the TNC and, if there is more than one modem, whether or not they are software selectable. If more than one of a type is provided (for example, two VHF 1200-baud modems), then the quantity of that type is indicated. If multiple modems are software selectable, that means there is a command in the TNC's command set that allows the user to select the modem (if a TNC has more than one modem, but the software selectable feature is not checked, then it may be assumed that the modems are hardware selectable, that is, via a front- or rear-panel switch).

Radio Ports—The quantity of radio ports and, if there is more than one, whether or not the ports are software selectable and simultaneously active. If multiple radio ports are software selectable, it indicates that there is a command in the TNC's command set that allows the user to select the radio port (if a TNC has more than one radio port, but the software-selectable feature is not checked, then it may be assumed that the radio ports are hardware selectable, ie, via a front- or rear-panel switch). If multiple radio ports are "active simultaneously," it indicates that connections and communications may be carried on by each port at the same time (if a TNC has more than one radio port, but the active simultaneously feature is not checked, then it may be assumed that the radio ports can only be used one at a time).

Front Panel Indicators—The status indicators provided by the TNC: Connection (typically shortened to CON), Data Carrier Detect (typically abbreviated as DCD), Power (typically PWR), Receive Audio (RCV), Status (STA), Transmitted Data (TXD), Transmitter On (PTT or SEND), Tuning Indicator and Other (other indicators, if any, are listed under *Notes*).

Gateway—Whether or not the TNC supports a gateway between its multiple radio ports (if it has multiple radio ports).

Host Mode—Whether or not the TNC supports a *host mode*. (A host mode allows a TNC to communicate with the computer in a language that is more efficient than the English language used by the TNC to communicate with a user.)

KISS—Whether or not the TNC supports the KISS mode. The KISS mode, for *keep it simple, stupid*, is required if the user wishes to use the KA9Q TCP/IP software package for packet-radio networking.

Mailbox—Whether or not the TNC provides a mailbox function, either of the personal or public (read PBBS) variety.

Network Node—Whether or not the TNC provides the ability to serve as a network node (other than the standard AX.25 digipeater variety).

QST Review—The issue of *QST*, if any, in which the TNC was reviewed.

Availability—Whether the TNC is currently available as new or used equipment.

Notes—Key to Notes:

A—CW mode also supported.
B—Baudot RTTY mode also supported.
C—ASCII RTTY mode also supported.
D—AMTOR mode also supported.
E—FAX mode also supported.
F—Navtex mode also supported.
G—Other indicators: Command Mode, Converse Mode, Multiple-Connection, Packet Mode and Transparent Mode.
H—Other indicators support non-packet-radio modes.
J—Other indicators: Command Mode, Converse Mode, Multiple-Connection, and Packet Mode.
K—Other indicators: CW Identification.
L—Kit version available only.
M—Kit or assembled versions available.
N—Maximum data rate of radio port is 1200 bit/s.
O—CMOS and NMOS versions available.
P—Other indicators: CW Identification, Reset and Spare.
Q—2400 bit/s MSK and PSK modems optional.
R—Connection, Transmitter On and Status indicators provided for each port.

S—KPC-1 with original TNC-1-compatible firmware.
T—KPC-1 with upgraded TNC-2-compatible firmware.
U—2400 bit/s PSK modem included.
V—Receive Audio and Transmitter On indicators provided for each port.
W—Other indicators: Mailbox and Repeater.
X—SSTV mode also supported.
Y—CW memory keyer also included.
Z—Parallel output port included.
a—Parallel output port optional.
b—Real-time hardware clock optional.
c—Connection, Data Carrier Detect, Status and Transmitter On indicators provided for each port.
d—Other indicators: Auxiliary, Personal Message System, Port 1, Port 2 and Received Data.
e—TNC 1 with original TNC-1 firmware.
f—TNC 1 with TNC-2 upgrade kit installed.
g—Commodore C-64 specific.
h—Menu-driven command set.
i—IBM PC/clone half-height expansion card.
j—Terminal-emulation software included.
k—TCP/IP software included.
m—2400-baud modem optional.
n—Intended to be used with two external HF modems.
o—IBM PC/clone expansion card.
p—VADCG V1/V2 software optional.
q—File-transfer software optional.
r—4800-baud modem optional.
s—IBM PC/clone ¾-height expansion card.
t—May be powered externally also.
u—Front panel indicators simulated on computer display.

Brand and Model	Type	Command Set	Power Requirements		Size (W x D x H in.)
GENERAL PURPOSE					
AEA PK-232	TNC 2 x	TNC 2 +	13 V dc	700 mA	8 x 11 x 2.5
AEA PK-80	TNC 2	TNC 2	12 - 15 V dc	400 mA	6 x 10 x 1.7
AEA PK-87	TNC 2 +	TNC 2 +	12 V dc	495 mA	9.5 x 5.8 x 2
AEA PK-88	TNC 2 +	TNC 2 +	13 V dc	500 mA	7.5 x 6.1 x 1.5
AEA PKT-1	TNC 1	TNC 1	12 V dc	1.1 A	11.8 x 8.5 x 3.5
Bill Ashby & Son PAC/NET System	VADCG	VADCG	8 - 10 V dc	500 mA	4.5 x 6 x 1
California Packet Concepts TNC II	TNC 2	TNC 2	12 V dc	150/350 mA†	6 x 10 x 1.7
GLB PK-1	TNC 1	GLB	12 V dc	200 mA	4.5 x 9.5 x 2
GLB PK-1L	TNC 1	GLB	9 - 15 V dc	25 mA	4.6 x 5.9 x 1
GLB TNC2-A	TNC 2	TNC 2	10 - 15 V dc	110/260 mA†	6 x 10 x 1.7
Heath HD-4040	TNC 1	TNC 1	120 V ac	1.0 A	13.7 x 7.8 x 2.4
Heath HK-21	TNC 2 +	TNC 2 +	9 - 13 V dc	40 mA	2.5 x 4.3 x 1
Heath HK-232	TNC 2 x	TNC 2 +	13 V dc	750 mA	8 x 11 x 2.5
Kantronics KAM	TNC 2 x	TNC 2 +	11 - 14 V dc	300 mA	5.9 x 9 x 1.9
Kantronics KPC-1	TNC 1 +	TNC 1	10 - 14 V dc	330 mA	5.9 x 8 x 1.9
Kantronics KPC-1	TNC 2 +	TNC 2 +	10 - 14 V dc	330 mA	5.9 x 8 x 1.9
Kantronics KPC-2	TNC 2 +	TNC 2 +	9 - 14 V dc	250 mA	5.9 x 8 x 1.9
Kantronics KPC-2400	TNC 2 +	TNC 2 +	10 - 15 V dc	330 mA	5.9 x 8 x 1.9
Kantronics KPC-4	TNC 2 +	TNC 2 +	11 - 14 V dc	200 mA	5.9 x 8 x 1.9
Kantronics UTU-XT/P	TNC 2 x	TNC 2 +	12 V dc	300 mA	5.9 x 8 x 1.9
MFJ MFJ-1270	TNC 2	TNC 2	10 - 15 V dc	200 mA	7.4 x 9.5 x 1.7
MFJ MFJ-1270B	TNC 2 +	TNC 2	12 V dc	350 mA	7.4 x 9.5 x 1.7
MFJ MFJ-1274	TNC 2 +	TNC 2	12 V dc	350 mA	7.4 x 9.5 x 1.7
MFJ MFJ-1278	TNC 2 x	TNC 2 +	12 V dc	500 mA	9.4 x 9.4 x 1.6
PacComm Micropower2	TNC 2 +	TNC 2	9 - 13.8 V dc	40 mA	5 x 7 x 1.3
PacComm Tiny-2	TNC 2 +	TNC 2	9 - 13.8 V dc	230 mA	5 x 7 x 1.3
PacComm TNC-200	TNC 2	TNC 2	12 - 14 V dc	150/350 mA†	6 x 9.5 x 1.9
PacComm TNC-220	TNC 2 +	TNC 2 +	12 V dc	500 mA	6 x 7.3 x 1.9
PacComm TNC-320	TNC 2 +	TNC 2 +	12 V dc	275 mA	6 x 7.3 x 1.9
TAPR TNC 1	TNC 1	TNC 1	117 V ac	1.0 A	12 x 7.5 x 4
TAPR TNC 1	TNC 1 & 2	TNC 1 & 2	117 V ac	1.0 A	12 x 7.5 x 4
TAPR TNC 2	TNC 2	TNC 2	12 V dc	350 mA	6 x 10 x 1.7
COMPUTER-SPECIFIC					
AEA PK-64	TNC 2 x	TNC 2 +	13 V dc	320 mA	10.3 x 5.5 x 2.3
DRSI PC*PA Type 1	TNC 2 +	TNC 2 +	powered by computer		4.2 x 5.8 x 0.5
DRSI PC*PA Type 2	TNC 2 +	TNC 2 +	powered by computer		4.2 x 5.8 x 0.5
DRSI PC*PA Type 3	TNC 2 +	TNC 2 +	powered by computer		4.2 x 5.8 x 0.5
HAPN HAPN-1	TNC 2	TNC 2	powered by computer		4.2 x 8.5 x 0.5
PacComm PC-110	TNC 2 +	TNC 2 +	powered by computer		4.2 x 5.8 x 0.5
PacComm PC-120	TNC 2 +	TNC 2 +	powered by computer		4.2 x 5.8 x 0.5
PacComm PC-320	TNC 2 +	TNC 2 +	powered by computer		4.1 x 10 x 0.6

† - CMOS/NMOS versions

	Computer Ports			Modems				Radio Ports	
Brand and Model	EIA-232-C/D	TTL	Other	VHF 1200 Baud	HF 300 Baud	Software Selectable	Quantity	Software Selectable	Simultaneously Active
GENERAL PURPOSE									
AEA PK-232	✓			✓	✓		2		
AEA PK-80	✓			✓			1		
AEA PK-87	✓			✓	✓		1		
AEA PK-88	✓			✓	✓		1		
AEA PKT-1	✓			✓			1		
Bill Ashby & Son PAC/NET System	✓								
California Packet Concepts TNC II	✓			✓			1		
GLB PK-1	✓			✓			1		
GLB PK-1L	✓			✓			1		
GLB TNC2-A	✓			✓			1		
Heath HD-4040	✓			✓	✓		1		
Heath HK-21	✓			✓			1		
Heath HK-232	✓			✓	✓		2		
Kantronics KAM	✓	✓		✓	✓		2		✓
Kantronics KPC-1	✓	✓		✓	✓	✓	1		
Kantronics KPC-1	✓	✓		✓	✓	✓	1		
Kantronics KPC-2	✓	✓		✓	✓	✓	1		
Kantronics KPC-2400	✓	✓		✓	✓	✓	1		
Kantronics KPC-4	✓	✓		✓			2		✓
Kantronics UTU-XT/P	✓	✓			✓		1		
MFJ MFJ-1270	✓	✓		✓			1		
MFJ MFJ-1270B	✓	✓		✓	✓		1		
MFJ MFJ-1274	✓	✓		✓	✓		1		
MFJ MFJ-1278	✓	✓		✓	✓	✓	2	✓	
PacComm Micropower2	✓	✓		✓			1		
PacComm Tiny-2	✓	✓		✓			1		
PacComm TNC-200	✓			✓	*		1		
PacComm TNC-220	✓	✓		✓	✓	✓	2	✓	
PacComm TNC-320	✓	*		✓	✓	✓	2	✓	✓
TAPR TNC 1	✓			✓			1		
TAPR TNC 1	✓			✓			1		
TAPR TNC 2	✓			✓			1		
COMPUTER-SPECIFIC									
AEA PK-64			✓	✓	*		1		
DRSI PC*PA Type 1			✓	✓	*		2		✓
DRSI PC*PA Type 2			✓	2			2		✓
DRSI PC*PA Type 3			✓		*		2		✓
HAPN HAPN-1			✓	✓			1		
PacComm PC-110			✓	✓	✓	✓	1		
PacComm PC-120			✓	2	✓	✓	2	✓	✓
PacComm PC-320	✓		✓	✓	✓	✓	2	✓	✓

✳ - optional

Brand and Model	Connection	Data Carrier Detect	Power	Receive Audio	Status	Transmitted Data	Transmitter On	Tuning Indicator	Other
GENERAL PURPOSE									
AEA PK-232		✓				✓	✓	✓	
AEA PK-80	✓	✓	✓		✓	✓			
AEA PK-87	✓	✓			✓	✓		✓	
AEA PK-88	✓	✓	✓		✓	✓		✓	
AEA PKT-1		✓		✓		✓	✓	✓	
Bill Ashby & Son PAC/NET System									
California Packet Concepts TNC II	✓	✓	✓		✓	✓			
GLB PK-1			✓						
GLB PK-1L									
GLB TNC2-A	✓	✓	✓		✓	✓			
Heath HD-4040		✓		✓		✓	✓		✓
Heath HK-21	✓	✓	✓		✓	✓			
Heath HK-232		✓				✓	✓	✓	
Kantronics KAM	✓			✓	✓	✓	✓		
Kantronics KPC-1			✓	✓		✓			
Kantronics KPC-1			✓	✓		✓			
Kantronics KPC-2	✓		✓	✓	✓	✓			
Kantronics KPC-2400	✓		✓	✓	✓	✓			
Kantronics KPC-4	✓		✓	✓		✓			
Kantronics UTU-XT/P	✓				✓		✓		
MFJ MFJ-1270	✓	✓	✓		✓	✓		*	
MFJ MFJ-1270B	✓	✓	✓		✓	✓			
MFJ MFJ-1274	✓	✓	✓		✓	✓	✓		
MFJ MFJ-1278	✓	✓	✓		✓	✓	✓		
PacComm Micropower2	✓	✓	✓		✓	✓			
PacComm Tiny-2	✓	✓	✓		✓	✓			
PacComm TNC-200	✓	✓	✓		✓	✓		*	
PacComm TNC-220	✓	✓	✓		✓	✓		*	
PacComm TNC-320	✓	✓		✓		✓	✓	✓	✓
TAPR TNC 1		✓		✓		✓	✓		✓
TAPR TNC 1		✓		✓		✓	✓		✓
TAPR TNC 2	✓	✓	✓		✓				
COMPUTER-SPECIFIC									
AEA PK-64		✓				✓	✓		
DRSI PC*PA Type 1									
DRSI PC*PA Type 2									
DRSI PC*PA Type 3									
HAPN HAPN-1									
PacComm PC-110									
PacComm PC-120									
PacComm PC-320	✓	✓	✓		✓	✓	✓	✓	✓

Front Panel Indicators

* - optional

Brand and Model	Gateway	Host Mode	KISS	Mailbox	Network Node	QST Review	Availability	Notes
GENERAL PURPOSE								
AEA PK-232	✓	✓				1/88	new	A B C D E F G H
AEA PK-80							used	
AEA PK-87	✓	✓					used	J
AEA PK-88	✓	✓	✓				new	J
AEA PKT-1						11/85	used	K
Bill Ashby & Son PAC/NET System							used	L
California Packet Concepts TNC II							used	M
GLB PK-1							used	N
GLB PK-1L							new	N
GLB TNC2-A							used	L O
Heath HD-4040						11/85	used	L P
Heath HK-21				✓			new	
Heath HK-232	✓	✓				1/88	new	A B C D E F G H L
Kantronics KAM	✓		✓	✓	✓	6/89	new	A B C D Q R
Kantronics KPC-1							used	N S
Kantronics KPC-1		✓	✓	✓			used	N T
Kantronics KPC-2		✓	✓	✓			new	
Kantronics KPC-2400		✓	✓	✓		11/87	new	U
Kantronics KPC-4	✓	✓	✓	✓			new	Q V W
Kantronics UTU-XT/P					✓		new	A B C D
MFJ MFJ-1270						9/86	used	
MFJ MFJ-1270B							new	
MFJ MFJ-1274							new	
MFJ MFJ-1278		✓	✓			7/89	new	A B C D E F X Y Z
PacComm Micropower2			✓				new	a b
PacComm Tiny-2			✳				new	
PacComm TNC-200			✳			6/87	new	M O
PacComm TNC-220			✳				new	M
PacComm TNC-320				✓			new	c d
TAPR TNC 1						11/85	used	L P e
TAPR TNC 1							used	L P f
TAPR TNC 2							used	L
COMPUTER-SPECIFIC								
AEA PK-64						6/86	used	A B C D g h
DRSI PC*PA Type 1	✓	✓	✓	✓			new	i j k m
DRSI PC*PA Type 2	✓	✓	✓	✓			new	i j k
DRSI PC*PA Type 3	✓	✓	✓	✓			new	i j k n
HAPN HAPN-1			✳				new	M h o p q r
PacComm PC-110							new	O h i
PacComm PC-120							new	O h i
PacComm PC-320				✓			new	c d s t u

✳ - optional

CHAPTER FIVE

Installation

An amateur packet-radio installation can be divided into three parts: the terminal equipment, the packet-radio equipment and the radio equipment.

The terminal equipment provides the direct interface to the user. The user types at the terminal keyboard and the terminal displays information for the user.

The packet-radio equipment provides the packet assembly and disassembly and *modulation* and *demodulation* functions. The packet-radio equipment may consist of a separate modem and a PAD, or it may be a TNC that includes both a PAD and a modem.

The radio equipment transmits and receives packets. It includes a transceiver (or separate transmitter and receiver), an antenna and any peripheral radio equipment (amplifier, preamplifier, tuner, feed line and so on).

This chapter describes these three basic components and how they are interconnected.

Terminal Equipment: The User Interface

In general, the terminal equipment that you will find in use at an amateur

Figure 5.1—The packet-radio installation at Amateur Radio station WA1LOU.

packet-radio station falls into one of two categories: dedicated terminals and computers that are emulating terminals.

Dedicated Terminal Equipment

Dedicated terminals, or simply *terminals* for short, are devices that are designed for the single purpose of communicating with computers. Terminals are available in a wide variety. Today, the most common terminal consists of some kind of video display, a keyboard and a serial interface (typically EIA RS-232-C/EIA-232-D compatible). This type of terminal is sometimes called a *video-display terminal* or *VDT*. The VDT may be a simple device that provides basic input and output functions (commonly called a *dumb terminal*), or it may provide numerous support functions as well as basic input and output (this device is commonly known as an *intelligent terminal*).

Some older terminals may use a printer instead of a video display for output, or they may use a paper-tape reader instead of a keyboard for input. Instead of an EIA-232 serial port, older terminals may use dc "loop" current for interfacing to external equipment. By their nature, the data rate of such devices is limited to slow or slower. High-speed line printers are still used today for hard-copy data output, but paper-tape reading equipment is considered obsolete.

Computers Emulating Terminals

Terminal-emulation software, which enables computers to emulate terminals, comes in a wide variety. Many computers have a number of communication programs available for them, with each program capable of emulating more than one type of terminal. With this combination of hardware and software, the variety seems infinite.

For packet-radio applications, communication software should, at a minimum, have a few simple commands for clearing the screen, moving the cursor, backspacing and tabbing. Such software should be capable of operating at a data rate that is compatible with the serial port of your packet-radio equipment. In addition, the software should be capable of saving received data in memory and/or in storage (on tape or disk). The software should also be capable of sending data that has been previously stored. Simultaneous hard-copy printing of what the terminal receives and sends is also a good feature.

The drawback with most communications software is that it is designed to operate primarily with telephone-line modems, not packet-radio modems (TNCs). As a result, these programs include features that are useful for telephone data communications, but which are useless to the packet-radio operator. Most of these programs also lack features that the packet-radio operator would find useful. All is not lost, however. Communications software designed specifically for packet-radio applications has been written for some of the more popular computers. The accompanying sidebar, "Packet-Radio Terminal-Emulation Software," lists what is available.

Packet-Radio Terminal-Emulation Software

There is a large variety of packet-radio communications software written for a number of popular personal computers. Here is a list of some of the software that is available.

Apple II

APR—An Apple II/II+/IIe/IIc/IIgs program for TNC 2s that is available by sending a blank 5.25- or 3.5-inch diskette and a postage-paid, self-addressed diskette mailer to Larry East, W1HUE, 119-7 Buckland St, Plantsville, CT 06479.

Comprehensive—An Apple II/II+/IIe program from W1EO, 39 Longridge Rd, Carlisle, MA 01741.

Apple Macintosh

Macket—Available from S. Fine Software, PO Box 6037, State College, PA 16801.

MacPacket—A program for TAPR TNCs (and clones) and Kantronics TNCs from Brincomm Technology, 3155 Resin St, Marietta, GA 30066.

MacRATT—A program for the AEA PK-232 TNC from Advanced Electronic Applications, Inc (AEA), PO Box C-2160, Lynnwood, WA 98036.

MacTTY—Available from Summit Concepts, Suite 102-190, 1840 41st Av, Capitola, CA 95010.

MFJ-1287—A program for the MFJ-1278 TNC from MFJ Enterprises, Inc, PO Box 494, Mississippi State, MS 39762.

Atari

Packet—A program for Atari 8-bit computers from Electrosoft, 1656 S California St, Loveland, CO 80537.

Commodore C-64/C-128

C64 Packet Talker—This unique "terminal emulator" for the C-64 converts all packet-radio messages to voice. It is available from Engineering Consulting, 583 Candlewood St, Brea, CA 92621.

Com Pakratt—A C-64 program for the AEA PK-232 TNC from Advanced Electronic Applications, Inc (AEA), PO Box C-2160, Lynnwood, WA 98036.

KANTERM 64/128—A C-64/C-128 program for Kantronics TNCs from Kantronics, 1202 E 23rd St, Lawrence, KS 66046.

MAXPAK-64—A C-64/C-128 program from PacComm Packet Radio Systems, 3652 West Cypress St, Tampa, FL 33607.

MFJ-1282—A C-64/C-128 program on disk for the MFJ-1278 TNC from MFJ Enterprises, Inc, PO Box 494, Mississippi State, MS 39762.

MFJ-1283—A C-64/C-128 program on tape for the MFJ-1278 TNC from MFJ Enterprises, Inc, PO Box 494, Mississippi State, MS 39762.

Pacterm—A C-64/C-128 program for Kantronics TNCs from Kantronics, 1202 E 23rd St, Lawrence, KS 66046.

TNC64—A C-64 program for the TNC 1 and 2 from the Texas Packet Radio Society, PO Box 831566, Richardson, TX 75083-1566.

TNCLINK-64/128—A C-64/C-128 program from Zeltwanger Electronics, PO Box 4995, Natick, MA 01760.

Commodore VIC-20

MFJ-1283—A program for the MFJ-1278 TNC from MFJ Enterprises Inc, PO Box 494, Mississippi State, MS 39762.

CP/M

CPK—A program to control the GLB PK-1 TNC from GLB Electronics, 151 Commerce Parkway, Buffalo, NY 14224.

IBM PC

Aries-1—An IBM PC/AT/XT and PS/2 program for the AEA PK-232 and Kantronics KAM TNCs from Ashton, PO Box 1067, Vestal, NY 13851.

arpTRM2—An IBM PC program for the AEA PK-232 TNC from Lloyd Computer Services, VE3BKB, 7 Westrose Ave, Toronto, ON M8X 1Z9, Canada.

CompRtty—An IBM PC program for the Heath HK-232 and AEA PK-232 TNCs from David A. Rice, KC2HO, 144 N Putt Corners Rd, New Paltz, NY 12561.

DIGIPAC I/DIGIPAC II—DIGIPAC I and II are programs written for IBM PCs and ATs. DIGIPAC-II is a combination of DIGIPAC I and MESSAGE-PAC, a program that allows the user to compose messages in the standard ARRL Radiogram format. They are available from Kalt & Associates, 2440 E Tudor Rd, Anchorage, AK 99507.

Ham-Com—An IBM PC program from PacComm Packet Radio Systems Inc, 3652 West Cypress St, Tampa, FL 33609.

Hamcom—An IBM PC program for the AEA PK-232 TNC from Dan Diehlman, AE6G, 5478 N Bond, Fresno, CA 93710.

Ham-Pak—An IBM PC program for the Heath HK-232 TNC from Heath Co, Benton Harbor, MI 49022.

KANTERM-PC—An IBM PC program for the Kantronics KAM and KPC-4 from Kantronics, 1202 E 23rd St, Lawrence, KS 66046.

LAN-LINK—An IBM PC program for the TNC 1, TNC 2, AEA PK-232 and Kantronics KAM TNCs from Joe Kasser, G3ZCZ, PO Box 3419, Silver Spring, MD 20901.

MFJ-1284—An IBM PC program for the MFJ-1278 TNC from MFJ Enterprises Inc, PO Box 494, Mississippi State, MS 39762.

Packet Terminal Program—An IBM PC program for the AEA PK-232, AEA PK-87 and Heath HK-232 TNCs. It may be downloaded from CompuServe's HamNet and is available from Lynn Taylor, WB6UUT, 463 Myrtle St, Laguna Beach, CA 92651.

PAC PRO—An IBM PC program for the TNC 1 and 2 from PacComm Packet Radio Systems Inc, 3652 West Cypress St, Tampa, FL 33609.

Pacterm—An IBM PC program for Kantronics TNCs from Kantronics, 1202 E 23rd St, Lawrence, KS 66046.

PAK-COMM—An IBM PC/AT/XT and PC jr program from Kalt & Associates, 2440 E Tudor Rd, Anchorage, AK 99507.

PC-PACKET—An IBM PC program for TNC 1, TNC 2 and GLB PK-1 TNCs from PacComm Packet Radio Systems, 3652 West Cypress St, Tampa, FL 33607.

PC-Pakratt—An IBM PC program for the AEA PK-232 from Advanced Electronic Applications, Inc (AEA), PO Box C-2160, Lynnwood, WA 98036.

PK232COM—An IBM PC program for the TNC 1, TNC 2 and AEA PK-232 TNC from Joe Kasser, G3ZCZ, PO Box 3419, Silver Spring, MD 20901.

RTP+—An IBM PC program from N4PY Software, Rte 3, Box 260, Franklinton, NC 27525.

WB8COX software—An IBM PC program for the TNC 1 and 2 running TAPR or WA8DED firmware. It is available by sending a blank, formatted diskette and a postage-paid, self-addressed diskette mailer to Tom Bray, WB8COX, 3373 E Fairfax Rd, Cleveland, OH 44118.

WD6FPY software—An IBM PC program for the TNC 1 and 2 running TAPR or WA8DED firmware. It may be downloaded from CompuServe's HamNet.

Yet Another Packet Program (*YAPP*)—An IBM PC program written by Jeff Jacobsen, WA7MBL. It may be downloaded from CompuServe's HamNet, and is also available for $1 from TAPR, Box 12925, Tucson, AZ 85732.

Tandy Color Computer

CocoPacket—Available from Brian Carling, 5131 Raywood Ln, Nashville, TN 37211.

CoCoPACT/CoCoPACT3—Available from Monty Haley, WJ5W, Rte 1, Box 210-B, Evening Shade, AR 72532.

Tandy TRS-80

Pacterm—A Model III/IV/4P program for Kantronics TNCs from Kantronics, 1202 E 23rd St, Lawrence, KS 66046.

Texas Instruments TI-99/4A

Mass Transfer—A general purpose terminal program on disk from Stuart Olson, 6625 W Coolidge St, Phoenix, AZ 85033.

Using a dedicated terminal or using a computer emulating a terminal both have advantages and disadvantages for packet-radio applications. Expense is always a consideration. On one hand, a good, used terminal may be less expensive than a new but barely adequate computer. On the other hand, a good, used computer may be less expensive than a new but barely adequate terminal.

The function of a terminal is to communicate. If you dedicate a terminal to packet-radio communications, it is doing the job it was intended to do. A computer can serve a variety of functions, however, and dedicating it to packet-radio applications may underutilize its abilities and be a waste of hardware and money.

Terminals are designed specifically for communications, while computers are not. This means that computers are not necessarily good communications tools. How good a communications tool a computer is depends on its communications software. One great advantage computers have over terminals is their ability to store data in memory and/or in a storage medium (on tape or disk). Most terminals have no means of storing data.

All of these considerations must be weighed when you decide what to use to communicate with your packet-radio equipment.

Packet-Radio Equipment: PADs, Modems and TNCs

PADs, modems, and TNCs were discussed in Chapters 3 and 4. A quick review of this equipment is in order. What follows is a breakdown of the major hardware differences between this equipment.

1) There are PADs, also known as TNCs, that require external modems. (A PAD never includes a built-in modem, but a TNC may or may not include a built-in modem.)

2) There are TNCs that include modems designed for VHF applications (1200 bauds, Bell-202 compatible). Most TNCs today are of this type.

3) There are TNCs that include modems that may be selected for 1200-baud VHF and 300-baud HF applications.

4) There are TNCs that include separate modems for VHF and HF applications. Separate VHF and HF radio ports permit the simultaneous connection of VHF and HF radio equipment.

   a) There are TNCs in this category that permit simultaneous VHF and HF packet-radio communications.

   b) There are TNCs in this category that permit gateway operation between the radio ports.

5) There are TNCs that include modems that operate at data rates other than 300 and 1200 bauds.

6) There are TNCs that are designed to be used only with specific computers.

7) There are TNCs that operate in other Amateur Radio modes.

8) There are TNCs that include more than one of these listed features.

In addition, there are external HF modems available that may be added to those TNCs that do not include HF capabilities, or to TNCs that include HF capabilities that are barely adequate. Typically, such external modems have filters for improved HF reception and front-panel displays to facilitate HF signal tuning. A switch permits bypassing the HF modem to permit you to use your TNC with its built-in modem without changing cables.

Three commercially available HF modems are the AEA PM-1, DRSI HF*Modem and the Pac-Comm PTU-200. In addition, AEA had an HF modem (the HFM-64) for its PK-64 TNC and Heath had one (the HD-4040-2) for its HD-4040 TNC.

RF Equipment: The Radio Connection

At the RF end of a packet-radio station is a lot of equipment. Some of this equipment is of little concern to us. For example, as long as the antennas and feed line are capable of putting a signal on the desired packet-radio frequency, that satisfies our requirements. Other RF hardware needs closer inspection, however.

Our primary concern is the radio equipment's receive-to-transmit and transmit-to-receive *turnaround times*. This is the amount of time that it takes for a transmitter to be ready to transmit and a receiver to be ready to receive after a switch between the transmit and receive modes occurs. A TNC can switch between the transmit and receive modes very quickly, so quickly that it usually must wait for the RF equipment before it can continue to communicate. According to Tucson Amateur Packet Radio (TAPR), most amateur radios have receive-to-transmit and transmit-to-receive turnaround times between 150 and 400 milliseconds (ms), which dramatically reduces the amount of data that can be sent and increases the chance that two or more stations will interfere with one another. Such delays slow down what is intended to be a fast mode of communications.

A number of factors affect the length of this delay. The actual physical switching of an antenna, internally in a transceiver or externally with a separate transmitter and receiver, affects the turnaround time. The older the transceiver, the more likely that the switching is performed mechanically by some kind of relay. If a separate transmitter and receiver are used with one antenna, there is also likely to be a mechanical relay performing the switch. In addition, if an external power amplifier and/or receive preamplifier is used, more mechanical switching is likely to be involved.

With newer equipment, the switching is more likely to be accomplished electronically. This speeds up the process, but this improvement may be compromised by the frequency synthesizer circuitry that is used by the newer RF equipment. After switching between the transmit and receive modes, all synthesizers require some time to lock on frequency before they are ready to transmit or receive. Older RF equipment does not use frequency synthesis and does not have this delay. Some new equipment is being designed with packet radio in mind and synthesizers that can lock more quickly are now being offered. If you are out hunting for a new transceiver for packet-radio applications, keep this feature in mind.

Another problem cited by TAPR is that the modem-to-radio interface of most of the radios used for packet radio depends on audio response filters and audio levels intended for microphones and speakers. More often than not, this leads to incorrect deviation of the transmitted signal, noise and hum on the audio, etc. Splatter filters and deviation limiters distort frequency response and further reduce the performance of the packet-radio system. You are stuck in this environment unless you want to modify the radio. The problem is that trying to perform surgery on your typical VHF/UHF FM voice transceiver is difficult to impossible because of the use of LSI, surface mounting and miniaturization.

Instead of using an average Amateur Radio for packet radio (and the compromises this involves), there are alternatives that solve many of the RF equipment problems that have been discussed. The solution comes in the guise of high-speed RF equipment that is optimized for packet-radio operation. Descriptions of four variations of the solution follow.

AEA RFM-220 Radio Modem

The RFM-220 is a 1- to 25-W, 220-MHz RF modem that is connected to a TNC to provide data rates of up to 19,200 bauds using FSK and 300 to 1200 bauds using *audio-frequency-shift keying* (*AFSK*). The CPU-controlled synthesizer provides 100 memory channels with memory-storage and band-scanning functions. The transmit and receive turnaround times are 5 ms and the receiver's front end includes a GaAsFET and multiple helical resonators. Besides packet radio, the RFM-220 will also operate in the FM voice mode.

GLB Netlink 220 Data Transceiver

The Netlink 220 is a high-speed (up to 19,200 bauds) 220-MHz data transceiver that is compatible with the TNC 2. It features transmit and receive turnaround times of 1 ms and an FSK modem that uses a 25-kHz bandwidth at 19,200 bauds. This crystal-controlled transceiver has an output of 2 W. A frequency-tracking system is used to keep the received signal precisely centered in the receiver passband—the frequency last received is "remembered" between packets in order to avoid the need to acquire and center an off-frequency signal at the start of every received transmission.

PacComm NB-96 Integrated Packet Radio

The heart of The PacComm Narrowband 9600-Baud Packet Radio System, or The NB-96 Series for short, is PacComm's commercial 9600-baud modem design, which is licensed from James Miller, G3RUH. The modem features digital generation of the transmit audio waveform, with precise shaping that compensates exactly for the amplitude and phase response of the receiver. This results in a "matched filter" system; that is, the received audio offered to the data detector has the optimum characteristic for minimum errors. It also allows very tight control of the transmit audio bandwidth. This modem will provide 9600-baud packet-radio operation on 2 meters, as well as other VHF and UHF bands. The modem is included in a digital transceiver that consists of a commercial grade, 2- to 5-W RF deck and, optionally, a TNC. It is available for 144, 220, 440 and 920 MHz.

TAPR packetRADIO

At the time of this writing, TAPR is beta-testing their packetRADIO, a 25-W, 5-channel, crystal-controlled digital radio that will operate at 1200 bauds using AFSK and 9600 bauds using FSK on 2 meters. TAPR's packetRADIO switches between the transmit and receive modes in less than 1 ms and is capable of full-duplex operation with an optional second local-oscillator board. It will be available with or without an internal TNC.

Physical Connection: All Together Now

The actual physical installation of a packet-radio station is straightforward. Basically, you connect your TNC to the terminal equipment and to the RF equipment (refer to Figure 5.2 for a typical installation).

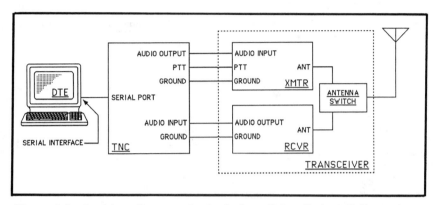

Figure 5.2—A wiring diagram of a typical packet-radio installation.

TNC-to-Terminal Connection

Most TNCs are designed to be connected to terminal equipment by means of a serial port that is compatible with EIA standards RS-232-C or EIA-232-D. In most cases, the omnipresent 25-pin subminiature D-type connector provides the actual physical connection to the TNC. If your terminal or computer also has an EIA-compatible interface, the connection is accomplished by means of a 25-wire cable with the appropriate 25-pin connectors at each end. Appropriate, in this case, refers to connector gender. According to industry standards, a DTE has a male connector on its serial port while a DCE has a female connector. The DTE in this case is your terminal or computer and the DCE is your TNC. This means that the appropriate 25-wire cable would have a male 25-pin connector at the TNC end and a female 25-pin connector at the terminal end. This standard is not always adhered to, however.

Cables containing 25 wires are expensive. As the sidebar "EIA RS-232-C/EIA-232-D" indicates, all 25 pins of the interface are not used by your TNC. Interconnections between pins 2, 3, 4, 5, 6, 7, 8 and 20 will be adequate for almost all applications, including telephone-line data communications. An 8-wire cable is certainly less expensive than a 25-wire cable.

Some computers do not have an EIA-compatible serial port; this makes connection to a TNC more difficult. Some TNCs can now be connected to computers in other ways. For example, TTL interface connections are now possible with some of the latest generation of TNCs. This makes it possible to connect a TNC directly to such computers as the popular Commodore line without adding an EIA interface to the computer. Also, some TNCs are contained on cards that may be installed inside a computer, such as IBM PC and compatible computers.

If your computer does not have either a TTL or an EIA interface, you will have to add one. EIA interfaces are often available as optional equipment or from third-party sources.

EIA RS-232-C/EIA-232-D

RS-232-C/EIA-232-D is a standard recommended by the EIA (Electronic Industries Association) for the interface between data terminal equipment (DTE) and data communication equipment (DCE) employing serial binary data interchange. RS-232-C was published in August 1969 and EIA-232-D was published in January 1987. EIA-232-D is a revision of RS-232-C to make it more compatible with international standards CCITT V.24 and V.28 and ISO IS2110. This standard is the first level, the Physical layer, of the ISO Open Systems Interconnection Model described in Chapter 3.

In the following table, the bracketed information indicates EIA RS-232-C items that have been revised by EIA-232-D.

Pin Number	Designation EIA	CCITT	Signal Name
1	[AA]	[101]	[Protective Ground]
	—	—	Shield
2	BA	103	Transmitted Data
3	BB	104	Received Data
4	CA	105	Request to Send
5	CB	106	Clear to Send
6	CC	107	[Data Set Ready] DCE Ready
7	AB	102	Signal Ground
8	CF	109	Received Line Signal Detector
9	—	—	Reserved for DCE testing
10	—	—	Reserved for DCE testing
11	—	—	Unassigned
12	SCF	122	Secondary Received Line Signal Detector
13	SCB	121	Secondary Clear to Send
14	SBA	118	Secondary Transmitted Data
15	DB	114	Transmitter Signal Element Timing (DCE Source)
16	SBB	119	Secondary Received Data
17	DD	115	Receiver Signal Element Timing
18	[—]	[—]	[Unassigned]
	LL	141	Local Loopback

19	SCA	120	Secondary Request to Send
20	CD	108.2	[Data Terminal Ready] DTE Ready
21	[CG]	[110]	[Signal Quality Detector]
	CG/RL	110/140	Signal Quality Detector/Remote Loopback
22	CE	125	Ring Detector
23	CH/CI	111/112	Data Signal Rate Selector (DTE/DCE Source)
24	DA	113	Transmitter Signal Element Timing (DTE Source)
25	[—]	[—]	[Unassigned]
	TM	142	Test Mode

A description of the EIA RS-232-C/EIA-232-D signals that are of most concern in a packet-radio installation follows:

Transmitted Data, pin 2, is intelligence from the DTE that is intended for transmission by the DCE (TNC) over the communication medium (RF).

Received Data, pin 3, is intelligence from the DCE (TNC) that was received over the communication medium (RF) and demodulated by the DCE (TNC).

Request To Send, pin 4, informs the DCE (TNC) that the DTE has data for transmission in order to prepare the DCE (TNC) to receive that data.

Clear To Send, pin 5, informs the DTE that the DCE (TNC) is ready to receive data. This signal is sent in response to the DTE's Request To Send.

DCE Ready, pin 6, formerly called Data Set Ready, informs the DTE that the DCE (TNC) is prepared for data communications.

Signal Ground, pin 7, provides a common ground reference for all the other interface signals except Shield, pin 1.

Received Line Signal Detector, pin 8, commonly called *Data Carrier Detect* or just *Carrier Detect*, informs the DTE that the DCE (TNC) is receiving a "suitable" carrier over the communication medium (RF).

DTE Ready, pin 20, formerly called Data Terminal Ready, informs the DCE (TNC) that the DTE is prepared for data communications.

These signals interact or handshake with each other to control the flow of data. The handshaking protocol used by a TNC 2 consists of the following parts.

1) When the TNC (DCE) is turned on it sends DCE READY to the DTE.

2) When the DTE is ready to receive data, it sends DTE READY to the TNC (DCE). This causes the TNC to send RECEIVED DATA to the DTE if there is any data to send.

3) When the TNC (DCE) is ready to receive data from the DTE, it sends CLEAR TO SEND to the DTE. This causes the DTE to send TRANSMITTED DATA to the TNC (DCE) if there is any data to send.

In most cases, the connection of a TNC to RF equipment is a matter of making a few simple connections.

The audio output of the TNC is connected to the audio input of your transmitter/transceiver. Typically, the audio input of your radio equipment is a microphone connector, but some transceivers have separate audio inputs for AFSK tones. If such a connection is available, it's better to use that connection rather than the microphone input, because it means you will not have to disconnect the packet-radio equipment when you want to use the radio in the voice mode. In addition, the transmitter/transceiver may have circuitry that processes the AFSK input signals in some way, and such processing would probably be beneficial to your packet-radio signal as well.

The push-to-talk (PTT) line from your TNC is connected to a PTT connection on your transmitter/transceiver. Usually, PTT is available at the radio's microphone connector, but the PTT line is sometimes brought out to another jack as well. Again, connection to the optional PTT jack is preferable; this avoids cable changes when you switch modes.

The audio output of your receiver/transceiver is connected to the audio input of your TNC. Typically, the audio output of your radio is a speaker or headphone connector, but some radios have optional audio outputs (sometimes labeled "AFSK out"). Again, connection to such an optional audio output avoids cable changes, and the receiver/transceiver may provide some filtering or processing of the AFSK output signals. If your rig does not have separate AFSK jacks, the phone patch input and output jacks often provide an acceptable alternative.

In addition to these three connections, there must be a ground connection between your TNC and the transceiver (or transmitter and receiver).

Some transmitters/transceivers, typically VHF and UHF hand-held transceivers, use a common conductor for audio input and PTT. Simply connecting the TNC's audio output and PTT leads to the common conductor on the radio will not work. To make the connection successfully, a capacitor and resistor are required, as shown in the wiring diagram provided in Figure 5.3.

To prevent RFI, all cables should be shielded. If shielding does not prevent RFI, the cables from the TNC to the radio should be wound around a toroid. If RFI is still a problem, wind the cabling between the TNC and the terminal, and all ac line cables, around toroids, too.

While we are on the topic of interference, we should mention that there is a problem with the design of the TAPR TNC 2 that causes the TNC's clock to place a *birdie* around 145.0 MHz. If the birdie is interfering with your packet-radio reception, you can make it migrate by replacing C47 with a 60-pF trimmer capacitor (on early versions of the TNC 2; later versions already have the trimmer capacitor installed). Tune the capacitor slightly to pull the

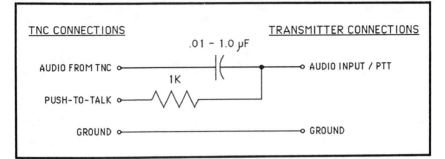

Figure 5.3—The TNC-to-transmitter wiring diagram for transmitters that use a common conductor for the PTT and audio input connection.

birdie off your favorite 2-meter packet-radio channel. (C47 is located next to the crystal, Y1, near the center of the TNC printed-circuit board.)

Does It Work?

One of the best ways to find out if your installation works is to give it a test under fire. FCC regulations permit Amateur Radio operators to test their equipment on the air. Try connecting to yourself through a local digipeater and sending some test data ("the quick brown fox" works just as well on packet radio as it does on RTTY). If you are able to connect with yourself and successfully receive the test data, your installation is working. If you don't know how to connect with yourself, read Chapters Six and Seven to learn how to configure and operate your TNC.

CHAPTER SIX

Selecting TNC Parameters

Y
ou have connected a TNC to a terminal and transceiver and are
anxious to let your first packet fly through the air. Before that happens, you have to make sure that your TNC is compatible with your
terminal and transceiver.

Whether your terminal is compatible or not depends on the hardware and
software. There is not much you can do about the hardware (besides getting
another terminal). If the terminal is actually a computer running terminal-
emulation software, then the compatibility depends on the flexibility of that
software. (The computer [or terminal] must also provide an I/O port which
is compatible with the TNC, as discussed in Chapter 5. If it does not, you
may be able to buy or build an interface to provide the proper signals for
each device.) If the software is not adequate, you can try a different program.

The transceiver is less flexible. If your transceiver is not suitable, you
will probably have to get a different transceiver (unless you are adept at
modifying LSI and microprocessor circuits).

Luckily, the TNC is very flexible. It may be adapted for use with almost
any terminal and transceiver that can be connected to it. What follows is
a checklist of parameters that you may set to make your TNC compatible
with your terminal and transceiver.

Data Rate

Data rate is the speed at which information is transferred. This speed
may be measured in bits per second or bauds. In most applications, a baud
is equal to one digital bit of information per second. As a result, the terms
data rate, *baud rate* and *bit rate* are used interchangeably (refer to the sidebar "Baud Rate vs Bits Per Second"). The TNC communicates with a terminal by means of its serial port (usually a female 25-pin "D-type" connector)
and with a transceiver by means of its radio port (usually a female 5-pin DIN
connector). A port is a circuit that allows a device to communicate with external equipment. A serial port transfers digital information bit-by-bit (serially), as opposed to transferring information character-by-character or
byte-by-byte (the bits composing each character are transferred in parallel).
The data rate of the radio port is independent of the serial-port data rate.
The rates are selected either by hardware or software. The radio-port data

Baud Rate vs Bits Per Second

There seems to be some confusion among radio amateurs as to the meaning of the terms "bauds" and "bits per second" as used to describe data-transmission rates. The two terms are *not* interchangeable. The term bauds is used to describe the *signaling* (or *symbol*) *rate*. This is a measure of how fast individual signal elements *could be* transmitted through a communications system. Specifically, the baud is defined as the reciprocal of the shortest element (in seconds) in the data-encoding scheme. For example, in a system where the shortest element is 1 ms long, the signaling rate would be 1000 elements per second. Instead of using "elements per second," the term "baud" is used. (Incidentally, this is why it is not actually correct to refer to the "baud rate;" since baud already means elements per second, "baud rate" means "elements per second rate," something like "miles per hour speed.") Continuous transmission is not required, since signaling speed is based only on the shortest signal element.

Signaling rate in bauds says nothing about actual *information transfer rate*. The maximum information transfer rate is defined as the number of equivalent binary digits transferred per second; this is measured in *bits per second*.

So far, everything seems fairly simple. The complications arise when more sophisticated data-encoding schemes are used. When binary data encoding is used, each signaling element represents one bit. In a quadriphase system, a phase transition of 90 degrees represents a level shift. There are four possible states in a QPSK system; since two binary bits are required to represent four possible levels, each state can represent two binary bits. If 1000 elements per second are transmitted in a quadriphase system where each element can represent two bits, the actual information rate is 2000 bit/s.

This scheme can be extended. It is possible to transmit three bits at a time using eight different phase angles (bit/s = 3 × bauds). In addition, each angle can have more than one amplitude. A standard 9600-bit/s modem uses 12 phase angles, four of which have two amplitude values. This yields 16 distinct states; each state can then represent four binary bits. Using this technique, the information transfer rate is four times the signaling speed. This is what makes it possible to transfer data over a phone line at a rate that would produce an unacceptable bandwidth using binary encoding. This also makes it possible to transfer data at 2400 bit/s on 10 meters, where FCC regulations allow only 1200-*baud* signals.

When are transmission speed in bauds and information rate in bit/s equal? Three conditions must be met: binary encoding must be used, all elements used to encode characters must be equal in width and synchronous transmission at a constant rate must be used. In all other cases, the two terms are not equivalent. Each term is important at a different location in a communications link. Information transfer rate is most important to the communicator; how the information gets where it is going makes no difference. The link designer, however, need only worry about the signaling rate; the number of "bits per baud" is unimportant at this level.—*Bruce Hale, KB1MW*

rate determines how fast you communicate with other packet-radio stations over the air. The terminal-port data rate determines how fast your TNC communicates with your terminal.

Serial-Port Speed

The data rate of the TNC's serial port and the data rate of the terminal connected to the TNC must be the same. If the terminal has selectable data rates, you should set the terminal (and the TNC's serial port) to the highest data rate that allows successful communication between the terminal and the TNC. A data rate of 2400 or 4800 bauds is acceptable. When you send a command to the TNC at these data rates, you will see the responses instantly, and messages received over the air will be printed almost the instant they are received by the TNC. (Higher data rates provide even quicker communication. Some TNCs do not operate reliably at these rates, however, so you will need to experiment to see if the TNC can handle it.)

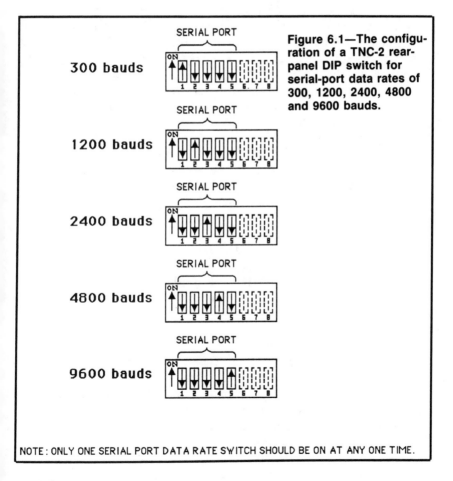

300 bauds — SERIAL PORT

1200 bauds — SERIAL PORT

2400 bauds — SERIAL PORT

4800 bauds — SERIAL PORT

9600 bauds — SERIAL PORT

Figure 6.1—The configuration of a TNC-2 rear-panel DIP switch for serial-port data rates of 300, 1200, 2400, 4800 and 9600 bauds.

NOTE: ONLY ONE SERIAL PORT DATA RATE SWITCH SHOULD BE ON AT ANY ONE TIME.

The serial port of a TNC 2 may be set to data rates of 300, 1200, 2400, 4800 and 9600 bauds. Figure 6.1 shows how to position the TNC's rear-panel DIP switch for each of these data rates. Make sure that the TNC is turned off when you select the serial-port data rate.

A TNC 1 may be set to serial-port data rates of 50, 75, 110, 135, 150, 300, 600, 1200, 1800, 2400, 3600, 4800, 7200, 9600 and 19200 bauds. To select the desired serial-port data rate, at the command prompt type:

cmd: Abaud n <CR>

where n is the desired serial-port data rate and <CR> is a *carriage return*. This same command is used to select the serial-port data rate in certain TNC-2 work-alikes, but their data rate selection is limited to those available to the TNC 2 (300, 1200, 2400, 4800 and 9600 bauds).

Radio-Port Speed

The data rate of the TNC's radio port is the rate used to transfer packets over the air. Below 28 MHz, 300 bauds is used exclusively (300 bauds is also the legal limit below 28 MHz). Above 28 MHz, 1200 bauds is generally used. Speeds above 1200 bauds are permitted in the VHF and UHF spectrum, and some packet-radio communication does occur at 4800 and 9600 bauds. Unfortunately, the modems built into most TNCs are designed for 1200 bauds. Different modulation standards are used at different data rates, so operation at higher speeds requires modification of the internal modem or the addition of an external modem.

The radio port of a TNC 2 may be set to 300, 1200 or 9600 bauds. Figure 6.2 illustrates the position of the TNC's DIP switch for each of the three data rates. You may change the radio-port data rate with the TNC turned on.

To select the radio-port data rate of a TNC 1 and certain TNC-2 work-alikes, at the command prompt type:

cmd: Hbaud n <CR>

where n is the desired radio-port data rate.

Remember that you must not set the radio-port data rate to anything other than 1200 bauds unless the TNC's internal modem is designed for other data rates or you are using an external modem designed for a different data rate.

Turning on the TNC

The remainder of the TNC parameters are selected by using the TNC's built-in commands. To access those commands, you must turn on the TNC.

When you press the TNC's pushbutton power switch, a sign-on message similar to the display shown in Figure 6.3 should appear on your terminal. The message includes some or all of the following items:

1) the manufacturer and model of the TNC

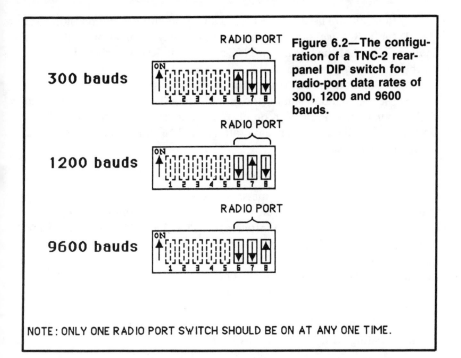

Figure 6.2—The configuration of a TNC-2 rear-panel DIP switch for radio-port data rates of 300, 1200 and 9600 bauds.

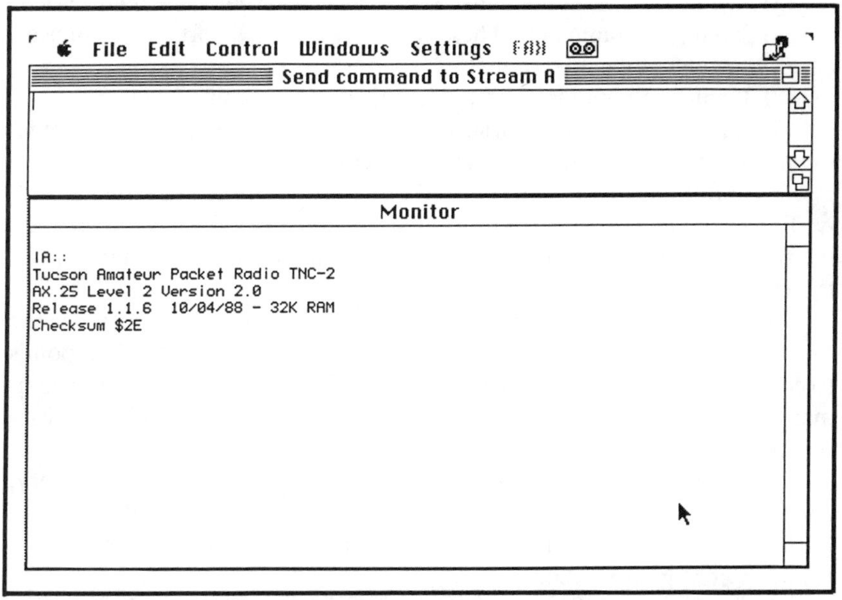

NOTE: ONLY ONE RADIO PORT SWITCH SHOULD BE ON AT ANY ONE TIME.

Figure 6.3—A typical TNC sign-on message, as displayed on a terminal, indicates that the TNC is functioning and is interfaced properly with its associated terminal.

2) the software used by the TNC, its version number and revision level

3) the TNC *checksum* (the checksum, or check summation, is the sum, in *hexadecimal* of the bits in the TNC software in ROM; it should be equal to the checksum published in the TNC manual)

4) the amount of RAM installed in the TNC

5) the command prompt (**cmd:**), indicating that the TNC is waiting to fulfill your wishes. If the sign-on message is unreadable, turn off the TNC and check that the serial-port data rate of the TNC and the data rate of the terminal are the same.

Commanding the TNC

After the TNC's sign-on message is displayed, the TNC should be in the command mode, as indicated by the command prompt (**cmd:**).

As of Version 1.1.6 of the software, the TNC 2 has 120 commands. These commands may be divided into seven categories:

1) Character commands. These select the special alphanumeric characters used by the TNC for various functions.

2) Identification commands. These determine how a packet-radio station is identified.

3) Link commands. These relate to functions and parameters used for communicating with other stations over the air.

4) Monitor commands. These relate to monitoring packet-radio activity and the status of the TNC.

5) Reinitialization commands. These cause the TNC to be reinitialized.

6) Serial-port commands. These configure the TNC port that is connected to your computer or terminal.

7) Timing commands. These select the TNC's timing parameters.

Within these seven categories, there are two types of TNC commands: *immediate commands* and *configuration commands*.

An immediate command causes the TNC to perform a task immediately. For example, the "CONNECT" command causes the TNC to initiate the transmission of a connect request to another station immediately after the command is invoked.

A configuration command sets a TNC parameter. For example, the "CONOK" (Connect Okay) command determines how the TNC responds to connect requests from other stations. If CONOK is enabled (by the command CONOK ON), the TNC accepts connect requests. If CONOK is disabled (CONOK OFF), the TNC rejects connect requests.

Appendix A lists all of the TNC-1 and TNC-2 commands by category, and includes a brief description of the function of each command. The table in the Appendix shows the default selection and the selectable parameters for each configuration command.

The default selection of each configuration parameter is the selection that is programmed in the TNC's permanent memory (ROM). When a TNC is turned on for the first time, or whenever the RESET command is invoked, all of the configuration parameters are set to these default selections.

Each configuration parameter may be set to a user-selected value. Whenever the user changes the value of any parameter (by invoking a configuration command), the new selection is stored in the TNC's temporary memory (RAM). When a TNC 2 is turned off, the RAM retains the user's settings by means of a built-in battery. A TNC 1 uses nonvolatile RAM, a hybrid combination of ROM and PROM, to store parameters. When the TNC is turned on again, the configuration selections are restored to the user-selected values.

Entering commands is a simple matter of typing the command at the command prompt. If you are entering a configuration command, you must type a parameter after the name of the command. The command is interpreted by the TNC when you type a carriage return <CR>. Note that commands may only be entered when the command prompt (**cmd:**) is displayed by your computer or terminal. For example, to command the TNC to disconnect from a connected station, you would type DISCONNE and a carriage return at the command prompt. This operation is represented as:

cmd: DISCONNE <CR>

Another example: To configure the TNC 2 to send the bell control character <BELL> whenever a connection is established, at the command prompt you type CBELL, followed by the parameter ON and a carriage return. This operation is represented as:

cmd: CBELL ON <CR>

To save some time entering commands, most of the commands may be entered using a shortened name. For example, instead of typing DISCONNE for the disconnect command, you can simply type the letter D. Similarly, instead of entering CBELL ON to enable the connection bell control character, you can type CB ON and save a few keystrokes. Note that the parameter selection OFF may be shortened to OF with a TNC 2 or to the letter O with a TNC 1. The parameter selection ON is always spelled out completely, however.

Throughout this book, each command will appear partially in upper-case characters and partially in lower-case characters. The uppercase portion will represent the shortened version of the command and the upper- and lower-case portions together will represent the long version of the command. For example, the disconnect command will be represented as:

cmd: Disconne <CR>

where D is the shortened version of the command and DISCONNE is the long version.

Enabling the connection bell control character would be represented as:

cmd: CBell ON <CR>

where CB is the shortened version of the command and CBELL is the long version.

Note that if the command appears completely in uppercase characters, there is no shortened version of that command. While we are on the subject of upper- and lower-case characters, note that the TNC does not care which case you use to *enter* a command; upper- or lower-case characters are acceptable.

Now that you know how to command the TNC, let's set up the TNC to suit the needs of your station equipment.

Fine Tuning the Serial Port

You communicate with the TNC through a terminal (or through a computer that emulates a terminal by running data communications software). For this discussion, both terminals and computers running terminal-emulation software will be identified as *terminals*. Once the correct serial-port speed is selected, the TNC is often compatible with the terminal without requiring any other changes. Some terminals and some applications, however, have special requirements that may be addressed using the TNC's configuration commands. The following parameters are the most critical for proper terminal-to-TNC interfacing.

Echo

The *echo* function echoes keystrokes. When you type a character on the terminal keyboard, the TNC sends the same character back to be printed on the terminal's display so that you can see what you have typed. The echo function is enabled by default in the TNC, based on the assumption that the terminal does not echo characters. If the terminal also provides the echo function, each character that is typed on the terminal's keyboard will be printed twice on the display, because both the terminal and the TNC are echoing the character. For example, if you type HI OM and the terminal prints HHII OOMM, duplicate character echoing is occurring (see Figure 6.4). If this is the case, the echo function of either the TNC or terminal should be disabled.

To disable the TNC's echo function, at the command prompt type:

cmd: Echo OFF <CR>

If you need to enable the TNC's echo function later, at the command prompt type:

cmd: Echo ON <CR>

Automatic Line Feed

The *automatic line feed* function causes the TNC to send a *line feed*

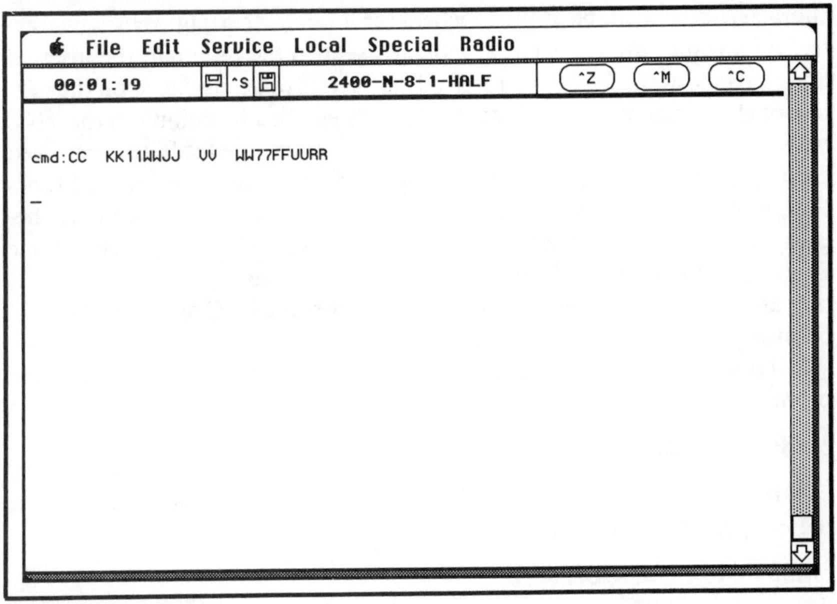

```
  File   Edit   Service   Local   Special   Radio

  00:01:19      |▣| ^S |▣|       2400-N-8-1-HALF       ( ^Z ) ( ^M ) ( ^C )


cmd:CC  KK11WWJJ  UU  WW77FFUURR

_
```

Figure 6.4—Double display of characters indicates that both the TNC and terminal are providing the echo function.

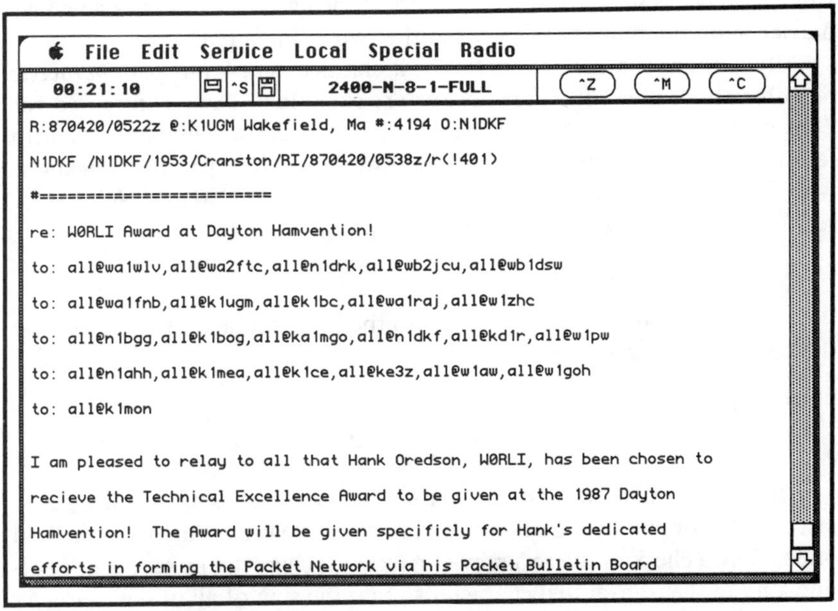

```
  File   Edit   Service   Local   Special   Radio

  00:21:10      |▣| ^S |▣|       2400-N-8-1-FULL       ( ^Z ) ( ^M ) ( ^C )

R:870420/0522z @:K1UGM Wakefield, Ma #:4194 O:N1DKF

N1DKF /N1DKF/1953/Cranston/RI/870420/0538z/r(!401)

#=========================

re: W0RLI Award at Dayton Hamvention!

to: all@wa1wlv,all@wa2ftc,all@n1drk,all@wb2jcu,all@wb1dsw

to: all@wa1fnb,all@k1ugm,all@k1bc,all@wa1raj,all@w1zhc

to: all@n1bgg,all@k1bog,all@ka1mgo,all@n1dkf,all@kd1r,all@w1pw

to: all@n1ahh,all@k1mea,all@k1ce,all@ke3z,all@w1aw,all@w1goh

to: all@k1mon


I am pleased to relay to all that Hank Oredson, W0RLI, has been chosen to

recieve the Technical Excellence Award to be given at the 1987 Dayton

Hamvention!  The Award will be given specificly for Hank's dedicated

efforts in forming the Packet Network via his Packet Bulletin Board
```

Figure 6.5—A blank line between each displayed line of characters indicates that both the TNC and the terminal are providing the automatic line feed function.

character <LF> to the terminal whenever it sends a carriage return character. As a result, after a carriage return is sent to the terminal, the inserted line feed causes the following received characters to be displayed on the next line of the terminal display. This function is enabled by default in the TNC because many terminals do not automatically insert line feeds after received carriage returns. If your terminal does provide the automatic line feed function, a blank line will be displayed between each line of displayed data, because the terminal is receiving two line feeds after each carriage return: one from the TNC and one from the terminal itself (see Figure 6.5). If this is the case, the automatic line feed function of either the TNC or terminal should be disabled.

To disable the TNC's automatic line feed function, at the command prompt type:

cmd: AUtolf OFF <CR>

If you need to enable the TNC's automatic line feed function later, at the command prompt type:

cmd: AUtolf ON <CR>

Character Length

The TNC and the terminal must "speak the same language" for successful communication. If the terminal is sending 8-bit characters to the TNC while the TNC is sending 7-bit characters to the terminal, there is a language barrier and communication between the two is impaired.

By default, the TNC is set for 7-bit characters or 7 *bits per character*; most terminals use 7-bit characters or are capable of being configured for 7-bit characters. This TNC setting may be changed for compatibility with terminals that use 8-bit characters exclusively, or for special applications where transferring the character's eighth bit is required. The TNC may be set for 8-bit characters at the command prompt by typing:

cmd: AWlen 8 <CR>

If you need to set the TNC back to the 7-bit character length later, at the command prompt type

cmd: AWlen 7 <CR>

Parity

In a similar vein, the TNC and the terminal must be using the same *parity* method, or communication between the two is impaired. Parity is a method of enabling a check of the accuracy of a received character by setting or resetting a bit in the transmitted character so that the sum of all of the *character bits* is even or odd, depending on the type of parity in use. By default, the TNC is set for even parity, because that's what most terminals use. If odd parity or no parity is required by your terminal or by some special application, a TNC 2 may be reconfigured at the command prompt by typing:

cmd: PARity 1 <CR>

for odd parity, and

cmd: PARity 0 <CR>

or

cmd: PARity 2 <CR>

for no parity.

To reselect even parity later (for example, to connect the TNC to a terminal that uses even parity exclusively), at the command prompt type:

cmd: PARity 3 <CR>

A TNC 1 uses a different numbering scheme for the PARity command: 0 equals odd parity, 1 equals even parity, 2 equals mark parity, 3 equals space parity, and 4 equals no parity.

Screen Width

For the most intelligible terminal display, the TNC should be set for the maximum number of columns or characters that can be displayed by the terminal on each line. Since many terminals are capable of displaying 80 columns per line, the TNC is set for 80 columns per line by default. Each time the TNC sends 80 characters to the terminal, it then sends control characters that cause the terminal to begin displaying new characters received from the TNC on the next line. Most terminals require a carriage return/line feed sequence (<CR> <LF>).

If the terminal displays more or fewer than 80 columns per line, this TNC parameter may be changed at the command prompt by typing:

cmd: ScreenIn n <CR>

where n is a number from 0 to 255 equal to the maximum number of columns or characters displayed per line by the terminal. For a TNC 1, the name of the command is shortened to ScreenI.

Other Serial Port Parameters

The echo and automatic line feed functions, screen length, character bit length and parity are the most critical parameters that need to be selected to make the TNC compatible with a terminal. Setting these parameters correctly should make the majority of terminals work correctly with your TNC. There are still other parameters that may be selected for special applications or for terminals that require more grooming.

8bitconv is a TNC 2-only command that strips or passes the eighth bit of characters sent by the terminal to the TNC in the Converse Mode. Eighth-bit stripping is OFF by default. EScape selects either the dollar sign, $, or *escape* control character, <ESC>, as the character to be sent to the terminal from the TNC whenever the escape character is used. EScape ON selects the dollar sign; EScape OFF selects the escape character (1B hex). EScape is OFF by default.

LCok is provided for terminals that can only display uppercase characters. It enables or disables the translation of lowercase characters to uppercase before they are sent to the terminal. LCok ON enables lowercase characters. With LCok OFF, received lowercase characters are converted to uppercase before the TNC sends them to the terminal. LCok is ON by default; ie, lowercase characters are not converted to uppercase for display by the terminal.

LFIgnore is a TNC 2-only command that causes the TNC to ignore line feeds in the Command Mode and Converse Mode, but not in the Transparent Mode. LFignore is ON by default.

Three commands are available to compensate for terminals with slow displays requiring extra time before they start printing on a new line. This is accomplished by inserting time-consuming, but non-printing, *null* control characters, <NUL>, before each new line is started. NUcr ON tells the TNC to send the null control character to the terminal after each carriage return; NUcr OFF disables nulls (this is the default condition). NULf enables or disables sending the null control character to the terminal after each line feed; it is disabled (OFF) by default. The "NULLS" command selects the number of null control characters to be sent when the NUcr and/or NULf functions are enabled.

Flow Control

Four commands are available to select various types of *flow control*. The flow control commands determine the way the TNC or terminal stops and starts sending characters.

When *software flow control* is selected, the transfer of characters between the terminal and TNC is stopped or restarted by the use of control characters typed at the terminal keyboard or sent from the TNC. When *hardware flow control* is selected, the transfer of characters between the terminal and TNC is controlled by TNC- and terminal-originated signals on the EIA terminal-to-TNC hardware interface.

Xflow selects software (*XON/XOFF*) flow control or hardware (EIA interface signal Request-to-Send) flow control. Xflow ON (the default setting) selects software flow control.

TRFlow is a TNC-2-only command that enables or disables terminal software flow control in the *Transparent Mode*. With TRFlow OFF (the default setting), only hardware flow control can be used in the Transparent mode. With TRFlow ON, the *start character* and *stop character* can be used to control the flow of characters from the TNC to the terminal.

TXFlow enables or disables TNC software flow control in the Transparent Mode. TXFlow works like TRFlow; when it is OFF only hardware flow control is available. TXFlow ON allows the start and stop characters to control the flow of characters from the terminal.

Type-in flow control causes the TNC to stop sending characters to the terminal whenever a character is entered at the terminal keyboard; this prevents displayed received characters from interfering with the display of keyed characters. The Flow command enables or disables this function; with Flow ON (the default setting) the TNC stops sending when you are typing at the terminal.

Control Characters

Thirteen commands are provided to change the values of the characters that may be used to control the interface between the terminal and the TNC, and to control the TNC itself. The default selection for many of the control characters is the standard ASCII value used by most terminals. These values may be changed, however, for terminals that use other ASCII values, or for special applications. Appendix B lists each control character available for use by the TNC, lists the command that can be invoked to change its value, and describes its function.

Fine Tuning The Radio Port

The radio port of the TNC controls the transceiver, sends data for transmission to the radio, and collects audio from the radio for the TNC. There are only a few connections between the radio port and its associated radio: transmit audio, receive audio, push-to-talk (PTT) and ground connections usually are enough to allow a TNC to successfully send and receive packets through a radio. Timing is a very important part of the TNC's success, however. Just like a good comedian, a good TNC has to have good timing in order to get its message across. And just as a good comedian adjusts his timing to get the best response from different audiences, the timing of the TNC can be adjusted to get the message across using different parts of the radio spectrum under different operating conditions and with different equipment.

When you turn on a TNC for the first time, its timing parameters are set to default values that are optimized for VHF operation using frequency modulation (and a modern transceiver). Most packet-radio activity is on 2-meter FM, and most packet-radio operators will never use any other mode or band, so they will never have to change the TNC's timing parameters. Some packet-radio operators do explore other Amateur Radio bands, however, and when they do, they have to make adjustments to their TNCs. The following paragraphs discuss the timing and timing-related parameters of the TNC that need to be adjusted for optimal operation on the various ham bands.

Data Rate

The most important timing parameter that needs adjustment when you change bands is the TNC's radio-port data rate. The manner of selecting the TNC's radio-port data rate was discussed earlier in this chapter.

By default, the TNC data rate is 1200 bauds, because this is the data rate that is used on 2-meter FM. The FCC allows 1200-baud operation anywhere above 28 MHz, so you may operate on 10 meters or 23 centimeters without adjusting this timing parameter. If you wish to operate below 28 MHz, however, the maximum legal data rate is 300 bauds; this means that an adjustment of the radio-port data rate is necessary (not to mention the modification of the TNC's internal modem or the addition of an external modem if the TNC is not designed for 300-baud operation).

Some packet-radio operators are transferring packets at higher data rates on 220 and 430 MHz. Operation at 2400, 4800 and 9600 bauds is occurring successfully at these frequencies, so the radio-port data rate must be adjusted upwards for compatibility with these operations. The use of an external modem is required at these higher data rates. Also note that a TNC 1 can be configured for operation at all three of these higher data rates, whereas a TNC 2 can be configured only for 9600-baud operation.

Receive-to-Transmit Turnaround Delay

When a transceiver's transmitter is keyed, there is a slight delay before intelligence can actually be sent over the air, because various circuits in the transceiver require time to switch from the receive mode to the transmit mode. The length of this delay varies, depending on the design of the transceiver. For example, transceivers using mechanical relays take longer to switch from the receive mode to the transmit mode than do transceivers using diode switching. Although the turnaround time seems instantaneous to the user, there is a small delay. The TNC must compensate for this delay, because it is ready to send intelligence (packets) as soon as it keys the transmitter.

By default, the receive-to-transmit turnaround delay is set to 300 ms in a TNC 2 and 160 ms in a TNC 1. The turnaround delay may be adjusted at the command prompt by typing:

cmd: TXdelay n <CR>

where n (in a TNC 2) is a number from 0 to 120 representing a turnaround time in 10-ms increments. [For example, to select a delay of 360 ms in a TNC 2, set n to 36 (360 ms/10 ms = 36).] In a TNC 1, n is a number from 0 to 16 representing a turnaround time in 40-ms increments. [For example, to select a 360-ms delay in a TNC 1, set n to 9 (360 ms/40 ms = 9).]

If the default turnaround time is not long enough, you will have to lengthen the delay. Otherwise, your TNC will not be able to send complete packets through your transceiver. It is also important to shorten the delay if the default turnaround time is too long—an overly long delay wastes valuable time on the packet-radio channel. Shortening the delay promotes more efficient packet-radio communications.

Maximum Number of Unacknowledged Packets and Packet Length

The *MAXframe* and *Paclen* parameters are two critical TNC parameters that should be adjusted depending on the operating conditions (propagation and channel activity).

MAXframe selects the maximum number of outstanding unacknowledged packets the TNC will allow at any one time. In other words, if MAXframe is set to 4, the TNC may send as many as four packets without receiving acknowledgments for any of them. Once the MAXframe limit is reached, however, the TNC will not send a new packet until one of the outstanding packets is acknowledged.

Paclen selects the maximum number of bytes of data in each packet. The TNC will never send a packet longer than the selected Paclen value. As data is entered from the terminal to the TNC, the TNC counts each byte of data. When the Paclen value is attained, the TNC makes up a packet containing the data, sends it over the air and begins counting the number of bytes of data for the next packet. The TNC will only send packets shorter than the selected Paclen value when it is specifically commanded to do so; a packet is forced whenever the *SEndpac* control character (<CR> is the default selection) is typed.

The default values for the MAXframe and Paclen parameters (4 outstanding packets, each 128 bytes long) are selected for good VHF operating conditions. When you are operating on HF or when VHF operating conditions are less than optimal (when there is a high level of channel activity), the MAXframe and Paclen values should be reduced as operating conditions warrant.

At 300 bauds, it takes approximately four times as long to send the same packet as it does at 1200 bauds. Even if you reduce the packet length by half, it still takes approximately twice as long to send a packet containing 64 bytes of data at 300 bauds as it does to send a packet containing 128 bytes of data at 1200 bauds. This means that your packet is on the air approximately twice as long, and the chances of it being interfered with are twice as great. Add to this the fact that HF conditions are usually not optimal for packet-radio operation, and you may end up with a lot of long unacknowledged packets hanging out there in the ether. The best thing to do is to shorten the Paclen parameter and set the MAXframe parameter to 1 to force the TNC to send one short packet, wait for an acknowledgment and then deal with the next short packet.

To change the value of the MAXframe parameter, at the command prompt type:

cmd: MAXframe n <CR>

where n is a number from 1 to 7 representing the maximum number of outstanding unacknowledged packets.

To change the value of the Paclen parameter, at the command prompt type:

cmd: Paclen n <CR>

where n is a number from 0 to 255 in a TNC 2, or 1 to 255 in a TNC 1, representing the maximum number of bytes of data in each packet. In a TNC 2, 0 actually represents 256 bytes.

Number of Packet Retries

When a TNC sends a packet, it waits a preset time for an acknowledgment that the packet was received without error by the intended receiving station. If the time limit is reached, the TNC again tries to obtain an acknowledgment from the receiving TNC. (The actual process of obtaining this acknowledgment is outside the scope of this chapter. If you are interested, the process is detailed in the *AX.25 Amateur Packet-Radio Link-Layer Protocol, Version 2.0, October 1984*, available from ARRL Headquarters.) After the maximum number of retries, the sending TNC enters the disconnected state. The *FRack* parameter sets the amount of time between retries, and the *REtry* parameter controls the number of allowable retransmission attempts.

The REtry and FRack parameters should be adjusted upward or downward, depending on the operating conditions. If conditions are good (good propagation and a low level of activity on the channel), the REtry and FRack parameters may be adjusted downward; if a packet cannot get through after one or two attempts under good conditions, there is probably an insurmountable problem with the link. For example, the intended receiving station may have gone off the air, so you might as well abandon the effort immediately.

If conditions are marginal (marginal propagation or a medium level of activity on the channel), the REtry and FRack parameters may be adjusted upward because it may only take a little longer to get the packet through to the intended receiving station. If conditions are poor (poor propagation and/or a high level of activity on the channel), you should abandon the effort until conditions improve. You have two strikes against you: It is very difficult to get the packet through to the intended receiving station because of poor propagation, and your packets are likely to collide with other packets because of the crowded channel.

By default, the REtry parameter value is set to 10 retries, but that may be changed at the command prompt by typing:

cmd: REtry n <CR>

where n is a number from 0 to 15. Zero represents an infinite number of retries and 1 to 15 represents the maximum number of retries that will be attempted before the TNC stops repeating a packet. Note that the REtry parameter does not include the initial transmission of the packet; it only represents the number of retries after the initial packet transmission.

By default, the FRack parameter value is set to 3 seconds in a TNC 2 and 4 seconds in a TNC 1, but this may be changed at the command prompt by typing:

cmd: FRack n <CR>

where n is a number from 1 to 15 in a TNC 2, or 1 to 16 in a TNC 1, representing the number of seconds that the TNC will wait for a packet acknowledgment before it again tries to obtain an acknowledgment. Note that the TNC automatically adjusts this value higher, depending on the number of digipeaters used in the selected path of the packet, according to the formula:

$$FRack \times (2 \times dr + 1) = adjusted\ FRack$$

where dr is the number of digipeaters in the selected path. [For example, if FRack is set to 4 seconds and 2 digipeaters are in the selected path, the adjusted FRack value is 20 seconds (4 seconds $\times$ (2 $\times$ 2 digipeaters + 1)) = 20 sec).]

Digipeater Timing

When one station's packet collides with another station's packet, each station must take steps to rectify the problem. When one station's packet collides with a digipeater's packet, the digipeater is not responsible for requesting a retransmission; the station that originated the packet must keep track of the outstanding packets. In some cases, several digipeaters are used in a link, and a packet may be lost by any one of them.

All this means that digipeated packets are at a disadvantage. To help counteract this, a timing parameter is included in the TNC to give digipeated packets a break. When a TNC is digipeating packets, it sends its packets as soon as the channel is clear of activity. If a TNC is originating its own packets, however, it waits a selected time period (set by the *DWait* command parameter value) after the channel is clear before it sends its packets. As a result, when a channel is clear, the digipeater always transmits first. This reduces the chance of digipeated packets colliding with non-digipeated TNC packets. The default setting of the DWait parameter in a TNC 2 is 16, which represents 160 ms. In a TNC 1 the default setting is 2, which represents 80 ms. To change this timing parameter, at the command prompt type:

cmd: DWait n <CR>

where n, in a TNC 2, is a number from 0 to 250 representing a delay in 10-ms increments. [For example, to select a delay of 120 ms in a TNC 2, set n to 12 (120 ms/10 ms = 12).] In a TNC 1, n is a number from 0 to 15 representing a delay in 40-ms increments. [For example, to select a delay of 120 ms in a TNC 1, set n to 3 (120 ms/40 ms = 3).] Note that DWait should be similarly applied in areas where network nodes have replaced digipeaters.

To work effectively, all of the TNCs on a channel used by one or more digipeaters should be using the same DWait value. Unless you know that the packet-radio operators in your area are using a DWait value other than the default, you should leave your TNC set at the default value. Figure 6.6 shows an illustration of the relationship between the DWait and TXdelay parameters.

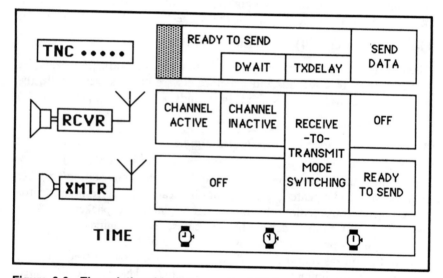

Figure 6.6—The relationship between the DWait and TXdelay TNC timing parameters.

Voice-Repeater Timing

If you plan to use a voice FM repeater for relaying your packet-radio transmissions, there are two TNC timing parameters that can be adjusted for optimal voice repeater operation. *AXDelay* inserts a delay between the time your transmitter is keyed and the time a packet is actually sent. This delay is in addition to the TXdelay mentioned earlier; AXdelay is used to allow the voice repeater to be keyed up and ready to relay your transmitted packet. Voice-repeater packet-radio operation is not common, so AXDelay is set to 0 ms by default. If you need to use a voice repeater for packet, a delay may be selected at the command prompt by typing:

cmd: AXDelay n <CR>

where n, in a TNC 2, is a number from 0 to 180 representing a delay in 10-ms increments. [For example, to select a delay of 480 ms in a TNC 2, set n to 48 (480 ms/10 ms = 48).] In a TNC 1, n is a number from 0 to 15, representing a delay in 120-ms increments. [For example, to select a delay of 480 ms in a TNC 1, set n to 4 (480 ms/120 ms = 4).] Figure 6.7 shows the relationship between the AXDelay and TXdelay parameters.

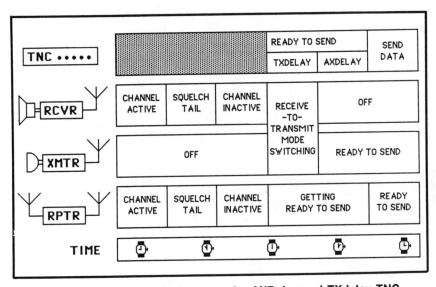

Figure 6.7—The relationship between the AXDelay and TXdelay TNC timing parameters.

Most voice repeaters continue transmitting unmodulated carrier for a certain amount of time after each repeated transmission to indicate to the repeated station that the repeater is functioning. This delay is called the *squelch tail* or *hang time,* and may be used in conjunction with the TNC's "AXHang" command to speed up voice-repeater packet-radio operation.

If the TNC is ready to send a packet and channel activity has been detected within the selected AXHang parameter value, the TNC keys its transmitter (keeping the repeater keyed) and sends data after the TXdelay parameter value has expired. This saves time, because the TNC does not wait for the AXdelay time in this case. Refer to Figure 6.8 for an illustration of the relationship between the AXHang and TXdelay parameters.

Again, voice-repeater packet-radio operation is not common, so AXHang is set to 0 ms by default. If you need to use an FM voice repeater, AXHang timing may be selected at the command prompt by typing:

cmd: AXHang n <CR>

where n, in a TNC 2, is a number from 0 to 20 representing a hang time in 100-ms increments. [For example, to select a hang time of 1200 ms in a TNC 2, set n to 12 (1200 ms/100 ms = 12).] In a TNC 1, n is a number 0 to 15 representing a hang time in 120-ms increments. [For example, to select a hang time of 1200 ms in a TNC 1, set n to 10 (1200 ms/120 ms = 10).]

How do you select the correct values for AXDelay and AXHang? In most cases, you do not know the length of a voice repeater's key-up delay and squelch tail, so unless another local packet-radio operator has already determined the best values for AXDelay and AXHang, you will have to experiment until you determine the appropriate values.

We've reviewed the most critical TNC timing and timing-related parameters that you need to check before you put your TNC on the air. Refer to Appendix A for other timing command parameters. Now, there is only one more thing left to do.

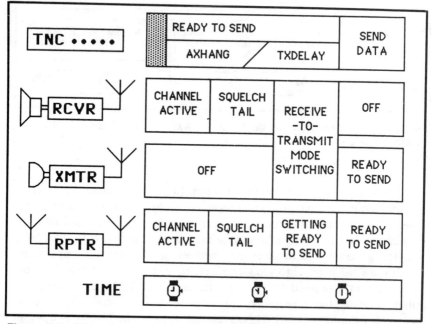

Figure 6.8—The relationship between the AXHang and TXdelay TNC timing parameters.

Station Identification

One last TNC parameter needs to be set, the call sign that identifies your station. To enter the call sign, at the command prompt type:

cmd: MYcall n <CR>

where n is the call sign of your station.

In packet radio, one Amateur Radio operator may have more than one packet-radio station on the air at the same time. A packet-radio operator may run a full-time digipeater, a packet-radio bulletin board system and his own packet-radio station. To differentiate these stations, the AX.25 protocol provides a Secondary Station Identifier (SSID), that is, a number (0 to 15). In most TNCs, the SSID is appended to the call sign with a hyphen. For example, my home station might be identified as WA1LOU-0, my packet-radio bulletin board system as WA1LOU-4 and my digipeater as WA1LOU-5. To enter the SSID in the TNC, use the "MYcall" command. For example, to enter my digipeater call sign in the TNC, at the command prompt, I type:

cmd: MYcall WA1LOU-5 <CR>

Note that if a call sign is entered without an SSID, the TNC assumes that the SSID is 0.

Before You Begin

Before you begin selecting the parameters of a new TNC or a reinitialized TNC, you should set your terminal for compatibility with the TNC's default selections for serial-port baud rate, character length (bits per character) and parity. Typically, 1200 bauds, 7 bit characters and even parity are the TNC's defaults. If you are working with a TNC 2 whose serial-port data rate is selected by means of a rear-panel DIP switch, however, there is no baud-rate default, so set the switch for 1200 bauds (see Figure 6.1). If the serial-port baud rate of the TNC 2 is software selectable, the default baud rate is likely to be 1200 bauds, but check the TNC's manual to see if this is the case. If it is not 1200 bauds, then set your terminal baud rate to be compatible with the TNC's default serial-port baud rate.

After the terminal and TNC are compatible, power up the TNC and its preamble should be displayed on your terminal in plain English (see Figure 6.3). To change the serial-port baud rate, character length and/or parity of the TNC and terminal, do so by changing the setting of the TNC first, then change the setting of the terminal one parameter at a time. For example, to change the serial-port baud rate to 9600 bauds, the character length to 8 bits and the parity to no parity, you would proceed according to the following steps:

1) Set your TNC for 8 character bits.
2) Set your terminal for 8 character bits.

3) Set your TNC for no parity.
4) Set your terminal for no parity.
5) Set your TNC for 9600 bauds.
6) Set your terminal for 9600 bauds.

Now, you can proceed to change any of the other TNC parameters as you desire.

After You Are Finished

That concludes the configuration of the TNC. It is now ready to launch its first packet. The next chapter will tell you how to make this happen.

CHAPTER SEVEN

Operating Procedures

Some packet-radio operating procedures are very similar to those used on other modes, but some are very different. In this chapter, we'll explore these similarities and differences.

Command, Converse and Transparent Modes

Before we talk about establishing a contact, we should discuss the various operating modes of a TNC. A TNC has three operating modes: the *command*, *converse* and *transparent* modes.

The command mode is the TNC state that allows the user to configure and control the TNC, while the converse and transparent modes are the TNC states in which packet-radio communications actually occur. In the command mode, the TNC sends the command prompt (**cmd:**) to the terminal to indicate that it is ready to accept user commands that configure TNC parameters

Figure 7.1—It's child's play! Learn a few commands and you can experience the new adventure called packet radio, as are the author's daughter, Hayley, and XYL, Laurie.

and control TNC functions. In the converse and transparent modes, the user sends and receives messages and files to and from other packet-radio stations.

So then, what's the difference between the converse mode and the transparent mode?

The converse mode is intended for most packet-radio communications. When you are in converse mode, most of what you type is sent as data to another station, while special characters may be interspersed in that data to command your TNC to perform a variety of functions. For example, to send a packet in the converse mode, you simply enter the text you wish to send followed by the Sendpac character (by default, this is a carriage return, <CR>). The text is transmitted to the other station, but the Sendpac character is not sent. This can be a drawback if you wish to send these special characters to the other station (rather than have them interpreted as commands by your TNC). (<CR> is a special case and is handled by the "CR" command.)

The solution to this problem is the transparent mode. In the transparent mode, no characters are interpreted as commands by your TNC, with one exception. As a result, any character can be imbedded in the data intended for transmission, except for a single special character, which is used to switch the TNC back to command mode. Even this character may be sent to the other station in the transparent mode, because it must be typed three times in a row (and within a certain time) in order to cause the TNC to switch modes. Thus, in the transparent mode, any data can be sent by the TNC.

To transfer the TNC to the transparent mode, at the command prompt type:

cmd: Trans <CR>

and to transfer the TNC to the converse mode, at the command prompt type:

cmd: CONVers <CR>

Making A Contact

In all modes of Amateur Radio communications, you must establish contact with another station before you can initiate communications. On packet radio, you connect to or make a connection with another station. To make a connection, you command the TNC to do so using the "Connect" command, at the command prompt, by typing:

cmd: Connect WA1LOU <CR>

where WA1LOU is the call sign of the station you wish to contact.

After you type the "Connect" command, the TNC sends connect-request packets to the desired station. The TNC also switches to the converse mode or the transparent mode, or remains in the command mode, depending on the selection of the *NEwmode* parameter.

NEwmode determines how the TNC acts when the "Connect" command is invoked and when a connection is ended. If NEwmode is enabled (the default selection), the TNC switches to the converse mode or transparent mode after the "Connect" command is invoked and switches back to the command mode after a connection is ended. If NEwmode is disabled, the TNC remains in the command mode until a connection is established (it then switches to converse or transparent mode) and the TNC does not switch to the command mode when a connection is ended. To enable or disable NEwmode, at the command prompt type:

cmd: NEwmode x <CR>

where x is ON to enable the NEwmode function, or OFF to disable it.

With NEwmode enabled, you may begin typing your first message to the station you wish to contact while the TNC is still trying to establish a connection with that station. If NEwmode is disabled, you cannot enter your first message until a connection is actually established. (Refer to Figure 7.2

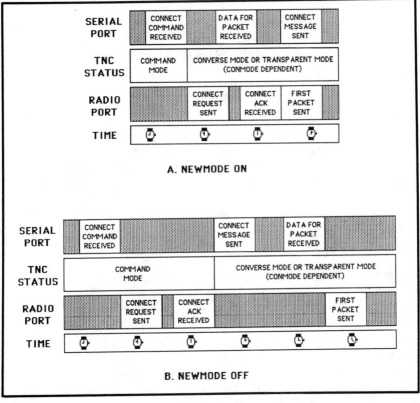

Figure 7.2—Enabling and disabling NEwmode causes the TNC to operate very differently. When NEwmode is enabled, communications can be initiated more quickly.

for an illustration of the difference between enabled and disabled NEwmode.)

The mode the TNC enters after the "Connect" command is invoked or after a connection is established is determined by the *CONMode* parameter. The TNC switches to the converse mode by default, but this may be changed at the command prompt by typing:

cmd: CONMode TRans <CR>

to cause the TNC to switch to the transparent mode. To reselect the converse mode, at the command prompt type:

cmd: CONMode COnvers <CR>

The TNC sends connect requests until an internal counter reaches 1 + the Retry parameter; the TNC then displays the *** **retry count exceeded** message and enters the disconnected state.

If your terminal displays:

*** retry count exceeded
*** DISCONNECTED

this means that the TNC was unable to make a connection with the addressed station.

If a connection is not established with the addressed station and your terminal displays:

*** WA1LOU busy
*** DISCONNECTED

this means that the TNC has received a frame from the addressed station indicating that it is busy. The addressed station may already be connected to another station (with the multiple-connect function disabled) or the addressed station may be configured to reject connect requests (with CONOk Off).

If a connection is established with the addressed station, your terminal displays:

*** CONNECTED to WA1LOU

where WA1LOU is the call sign of the addressed station.

It's Always Your Turn To Transmit

Once a contact is established and communication begins, there are standard procedures to indicate that you are finished transmitting and ready to receive a transmission from the other station. The letter K is used in CW communications and the word "over" is used in voice communications. In packet radio, however, the situation is a bit different, because packet-radio communication is virtually full duplex. When you are using landline telephone equipment (which is a full-duplex system), you don't need to say "over" to let the party on the other end of the line know that it is their turn to talk; both parties can talk at the same time if they want to. When you send a transmission via packet radio, you do not need to let the other station know it is his or her turn to transmit. The other station has probably sent a packet back to you already!

In other Amateur Radio modes, communications are half duplex—at any given time, one station transmits while the other station receives. In packet radio, transmissions are very short; therefore, connected stations are in the receive mode most of the time. In the receive mode, the operator is often typing a response to the other station's previous transmission. When he enters a carriage return, what he typed is transmitted, and the other station's next transmission is displayed on his terminal awaiting his next response.

This is almost full-duplex communication (packets can be travelling in both directions at once, and sometimes are!). As a result, you do not usually need to indicate when you are finished transmitting and are ready to receive the other station's transmission.

Old habits die hard, however, and you will see some stations using K, as on CW, or a string of greater-than signs (> > >) to indicate the end of a transmission. There is nothing wrong or illegal about using such indicators, but they are usually unnecessary in a packet-radio QSO. However, if a single packet is not a complete transmission and the packet-radio QSO is getting confusing, don't be afraid to use some sort of end-of-transmission indicator if it helps you communicate.

Breaking A Connection

To complete a contact on most Amateur Radio modes, you simply say "73" or "see you later" and call another station, call CQ or turn off the transceiver. In packet radio, one more step is required. After all of the good-byes are exchanged, your TNC is still connected to the other station's TNC. You or the operator at the other station must command the TNC to break this connection by invoking the "Disconnect" command. This poses a problem: To use the "Disconnect" command, the TNC must be in the command mode, but ever since the connection was established, the TNC has either been in the converse mode or the transparent mode. The solution is to switch back to the command mode.

In the converse mode, simply enter the *command-mode character*, which is <CTRL-C> by default. After the command-mode character is entered, the TNC enters the command mode and the command prompt is displayed on the terminal.

In the transparent mode, the command mode character must be entered three times in succession, in a timely manner according to the value of the *CMdtime* parameter (one second is the default value for the CMdtime parameter). To transfer from the transparent mode to the command mode, you must use the following sequence:

1) Wait longer than the CMdtime parameter (1 second) after the last keyboard entry.

2) Enter the command-mode character, <CTRL-C>, three times in succession, with the time between each entry being less than the CMdtime parameter (one second).

3) After the CMdtime parameter (1 second), the command prompt will be displayed at the terminal.

Once the command prompt is displayed, invoke the "Disconnect" command by typing:

For Either or Transparent Convers

cmd: Disconne <CR>

When the disconnection is completed, the terminal displays:

*** DISCONNECTED

and the TNC does or does not enter the command mode, depending on the selection of the NEwmode parameter described earlier.

You may change the command-mode character at the command prompt by typing:

cmd: COMmand n <CR>

where n is the hexadecimal or decimal value of the ASCII character selected to represent the command mode character (refer to Appendix D—ASCII Character Set for the hexadecimal and decimal values of each ASCII character).

You can also change the CMdtime parameter at the command prompt by typing:

cmd: CMdtime n <CR>

where n is a number from 0 to 250 (0 to 15 in a TNC 1) representing the transparent-mode time-out value in 1-second increments.

Monitoring Packet-Radio Activity

The TNC is a versatile monitor. In other modes of Amateur Radio communications, you limit reception by the judicious use of filters and related circuits that are built into your receiver. Even the best filters cannot block out very strong signals only a few kilohertz away from your operating frequency. A TNC, however, can be configured to reject signals from your next-door packet-radio neighbor operating on the same frequency you're using!

Do you want to know what other stations are on frequency? In other modes of Amateur Radio, you would have to sit by the receiver and compile a list of the stations you hear on the frequency. In packet radio, your TNC can provide you with a list of the stations monitored on frequency and can tell you at what time they were monitored as well.

A variety of monitoring commands are provided to configure the TNC to your monitoring requirements. Refer to Figure 7.3 for an illustration of how the various monitoring commands affect the display of monitored packets. The most important monitoring command is aptly named the "Monitor" command! This determines whether or not your terminal displays received packets while the TNC is in the command mode. By default, the monitoring function is enabled. This may be changed, however, at the command prompt by typing:

cmd: Monitor x <CR>

where x is ON to enable the monitoring function or OFF to disable the monitoring function.

If the monitoring function is enabled, received packets are displayed in the following format:

WA1LOU>KE3Z-2: Do you hear my signal on 221.11 MHz?

where WA1LOU-0 is the station originating the packet (SSIDs of 0 are not displayed), KE3Z-2 is the station of destination for the packet and "Do you hear..." is the data contained in the packet. The originating and receiving call signs are separated by the greater-than sign (>), and the call signs and data are separated by a colon (:).

Monitoring While Connected

The monitoring function normally allows you to monitor packets only while the TNC is not connected. When your station is connected to another

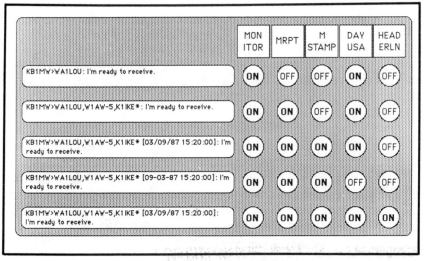

Figure 7.3—The display of monitored packets can be customized to your desires by selecting the proper monitoring functions.

station, your TNC will normally display only packets from the station to which you are connected. If you need to know what is going on among other stations on the frequency while you are connected to another station, use the "MCon" command. The "MCon" command enables the TNC to continue monitoring other channel activity during a connection. By default, the MCon function is disabled, but this may be changed at the command prompt by typing:

cmd: MCon x <CR>

where x is ON to enable the MCon function, or OFF to disable the MCon function.

Digipeater/Network-Node Pathfinding

If digipeaters or network nodes are used for passing packets in your area, it is often useful to know what digipeater and node paths are being used. The *"MRpt"* command enables the TNC to display the call signs of the digipeaters and nodes used by each monitored packet. By default, the MRpt function is enabled. This may be changed at the command prompt by typing:

cmd: MRpt x <CR>

where x is ON to enable the MRpt function, or OFF to disable the MRpt function.

If the MRpt function is enabled, received packets are displayed in the following format:

WA1LOU>KE3Z-2,W1AW-5,K1IKE*: Do you hear my signal on 221.11 MHz?

where WA1LOU is the station originating the packet, KE3Z-2 is the station of destination for the packet and "Do you hear..." is the data contained in the packet. W1AW-5 and K1IKE are digipeaters or nodes used to pass packets between WA1LOU-0 and KE3Z-2. The asterisk (*) after K1IKE indicates that K1IKE is the station that is actually being received by your TNC. Note that this facility is not available in a TNC 1.

Time-Stamped Monitoring

It is often useful to know when a packet was actually monitored. This is especially true if you "read the mail" later (by reading a printout or a saved file of monitored packets). The TNC 2 has a clock that can be used to time-stamp monitored packets. Before *time stamping* can be used, however, the TNC clock must be set using the *"DAytime"* command. To set the TNC clock, at the command prompt type:

cmd: DAytime yymmddhhmm <CR>

where yy are the last two digits of the year, mm is the numerical representation of the month (01 through 12), dd is the day of the month (01 through 31), hh is the hour of the day (00 through 23), and the second mm is the minute of the hour (00 through 59). For example, to set the TNC clock to August 11, 1989, 1:36 PM, at the command prompt type:

cmd: DAytime 8908111336 <CR>

where 89 represents the year; 08, the month; 11, the day of the month; 13, the hour of the day; and 36, the minute of the hour.

After you have set the TNC clock, you may check the time at the command prompt by typing:

cmd: DAytime <CR>

The date and time is displayed in the following format:

08/11/89 13:36:00

for August 11, 1989, 1:36 PM.

If you prefer to have the date displayed in the European format, with the day of the month preceding the month (11-8-89), rather than in the American format, where the day of the month follows the month (8/11/89), the *DAYUsa* function must be disabled (by default, the function is enabled). To change the DAYUsa function, at the command prompt type:

cmd: DAYUsa x <CR>

where x is ON to enable the DAYUsa function, or OFF to disable the DAYUsa function.

Please note that the TNC-2 clock is not intended to be an accurate timepiece. In most TNCs, it loses time. This loss of time can be compensated for by using the *"CLKADJ"* command to insert a correction factor in the TNC clock routine. The value of the correction factor must be determined by experimentation—try different values until you find one that provides the best clock accuracy. By default, the correction factor is 0; to insert a correction factor, at the command prompt type:

cmd: CLKADJ n <CR>

where n is a number between 0 and 65535 representing the TNC clock-correction factor.

Now that the TNC-2 clock is set, we can put it to use. The *"MStamp"* command controls the time stamping of monitored packets. Time stamping of monitored packets is disabled by default; this may be changed at the command prompt by typing:

cmd: MStamp x <CR>

where x is ON to enable the time stamping of monitored packets, or OFF to disable this feature. When time stamping is enabled, monitored packets are displayed in the following format:

WA1LOU > KE3Z-2 [03/08/87 12:34:45]: Do you hear my signal on 221.11 MHz?

where the date and time that the packet is received by the TNC is displayed between a set of brackets that precedes the colon (:) and the data portion of the packet.

With the call signs of the originating, destination and digipeater/node stations and the date and time being displayed along with the data contained in each packet, the length of a displayed packet often extends to a second line. To make the display more legible, the packet *header* (the call signs, date and time) may be displayed on one line, with the data on the line immediately following the header. This function is enabled by means of the *HEaderln* command, which is disabled by default. To change this, at the command prompt type:

cmd: HEaderln x < CR >

where x is ON to enable the separate-line display of packet headers and data, or OFF to disable the separate-line display function. After HEeaderln is enabled, the previous example of a monitored packet is displayed as:

WA1LOU > KE3Z-2 [03/08/87 12:34:45]:
Do you hear my signal on 221.11 MHz?

The TNC-2 clock can also be used to time-stamp connection messages. By default, this time stamping is disabled. This may be changed at the command prompt by typing:

cmd: CONStamp x < CR >

where x is ON to enable the time stamping of connection messages, or OFF to disable the time stamping. When this function is enabled, connection messages are displayed in the following format:

* * * CONNECTED to WA1LOU [03/08/87 12:34:45]

where the date and time that the connection was made is displayed between a set of brackets that follows the connection message.

Log of Monitored Stations

Do you wish to know what stations have been active on the frequency lately? The *"MHeard"* command allows you to obtain a list of the most recent 18 stations monitored by the TNC. To obtain this list, at the command prompt type:

cmd: MHeard < CR >

and the last 18 different stations monitored are displayed in the following format:

KG1O-9	07/30/89	15:29:24
K1IKE-1	07/30/89	15:29:23
W1AW-5	07/30/89	15:29:17
N2MH-11	07/30/89	15:27:13
WB2QBP-2	07/30/89	15:25:05
NR1L	07/30/89	15:18:27
KA1JES-1	07/30/89	15:18:22
WB2KMY-1	07/30/89	15:16:12
W1AW-4*	07/30/89	15:15:03
WA2SNA*	07/30/89	15:14:35
WA2SNA-1*	07/30/89	15:09:10
WA2S*	07/30/89	15:09:08
W1AW-11	07/30/89	15:08:14
WA2SNA-2	07/30/89	15:07:34
K3RLI-15	07/30/89	15:03:51
KA2FIR*	07/30/89	15:03:27
K2SK-1	07/30/89	14:50:48
N1BBI-15	07/30/89	14:44:07

where the asterisk (*) after a station indicates that that station was monitored through a digipeater or node. The date and time are displayed only if the TNC-2 clock has been set.

In order to start a new list, the old list of monitored stations logged by the TNC may be deleted. This is accomplished by invoking the "*MHClear*" command at the command prompt by typing:

cmd: MHClear < CR >

Discriminatory Monitoring

The "*LCAll*" command is used in conjunction with the "*BUdlist*" command to permit the TNC to limit station monitoring. These commands may be used to limit monitoring exclusively to certain stations or to limit monitoring to all stations except certain stations. This LCAlls-BUdlist combination is useful in eliminating the display of beacons that constantly bombard your TNC from certain stations. It is also useful to eliminate the display of messages from PBBSs that are being read for the umpteenth time. As many as eight stations can be selected or excluded in this way.

First, the call signs (and SSIDs) of the stations to be limited are entered into the TNC with the "LCAlls" command at the command prompt by typing:

cmd: LCAlls call sign1, ... call sign8 <CR>

where call sign 1 through call sign 8 represent the call signs of one to eight stations to be limited (the call signs must be separated by commas).

Next, the "BUdlist" command is used to select the desired discriminatory monitoring. BUdlist is disabled by default, and packets from stations included in the LCAlls list are not displayed. On the other hand, if BUdlist is enabled, only the packets from the stations included in the LCAlls list are displayed. To change the status of the BUdlist function, at the command prompt type:

cmd: BUdlist x <CR>

where x is ON to enable the Budlist function, or OFF to disable the function.

If no calls are entered in the LCAlls list, the status of BUdlist is inconsequential and the packets of all monitored stations are displayed. To check the LCAlls list, at the command prompt type:

cmd: LCAlls <CR>

and the LCAlls station list is displayed.

The TNC 1 does not use the "LCAlls" and "BUdlist" commands, but it has two other commands that provide some limitations to station monitoring. The "*MFrom*" command limits monitoring to packets sent from as many as 10 stations, while the "*MTo*" command limits monitoring to packets sent to as many as 10 stations.

The "MFrom" command is invoked at the command prompt by typing:

cmd: MFrom call sign1, ... call sign10 <CR>

where call sign 1 through call sign 10 represent the call signs of one to 10 stations with limited monitoring; the TNC 1 only displays packets sent from these stations and no others. Remember that the call signs must be separated by commas.

The "MTo" command is invoked at the command prompt by typing:

cmd: MTo call sign1, ... call sign10 <CR>

where call sign 1 through call sign 10 represent the call signs of one to 10 stations with limited monitoring; the TNC 1 only displays packets sent to these stations and no others.

The "MFrom" and "MTo" commands can be used simultaneously to limit the monitoring of a maximum of 20 stations. Also, ALL or NONE may be used with these commands instead of call signs to cause the TNC 1 to display packets sent from or sent to all or no stations respectively.

Other Monitoring Functions

Other on-the-air monitoring commands include the "*MAll*" command, which, when enabled, causes the TNC to display *unconnected packets* as well as connected packets. (Unconnected packets are used when more than two packet-radio stations are in communication with each other, or for CQs and beacon messages.) The *"MCOM"* command, when enabled, causes the TNC to display connect, disconnect, UA and DM frames in addition to I (information) frames. Finally, the *"MFilter"* command can be used to specify as many as four ASCII characters that are then filtered from monitored packets (in order to eliminate certain control characters that can disrupt your terminal's operation).

Monitoring The TNC

Besides on-the-air monitoring, there is a class of monitoring commands that are concerned with monitoring the status of the TNC. The most frequently used command of this class is the *"DISPlay"* command, which causes the terminal to display the status of all selectable TNC parameters. Since over a hundred different parameters may be displayed using this command, it is made more useful by optionally limiting the display of parameters to a certain class, such as timing parameters. To invoke this command, at the command prompt type:

cmd: DISPlay x <CR>

where x may be optionally included to limit the display of parameters to a certain class, as follows: A for asynchronous port parameters, C for special characters, H for health counters and LEDs, I for identification parameters, L for link parameters, M for monitor parameters and T for timing parameters.

In addition to the "DISPlay" command, there is a group of esoteric TNC monitoring commands that allow you to display such things as the number of frames discarded because of length or bad CRC. These monitoring commands are listed in Appendix A.

Multiple Connections

A TNC 2 can be connected with more than one station simultaneously. In fact, it may be connected with as many as 10 other stations at the same time! Multiple-connection capability was intended for such uses as traffic handling, *roundtable* communicating and multiple-user PBBS operation. Use your imagination and you can probably discover a new use for the multiple-connection function.

One way of describing how multiple connections work is to think of your TNC as having 10 channels or *streams* for the flow of data. The streams are labeled A through J; instead of using a front-panel channel selector to choose a stream, you command the TNC to select a stream for you.

You can limit the number of streams that can be used for multiple connections to any number between one and ten. If only one stream is available for use, you have effectively disabled the multiple-connection function. One available stream is the default selection. To enable the multi-connect function, at the command prompt type:

cmd: USers n <CR>

where n is a number between 1 and 10 representing the number of channels to be made available for communications (n must be greater than 1 to enable the multiple-connection function).

After the multiple-connection function is enabled, the TNC is initially tuned to stream A. To select a different stream, at the command prompt type:

cmd: |x <CR>

where | is the default value for the *streamswitch* character and x is a letter (A through J) representing the desired stream. For example, to select stream B type:

cmd: |B <CR>

After you switch streams, the terminal displays:

|Bcmd:

indicating that the TNC is now tuned to stream B. From that point on, any commands sent to the TNC are addressed to stream B until a new stream is selected. Note that the stream indication (|B) only appears after a stream switch occurs. When the command prompt is displayed again, there is no stream indication; after displaying the stream indication once, the TNC assumes that you know which stream you are addressing.

If there is activity on another stream, the stream indication will appear again, followed by the activity that has occurred on that stream. For example, if your TNC is connected to two stations, one on stream A and another on stream B, and the station on stream A disconnects while you are in the converse mode on stream B, the terminal displays:

|A * DISCONNECTED**

Or if the station on stream A sends you a message, the terminal displays:

|A Who are you talking to on the other channel?

In either case, your terminal is still addressing stream B and anything you type is directed to that stream. To answer the question received on stream A, you enter the streamswitch character, the letter representing the stream to which you wish to switch, and the text of your message, as follows:

|A I am connected to the bulletin board <CR>

You may enter this without a command prompt; you can switch streams directly from the converse mode (without returning to the command mode).

Sorting Out Multiple Connections

Trying to communicate on more than one stream can get a little confusing. The TNC provides some information to help you sort things out. To obtain the big picture of what is going on, use the *"CStatus"* command, at the command prompt, by typing:

cmd: CStatus <CR>

The terminal will display:

A stream - Link state is: CONNECTED to W1AW-4 VIA K1IKE
B stream - IO Link state is: CONNECT in progress
C stream - Link state is: DISCONNECTED
D stream - Link state is: DISCONNECTED
E stream - Link state is: DISCONNECTED
F stream - Link state is: DISCONNECTED
G stream - Link state is: DISCONNECTED
H stream - Link state is: DISCONNECTED
I stream - Link state is: DISCONNECTED
J stream - Link state is: DISCONNECTED

This display indicates the status of each stream. In this example, stream A is connected to station W1AW-4 through digipeater/node K1IKE, stream B is currently attempting to establish a connection, and streams C through J are disconnected. The "IO" designation indicates that input and output to and from the TNC is currently assigned to stream B; that is, anything sent between the TNC and the terminal is addressed to or received from stream B.

The TNC provides another way to sort out streams by inserting the call sign of the connected station after each display of the stream indicator. In the example above, the station on stream A sent you a message that was displayed as:

|A Who are you talking to on the other channel?

If the stream call sign indication function was enabled, that same message would have been displayed as:

|A:K8KA:Who are you talking to on the other channel?

Now when something occurs on another stream, you not only know the stream where that activity is occurring, but you also are reminded of the station that is connected to that stream. By default, the stream call sign indication function is disabled. This may be changed at the command prompt by typing:

cmd: STREAMCa x <CR>

where x is ON to enable the stream call sign indication function, or OFF to disable the function.

A Typical(!) Multiple Connection

One example of a multiple connection probably teaches more than a multi-page description. Here is an actual multiple-connection session (with annotations in parentheses), conducted on a quiet Saturday night between WA1LOU and two bulletin boards, W1AW-4 on stream A and KE3Z on stream B, on 145.01 MHz. In this session, the WA1LOU TNC is set for 10 users with the stream call sign indicator enabled and all time-stamping functions disabled.

cmd:C W1AW-4 V K1IKE

(:LOU initiates connection on default stream A)

*** CONNECTED to W1AW-4 VIA K1IKE

(:stream-A connection message)

Max. path length: 2 digis

(:stream-A bulletin-board preamble)

cmd:|B

(:LOU switches streams)

|B:cmd:C KE3Z V K1IKE

(:LOU initiates connection on stream B)

|A:W1AW-4:0055z, 119 msgs, last = 6895 >

(:stream A-bulletin-board command prompt)

|AL

(:LOU sends "List" command on stream A)

|B:KE3Z:*** CONNECTED to KE3Z VIA K1IKE

(:stream-B connection message)

Max. connect path: 2 digis

(:stream-B bulletin-board preamble)

|BL

(:LOU sends "List" command on stream B)

WA1LOU de KE3Z: 870419/0057z 26 msgs, last 505 >

(:stream-B bulletin-board command prompt)

*** None found.

(:stream-B bulletin-board response to "List" command)

WA1LOU de KE3Z: 870419/0057z 26 msgs, last 505 >

(:stream-B bulletin-board command prompt)

W

(:LOU sends "What" command on stream B)

|A:W1AW-4:*** Not found.

(:stream-A bulletin-board response to "List" command)

|AW

(:LOU sends "What" command on stream A)

0056z, 119 msgs, last = 6895 >
(:stream-A bulletin-board command prompt)

DOC   .TNC 4k > FASTOKEN.C64 4k > FASTOKEN.DOC 4k:
MON.TNC 4k
NTS   .DOC 4k
Drive A contains 20K in 5 files with 3860K free
(:stream-A bulletin-board response to "What" command)

0057z, 119 msgs, last = 6895 >
(:stream-A bulletin-board command prompt)

|BLM
(:LOU sends "List Mine" command on stream B)

|AB
(:LOU sends "Bye" command on stream A)

|B:KE3Z:Use W and directory ID:
WA = AMSAT/satellite info
WB = BBS help info
WC = TRS80 (all models) files
WD = Kenwood info
WE = ICOM info
WF = BASIC programs
WG = General info
(:stream-B bulletin-board response to "What" command)

|A:W1AW-4:WA1LOU Stan de W1AW: 73, CUL
*** DISCONNECTED
(:stream-A bulletin-board response to "Bye" command)

cmd:CS
(:LOU sends "CStatus" command to TNC)

|B:KE3Z:WA1LOU de KE3Z: 870419/0059z 26 msgs, last 505 >
(:stream-B bulletin-board command prompt)

*** None found.
(:stream-B bulletin-board response to "List Mine" command)

A stream -	**I Link state is: DISCONNECTED**
B stream -	**O Link state is: CONNECTED to KE3Z VIA K1IKE**
C stream -	**Link state is: DISCONNECTED**
D stream -	**Link state is: DISCONNECTED**
E stream -	**Link state is: DISCONNECTED**
F stream -	**Link state is: DISCONNECTED**
G stream -	**Link state is: DISCONNECTED**
H stream -	**Link state is: DISCONNECTED**
I stream -	**Link state is: DISCONNECTED**
J stream -	**Link state is: DISCONNECTED**

(:TNC response to "CStatus" command; note that TNC-to-terminal Input is assigned to stream A and TNC-to-terminal Output is assigned to stream B)

|A:cmd:
(:TNC command prompt with Input assigned to stream A)

|B:KE3Z:WA1LOU de KE3Z: 870419/0059z 26 msgs, last 505>
(:stream-B bulletin-board command prompt)

cmd:|B
(:LOU reassigns Input to stream B)

cmd:CONV
(:LOU invokes "CONVerse" mode command)

B
(:LOU sends "Bye" command on stream B)

*** DISCONNECTED
(:stream-A bulletin-board response to "Bye" command)

Multiple-connection communications will keep you hopping. It takes a little getting used to, but once you get the hang of it, it's fun!

Good Operating Procedures

When you start using a new mode of amateur communications, it's important to learn good operating procedures. Let's look at some of the "rules of the road" for good packet-radio operating.

Packet-Radio Activity Frequencies

Like other modes of Amateur Radio communication, such as RTTY, SSTV and CW, packet-radio operation uses certain portions of the Amateur Radio bands. This helps prevent interference between different modes of communications. Imagine the cacophony of CW, RTTY, SSTV and voice communications all occurring within a few kilohertz of each other! The gentlemen's agreement also provides a common meeting place for each communications mode. The operators of each mode do not have to search from one end of an amateur band to the other to find activity on their chosen mode; the operators of their mode can be found within a known set of frequencies.

Packet-radio operations are found within certain defined frequencies; it is considered good operating practice to operate within these frequencies. The following chapters on VHF/UHF and HF communications delineate the specific packet-radio frequencies. Indiscriminately choosing any frequency within the Amateur Radio bands to operate packet radio is no way to make friends, and a good way to make enemies. Stick with the band plans and it will be easier for everyone.

Avoiding Collisions

Whenever any Amateur Radio contact is established on a frequency where there is other activity, it is good operating practice to move the contact to another frequency where there is no activity in order to avoid interference with other stations on the active frequency.

Packet radio permits more than one contact to be conducted on the same frequency, because if there is interference (a *collision* between the transmitted packets of two or more stations), the interference is invisible to the receiving stations and each transmitting station keeps sending the packet until the receiving station is able to receive the packet perfectly. Unfortunately, as the number of transmitting stations on the same frequency increases, the number of packet collisions increases and so does the number of packet retransmissions. As a result, the time it takes to transfer information between the various stations on a frequency increases and all the QSOs slow down to a crawl.

This means that, although multiple contacts on the same frequency are possible in packet radio, it is still good operating practice to move a contact to another frequency where there is less activity, especially if the frequency of the initial contact is populated by PBBSs. With fewer stations on a frequency, there will be fewer packet collisions, fewer resulting retransmissions, and communications will move at a good clip.

CQ

Calling CQ is the traditional way of attracting another Amateur Radio station for communications, and this tradition is supported in packet radio. A packet-radio CQ is easily accomplished by sending some properly configured unconnected packets in the converse mode. By default, unconnected packets are CQ packets. To be sure that this is the case, at the command prompt type:

cmd: Unproto <CR>

and if unconnected packets are configured as CQ packets, the terminal displays:

UNPROTO CQ

If CQ is not displayed, at the command prompt type:

cmd: Unproto CQ <CR>

After configuring unconnected packets for CQ, transfer to the converse mode and enter a carriage return. Each carriage return causes the TNC to transmit an unconnected CQ packet. Your CQ packets can be received by other stations monitoring the frequency who can hear your signal direct (without using a digipeater or node). If someone is interested in communicating with you, they can respond to your CQ by initiating a connection.

Like any other packet, an unconnected packet can collide with other packets, so do not send too many CQ packets on a congested frequency.

If there is a lot of activity on frequency, it may be easier to establish a connection with a station on your MHeard list than by trying to elicit a response to a random CQ. If there is not much activity on frequency, however, a few random CQs may prove successful. Don't overdo it. Anyone who can hear your station will receive one of your first few CQ packets, so dozens of CQs are unnecessary.

Beacons: The TNC Public Announcement Function

Each TNC has a beacon function which permits a station automatically to send unconnected packets at regular intervals. The purpose of the beacon function is to announce that your packet-radio station is on the air. This function was included in the very early TNCs because there was very little packet-radio activity at that time. New packet-radio operators needed a way to let other packet-radio operators know they were on the air. Without the beacon function, some of the early packet-radio stations might never have found anybody to exchange packets with.

Times have changed. Today, there are thousands of packet-radio stations on the air. Most of these stations operate on a few select frequencies within the Amateur Radio spectrum. As a result, it is not very difficult to find another station to contact. By simply using the "MHeard" command you can obtain a list of recently monitored stations. It is very likely that more than one of the listed stations is still on the air and can be connected to your station. Even the newest TNCs still include the beacon function, however, and since it is there, it is still being used on the busiest packet-radio frequencies in the world.

The beacon function still serves a legitimate purpose on frequencies (or in localities) where there is little packet-radio activity. If you are operating a 902-MHz PBBS in Barrow, Alaska, by all means enable the beacon function on a five-minute interval. If you leave your TNC on 24 hours a day on 145.01 MHz in Chevy Chase, Maryland, however, do not beacon the fact that your station is on the air. Sending beacons in such packet-radio-congested areas is poor operating practice. It annoys stations trying to exchange packets on the frequency and does not win many friends. Disable the beacon function and leave a message on the local PBBS that your station is on the air. Where there is a fair amount of packet-radio activity, anything that can be announced with a beacon is better off being announced with a message on the local PBBS.

Again, beacons still serve a legitimate purpose on certain frequencies and/or in certain localities, so a short primer on the beacon function is in order.

The contents of the beacon (the beacon message or announcement) are stored in the TNC by means of the "BText" command. This message can contain a maximum of 120 characters in the TNC 2 and 128 characters in the TNC 1. BText is entered at the command prompt by typing:

cmd: BText x <CR>

where x is the contents of the beacon message.

The beacon function may be enabled in one of two ways. It may be enabled to transmit at regular specified intervals, or it may be enabled to transmit after a specified interval of packet-radio inactivity. The "beacon after" mode is preferred, because transmissions only occur when the channel is clear and has not been in use for some time. In the beacon-after mode, the beacon is transmitted once after the set amount of time passes with no channel activity. The TNC will not send the beacon again until it detects activity on the channel, and then only after the activity has again ceased for the set interval. In the regular interval mode, beacons are transmitted at regular intervals, even during the busiest periods.

To enable the inactivity beacon mode, at the command prompt type:

cmd: Beacon After n <CR>

where n is a number from 0 to 250 (0 to 255 in the TNC 1) representing intervals of packet-radio inactivity in 10-second increments. For example, to select a beacon interval of 10 minutes (600 seconds), set n to 60 (600 sec / 10 sec = 60). If n is 0, the beacon function is disabled.

To enable the regular-interval beacon mode, at the command prompt type:

cmd: Beacon Every n <CR>

where n is a number from 0 to 250 (0 to 255 in the TNC 1) representing the interval between beacon transmissions in 10-second increments. Again, if n is 0, the beacon function is disabled.

Conclusion

This chapter has spelled out the basic operating procedures for amateur packet radio. The following chapters take these basic operating procedures and fine tune them for the various types of packet-radio communications now occurring on the air: VHF/UHF communications, HF communications, time-shifting communications, network communications, space communications and other applications.

CHAPTER EIGHT

VHF and UHF Communications

The VHF and UHF spectrum is where most Amateur Radio packet-radio communication occurs today. Most of this activity is concentrated on 2 meters, usually on or near 145.01 MHz.

The level of growth of packet-radio activity today is similar to the growth of FM activity in the 1970s. Each represents the hottest mode of Amateur Radio operation in its respective decade.

What's the Attraction?

One attraction of both VHF/UHF packet radio and VHF FM is the ability to go a long way with only a little equipment. On VHF FM, you can cover a wide area with a 1-watt 2-meter hand-held transceiver. On packet, you can communicate all over the country with that same hand-held transceiver and a TNC.

The key to this wide coverage is the use of a repeater to retransmit your signal beyond the normal coverage of your station. Normally, an FM transmission is only repeated once (this is sometimes called "one hop"), so repeated FM communication is limited to intrastate propagation (unless you or the repeater are located on a state line or in a small state). In packet radio, as many as eight packet-radio digital repeaters (or digipeaters) or an unconstrained number of network nodes and switches may be used (sometimes called "multi hop"). This makes interstate communication possible on packet radio. (For a full description on how to use digipeaters, network nodes and other networking operations, refer to Chapter 11—Network Communications.)

In addition to the advantage in the number of repeaters, plus nodes and switches, that may be used on packet radio as compared to voice repeaters, any active packet-radio station may be used as a digipeater when needed.

HF or VHF?

One reason why VHF and UHF packet radio is more popular than HF packet radio is that higher data rates are permitted in the VHF and UHF spectrum. Below 28 MHz, the maximum permissible data rate is 300 bauds. Above 28 MHz, the legal limit starts at 1200 bauds and increases as the operating frequency increases. (The maximum data rate is 1200 bauds between 28 MHz and 50 MHz, 19.6 kilobauds between 50 MHz and 220 MHz, and

Novices on 220 MHz

ARRL Headquarters has received numerous inquiries concerning which frequency or frequencies Novices should use for simplex packet-radio operations in the 220-MHz band. The ARRL offers the following interim guidance, pending any future revision of the ARRL 220-MHz band plan.

Use 223.40 MHz as a national packet-radio simplex frequency except in those areas where frequency coordinators have coordinated repeaters or other uses on this frequency. Packet-radio simplex operations should not cause interference to repeaters or other uses already coordinated, and another simplex frequency that is not in use locally should be selected from the simplex frequency list below.

223.42	223.44	223.46	223.48	223.52	223.54
223.56	223.58	223.60	223.62	223.64	223.66
223.68	223.70	223.72	223.74	223.76	223.78
223.80	223.82	223.84	223.86	223.88	223.90

If duplex packet-radio operation is needed, use *input frequencies* and *output frequencies* in the 222.32-223.38 and 223.92-223.98 MHz bands, respectively, as assigned by the local frequency coordinator.

56 kilobauds between 220 MHz and 902 MHz. Above 902 MHz there is no speed limit.)

Although some amateurs are experimenting with 4800- and 9600-baud data rates, the most popular data rate currently in use in the VHF and UHF spectrum is 1200 bauds. The reason for the popularity of 1200 bauds is twofold. First, since the beginning of amateur packet radio, 1200 bauds has been the data rate that has been used by most amateurs on VHF and UHF. In order to be able to transfer packets with most other amateurs, you must use 1200 bauds. Second, since most amateurs want the capability to communicate with other amateurs, they want 1200-baud capability; as a result, most TNCs that have an internal modem have a 1200-baud modem (some also have 300-baud modems for HF capability, and others have higher-speed modems as well).

Another reason for the use of VHF/UHF is that current FCC Rules do not allow transmission of anything other than ASCII or RTTY codes below 50 MHz. You cannot legally send a file of binary data (for example, a program image) on HF, but you can do so on VHF/UHF.

FM and AFSK

As we mentioned earlier, the same hand-held transceiver that is used for FM voice communications may be used for VHF and UHF packet radio. Because of this, frequency modulation (FM) is used to put a signal on the air in most of the VHF and UHF packet-radio world, and audio-frequency-shift keying (AFSK) is used to put intelligence onto that FM signal. The FM signal is generated by the transceiver that is connected to the radio port of a TNC with an internal modem, or to the telephone-line connection of the external modem connected to a TNC without an internal modem. The AFSK is generated by the modem.

At 1200 bauds, amateurs use one of the modem standards developed for 1200-baud telephone data communications. This standard is known as Bell 202. The Bell 202 standard was selected because Bell 202 modems were readily available as surplus equipment when the Vancouver amateur packet-radio pioneers were looking for a 1200-baud modem to connect to their new, modem-less TNCs.

The Bell 202 standard is designed for half-duplex transmission and reception of asynchronous, binary, serial data at a maximum data rate of 1200 bits per second. The modem uses FSK modulation and demodulation techniques, with mark and space frequencies of 1200 Hz and 2200 Hz

Bulletin Boards and Mailboxes

Using PBBSs is a popular activity in packet-radio communication, so popular that an entire chapter (Chapter 10) in this book is devoted to it. Some PBBS operating procedures specifically relate to VHF and UHF operation, however, and a discussion of those procedures follows.

Much PBBS activity involves *uploading* and *downloading* mail and files. These activities are often very time consuming and, since so many stations actively share the same frequency in VHF and UHF packet radio, certain procedures should be followed to minimize the amount of time spent with a VHF or UHF PBBS.

Trying to maintain a multiple digipeater or network node contact with another live-operator station is very difficult because of the packet-collision problem. Considering the great amount of data that is passed to and from a PBBS, trying to maintain a multiple digipeater or node contact with a PBBS is next to impossible. Always use the minimum number of digipeaters and nodes necessary to communicate with a PBBS. If you can communicate with a PBBS directly, do so!

If you must use digipeaters or nodes, however, never use more than one or two. Some PBBSs have the capability to reject connections that use more than a set number of digipeaters and nodes. As packet-radio activity continues to grow, the trend has been to enable this capability with the maximum number set low (to one or two). Most areas now have at least one local PBBS, and you won't usually find anything of interest to you on a distant PBBS that isn't on your local PBBS. The next time you attempt a long-distance PBBS connection and are disconnected before things get going, you've probably been disconnected by the "maximum digipeaters" parameter.

When you use a PBBS, you can save time by sending multiple commands at once rather than using a separate packet to send each command. Normally, to send a command to a PBBS, you type the command followed by a carriage return, <CR>. The <CR> forces the TNC to send a packet which contains one command. To send multiple commands in a packet, you can enter a <CTRL-V> before each <CR> (except the last <CR>). The purpose of <CTRL-V> is to cause the TNC to ignore the character that follows it, but to pass that ignored character to the other station. In this case, <CTRL-V> preceding <CR> causes the TNC to ignore <CR> and, as a result, the TNC is not forced to send a packet by the ignored <CR>. That <CR> is transferred to the PBBS, however (the PBBS requires that each command be separated by a <CR>). For example, to send the RM, KM and L commands to a PBBS in one packet, you would type:

RM <CTRL-V> <CR> KM <CTRL-V> <CR> L <CR>

Note that the last <CR> is not preceded by a <CTRL-V>, because the TNC must not ignore it. The TNC must recognize the last <CR> in order to force the transmission of the complete packet containing the three commands.

During prime time (between 6 and 11 PM on weekdays and during waking hours on weekends), there is a lot of competition on the VHF and UHF packet-radio frequencies, and much of that involves trying to win the attention of the local PBBS. If your schedule permits, use the PBBS during nonprime-time hours. You will be pleasantly surprised by how easy it is to use the PBBS during the weekday while most people are at work or late at night and early in the morning while most people are asleep.

Good Operating Procedures

When you begin to operate any new Amateur Radio mode, it is important to learn good operating procedures. Let's look at some of the ways you can be an A-1 packet-radio operator.

Suggested Frequencies

If you have operated in the VHF or UHF spectrum for any amount of time, you are aware of the band plans that have come into use to guide amateurs as where to operate different modes on the same band. The band plans are based partly on the FCC regulations. For example, the FCC rules specify that only CW may be used between 144.0 and 144.1 MHz, and the 2-meter band plan adheres to that rule. Between 144.1 and 148.0 MHz, however, the FCC permits 12 different emission modes. As a result, the amateur band planners had the chore of dividing up the remaining 3.9 MHz of the 2-meter band for the different modes in order to avoid mass mode confusion.

With the growth in popularity of packet radio, the band planners (and the frequency coordinators, who actually administer the band plans) have had to make some adjustments to the plans to accommodate packet-radio activity. While some frequency coordinators are still standing on the side-

VHF/UHF TNC Parameters

When a TNC is turned on for the first time (or whenever the "Reset" command is invoked), all of the TNC's selectable parameters are set to their default selections. The default values are optimized for VHF and UHF operation. The following is a list of the critical parameters that optimize the TNC for VHF and UHF operation. They are listed here to provide a quick reference for reconfiguring the TNC for VHF and UHF operation (for example, after experimenting with different parameter values, or after using the TNC on HF).

Radio port data rate:

TNC 1: Hbaud = 1200

TNC 2: DIP switch position 7 = ON

MAXframe = 4 (maximum number of outstanding unacknowledged packets)

Paclen = 128 (number of bytes in each packet)

DWait (delays TNC transmissions in favor of digipeater transmissions):

TNC 1: DWait = 2
TNC 2: DWait = 16

AXDelay = 0 (when a voice repeater is used for packet-radio repeating, AXDelay should be set to a value equal to the repeater's receive-to-transmit turnaround time minus the value of TXdelay)

AXHang = 0 (when a voice repeater is used for packet-radio repeating, AXHang should be set to a value equal to the length of the repeater's squelch tail.)

lines waiting to see if packet radio is real or just a passing fancy before they make any changes, others have already made changes. Some coordinators have simply set aside some frequencies for packet-radio activity, while others have set aside certain frequencies for specific types of packet-radio operations (separate channels for PBBS operations, station-to-station operations, etc), often after consulting the packet-radio operators within their jurisdiction.

At this time, most VHF and UHF packet-radio activity occurs on the 144- and 220-MHz bands. On 2 meters, 145.010 MHz is the first place to look. In areas where there is a lot of packet-radio activity on 2 meters, activity has spread out onto the frequencies above and below 145.010 MHz, usually at 20 kHz intervals (below 145.010 MHz on 144.910, 144.930, 144.950, 144.970 and 144.990, and above 145.010 MHz on 145.030, 145.050, 145.070 and 145.090).

On 220 MHz, the most active packet-radio frequency in some areas is 221.110 MHz. This frequency is usually used strictly for forwarding messages or mail from one PBBS to another PBBS. Individual packet-radio stations

Table 8.1

Suggested Frequencies for Packet-Radio Activity

The following frequencies are recommended for packet-radio operation by the ARRL Digital Committee and ARRL Board of Directors, subject to local frequency coordinator recommendations. Specific use of these frequencies should be determined by local user groups. Additional frequencies (including any duplex operation) should be coordinated with local frequency coordinators. (The recommendations for the 33-cm band were adopted as interim guidelines for packet-radio frequencies, pending conclusion of a study by the ARRL Membership Services Committee on revising the current interim band plan.)

50.62 / 51.62 MHz	: locally coordinated duplex pair (high in, low out)
50.64 / 51.64	: locally coordinated duplex pair (high in, low out)
50.66 / 51.66	: locally coordinated duplex pair (high in, low out)
50.68 / 51.68	: locally coordinated duplex pair (high in, low out)
50.72 / 51.72	: locally coordinated duplex pair (high in, low out)
50.74 / 51.74	: locally coordinated duplex pair (high in, low out)
50.76 / 51.76	: locally coordinated duplex pair (high in, low out)
50.78 / 51.78	: locally coordinated duplex pair (high in, low out)
51.70	: national packet-radio simplex frequency
145.010 MHz	: automatic/unattended operation (inter-LAN use)
145.030	: automatic/unattended operation
145.050	: automatic/unattended operation
145.070	: automatic/unattended operation
145.090	: automatic/unattended operation
220.55 MHz	: 100-kHz-bandwidth channel
220.65	: 100-kHz-bandwidth channel
220.75	: 100-kHz-bandwidth channel
220.85	: 100-kHz-bandwidth channel
220.95	: 100-kHz-bandwidth channel
221.01	: 20-kHz-bandwidth channel
221.03	: 20-kHz-bandwidth channel
221.05	: 20-kHz-bandwidth channel
221.07	: 20-kHz-bandwidth channel
221.09	: 20-kHz-bandwidth channel
223.40	: National packet-radio simplex frequency
223.42	: locally coordinated Novice packet-radio simplex channel
223.44	: locally coordinated Novice packet-radio simplex channel
223.46	: locally coordinated Novice packet-radio simplex channel
223.48	: locally coordinated Novice packet-radio simplex channel

should not attempt to connect with stations conducting mail forwarding. Most often, the equipment used by these stations is configured to reject packets from individual users. In addition, communication between individual stations is not recommended on 221.110 MHz, in order to avoid interference with the mail-forwarding operations.

While packet-radio activity on the other VHF and UHF bands is sporadic, Table 8.1 is provided to show VHF and UHF frequencies where packet-radio activity is likely to occur. To minimize interference with other Amateur Radio modes, packet-radio communications should be limited to these frequencies. If you are in doubt, check with other local packet-radio users or your area frequency coordinator.

430.05 MHz	: 100-kHz-wide channel
430.15	: 100-kHz-wide channel
430.25	: 100-kHz-wide channel
430.35	: 100-kHz-wide channel
430.45	: 100-kHz-wide channel
430.55	: 100-kHz-wide channel
430.65	: 100-kHz-wide channel
430.85	: 100-kHz-wide channel
430.95	: 100-kHz-wide channel
431.025	: narrow-band channel
440.975	: 25-kHz-wide channel
441.000	: 25-kHz-wide channel
441.025	: 25-kHz-wide channel
441.050	: 25-kHz-wide channel
441.075	: 25-kHz-wide channel
1249.0 MHz	: 2-MHz-wide channel
1251.0	: 2-MHz-wide channel
1294.025	: 25-kHz-wide channel
1294.050	: 25-kHz-wide channel
1294.075	: 25-kHz-wide channel
1294.100	: 25-kHz-wide channel; National packet-radio *calling frequency*
1294.125	: 25-kHz-wide channel
1294.150	: 25-kHz-wide channel
1294.175	: 25-kHz-wide channel
1298.0	: 2-MHz-wide channel
1299.05	: 100-kHz-wide channel
1299.15	: 100-kHz-wide channel
1299.25	: 100-kHz-wide channel
1299.35	: 100-kHz-wide channel
1299.45	: 100-kHz-wide channel
1299.55	: 100-kHz-wide channel
1299.65	: 100-kHz-wide channel
1299.75	: 100-kHz-wide channel
1299.85	: 100-kHz-wide channel
1299.95	: 100-kHz-wide channel

On 33-cm (902-928 MHz), the recommended interim packet-radio band plan allocates two 3-MHz-wide channels (to accommodate 1.5 Mbit/s links) with 10.7-MHz spacing. This allocation may be accomplished with channels at 903-906 and 914-917 MHz.

Avoiding Collisions and Increasing Throughput

The channelized nature of packet-radio activity in the VHF and UHF spectrum demands that packet-radio stations be aware of what activity is on the channel in order to avoid interference whenever possible. Attempting to conduct a contact between individual stations on a frequency where there is a wide-coverage digipeater, network node or PBBS in operation frustrates all the stations on the channel, as collisions between packets are very likely to occur. Since it is easier to move the contact between individual stations to another channel than it is to move a digipeater, node or PBBS, it is good operating practice for the individual stations to move their connection to another channel where there is relative inactivity. Again, this is analogous to using FM voice *simplex* whenever possible, to avoid tying up a voice repeater that may be needed by other users.

Note that it is not necessary to disconnect when you move a contact from one frequency to another. When you decide to make a move and know where to go, simply tune your transceiver to the new frequency without disconnecting. Assuming that the other station did not get lost during the move, you should still be connected and can carry on communications without missing too many beats.

CQs and Beacons

Good operating procedures concerning the transmission of packet-radio CQs and beacons were discussed in the previous chapter. The only thing that needs to be added is that long-distance CQs and beacons are possible in the VHF and UHF spectrum, with the help of digipeaters and network nodes. As many as eight digipeaters and an unconstrained number of network nodes can be used to send your CQ or beacon message out into the packet-radio hinterlands. Under average VHF and UHF packet-radio operating situations (read: crowded), no more than one or two digipeaters or nodes should be used. As we mentioned earlier, it is difficult to maintain a connection through multiple digipeaters and nodes. The purpose of a CQ or beacon is to attract another station for communications, so why bother trying to attract another station over a multi-hop path when it would be difficult (or impossible) to maintain a connection with that same station over the same multi-hop path?

If you want to use one or more digipeaters to send a CQ or beacon, at the command prompt type:

cmd: Unproto CQ Via WA1UTQ,K1IKE,W1AW-5 <CR>

where WA1UTQ, K1IKE and W1AW-5 are the call signs of the digipeaters you wish to use to send a CQ or beacon. As with the "Connect" command, commas separate the digipeater station call signs. SSIDs must be included if the station's SSID is anything other than 0. Also, the order of digipeater call signs is critical and a maximum of eight digipeater stations may be used.

To send a CQ through one or more digipeaters, transfer to the Converse Mode and enter a carriage return. Each carriage return causes the TNC to transmit an unconnected CQ packet through the digipeaters selected with the "Unproto" command. (Sending CQs via a node is dependent on the type of node being used. Refer to Chapter 11—Network Communications for information concerning network nodes that provide the CQ.)

To send a beacon through one or more digipeaters, enter a beacon message using the "BText" command and enable the beacon function using the "Beacon Every/After" command, as described in the previous chapter. Each beacon will be transmitted through the digipeaters selected with the "Unproto" command.

Conclusion

The basic operating procedures for VHF and UHF packet-radio communications have been discussed in this chapter. Later chapters dealing with time-shifting communications, network communications, space communications and other applications will take these same basic procedures and utilize them in specialized VHF and UHF packet-radio modes of operation.

CHAPTER NINE

HF Communications

HF Amateur Radio communication, whatever the mode, means DX. The long-distance propagation provided by the HF radio spectrum makes transcontinental and transoceanic communications possible. DX communication also plays an important role in the overall packet-radio scheme. Long-distance packet-radio communications provide the means for packet-radio experimenters in different countries to exchange ideas and information concerning amateur packet-radio technology. In addition, packet-radio mail is forwarded and delivered over long distances using the HF bands.

300-Baud Equipment

Operating HF packet radio is quite different from VHF and UHF packet-radio operating. For one thing, only data using ASCII or RTTY codes is allowed below 50 MHz; you may not send "binary" files. Another significant difference is that the authorized maximum data rate in the HF radio spectrum is lower than in the VHF and UHF spectrum. The maximum data rate permitted below 28 MHz by present FCC regulations is 300 bauds. On 10 meters, 1200-baud packet radio is permitted.

Besides the lower data rate, another significant difference is the method of generating the packet-radio signals. On VHF, packet radio typically uses audio tones applied to the microphone input of an FM transmitter to generate an AFSK signal. On HF, the audio tones are applied to the microphone input of a single-sideband suppressed-carrier transmitter to generate what is essentially an FSK signal. At 300 bauds, TAPR TNCs use 1600-Hz and 1800-Hz tones (200-Hz shift), rather than the Bell-202 tones (1000-Hz shift) used at VHF and above.

Many of the TNCs manufactured today may be used at 300 bauds or 1200 bauds simply by changing a switch or invoking a software command. The majority of older TNCs include only the Bell-202 VHF/UHF standard modem, if they include a modem at all. The owners of these older TNCs either have to make modifications to the internal modem, if there is one, or add an external HF-compatible modem.

Modification of the modems in the TNC 1 and TNC 2 requires changing the values of one capacitor and one resistor (change TNC-1 C21 or TNC-2 C54 to 0.01 μF, and TNC-1 R46 or TNC-2 R93 to 220 kΩ). After the components are changed, the modem must be recalibrated, and the radio-port data rate must be changed to 300 bauds (TNC-1 command Hbaud 300 or TNC-2 DIP-switch position 6 ON). The disadvantage of modifying the internal modem is that the TNC then cannot be used for VHF and UHF operation without modifying and recalibrating the modem again.

Adding an external modem for HF operation provides a more convenient alternative. Commercial HF modems like AEA's PM-1, DRSI's HF*Modem, HAL's ST-7000 and Pac-Comm's PTU-220 are simple to install and use. Installation requires proper cabling between a TNC and the HF modem; after the proper connections are made, switching between the external HF modem and the TNC's internal modem is as simple as engaging or disengaging a front-panel push-button switch and changing the TNC's radio-port data rate. In addition, each manufacturer claims that the designs of their external HF modems are optimized for HF operation so that they provide better performance than a modified internal TNC modem.

Tuning A Signal

One of the most difficult parts of HF packet-radio operation is properly tuning a received signal. On VHF and UHF, tuning is simply a matter of turning the transceiver's frequency selector to a known active packet-radio channel and waiting for a packet to be displayed on your terminal.

On HF, tuning is more difficult. Tune your HF receiver very slowly across the part of the band that contains known packet-radio activity. Tune in as small an increment as possible (10-Hz increments are desirable) until your terminal begins displaying packets. When you tune on HF, do not change frequency until you hear the end of a packet. If you shift frequency in mid-packet, it is likely that the packet will not be received properly and will not be displayed on your terminal, even if you were on the correct frequency before or after the frequency change. Remember, each packet must be received correctly from beginning to end before the TNC will send it to your terminal for display.

Most TNCs that include HF modems (and most external commercial HF modems) include tuning indicators to simplify proper HF tuning. Kits are also available to add tuning indicators to those TNCs without one.

For example, on AEA's PM-1 HF modem, the tuning indicator consists of a 10-segment LED bar display. With the PM-1, you tune your receiver until the maximum number of segments are lit equally in either direction from the center of the display. Using a tuning indicator is much easier than adjusting the receiver's frequency in 10-Hz steps until a packet is successfully displayed.

Point-To-Point Communications

Most HF packet-radio communications are *point-to-point*. Very few digipeaters or network nodes are active on HF. There are several reasons for this, including the fact that FCC regulations do not allow unattended digipeater operation on HF. Another important reason is that an operating digipeater or node is technically passing third-party traffic. HF digipeater and node operation also compounds the *hidden transmitter* problem, where your TNC cannot hear a station (or stations) that the digipeater or node can hear. This leads to collision problems and general confusion. For all these reasons, it is best to disable your TNC's digipeater function on HF and to avoid using any active digipeaters or nodes you may hear.

The lack of digipeaters and network nodes on HF is really not a problem. On HF, point-to-point communications means interstate or international communications, depending on the time of day, time of year, operating frequency and the number of active sunspots.

Packet radio became popular during a period of low sunspot activity. As a result, through the middle of the 1980s most HF packet-radio activity was limited to 20 meters and below, with infrequent forays to 10 and 15 meters for local operations and experiments. As sunspot activity increased in the late 1980s, the frequencies above 20 meters became more reliable for DX

HF TNC Parameters

When a TNC is turned on for the first time or whenever the "RESET" command is invoked, all of the TNC's selectable parameters are set to their default selections, which are optimized for VHF and UHF operation.

To operate successfully on HF, certain critical parameters must be changed from the default values. These critical parameters are listed here to provide a quick reference for configuring the TNC for HF operation.

Radio port data rate:
    Below 28 MHz, 300 baud:
        TNC 1: Hbaud = 300
        TNC 2: DIP switch position 6 = ON

    28.0-50.0 MHz, 1200 baud:
        TNC 1: Hbaud = 1200
        TNC 2: DIP switch position 7 = ON

MAXframe = 1 (maximum number of outstanding unacknowledged packets)

Paclen = 64 or less (number of bytes in each packet)

DIGIpeat = OFF (disable TNC's digipeater function)

DWait = 0 (a digipeater timing function, unnecessary on HF)

TXdelay = minimum radio receive-to-transmit turnaround time

AXDelay = 0 (an unnecessary voice-repeater timing function)

AXHang = 0 (an unnecessary voice-repeater timing function)

propagation, and packet-radio DX activity blossomed, especially in the 10-meter band.

Although HF provides long-distance propagation for packet-radio, conditions can vary widely. Anyone who has operated on HF knows that one minute you may be in contact with a station halfway around the world, with excellent signals at both ends, and the next minute you may be talking to yourself as propagation shifts and closes the path to the other station. To compensate somewhat for the vagaries of HF propagation, certain critical TNC parameters may be changed. You cannot run a TNC in the same configuration on HF as on VHF or UHF, where propagation is more stable. The sidebar "HF TNC Parameters" summarizes the critical TNC parameters that should be changed for HF operation, while Chapter 6 fully describes how to select these parameters.

The DX Connection

Working packet-radio DX is not much different than working DX on any other mode. You tune to an active HF packet-radio channel with the monitoring function enabled and check for DX call signs. If you hear a DX station that you would like to contact, you wait patiently for the DX station to finish his current contact. After the DX station disconnects, you may send a connect request to that station; assuming that the propagation path is reciprocal, you should be able to make a DX connection.

More and more countries are permitting amateur packet radio, so a lot of interesting DX can be found on the HF packet-radio channels these days (refer to the sidebar "A DX Sampler" for an East Coast sampling). So many countries are joining the packet-radio ranks that the number of active

---

A DX Sampler

The following is a sample of stations monitored on 14 MHz at various times of the day from station WA1LOU, located in downtown Wolcott, Connecticut. All times are UTC. (This list was compiled using the TNC's "MHeard" command.)

A4XKC	16:40	GJ4YAD	17:42	LX1YZ	20:54
AL7FL	23:56	GM4VPA	19:48	OA4CK	18:18
CP5PM	18:02	GW4HDR	18:49	ON8NY	19:13
CT1AEX	19:22	HA5XA	17:26	PA0GX	16:40
DL1CB	15:29	HB9CBT	16:31	TF3KB	17:07
EA3EGI	23:56	HK7DPE	17:22	TI2ALG	23:24
EA8QS	23:08	HP1XAW	14:13	TR8LD	17:19
EI6EH	23:09	I4QHD	19:25	VE1PEI	15:45
F5LO	15:20	IS0VDG	16:32	YV5AVW	23:29
G4RQX	23:39	LA9EX	16:39	ZF1GC	14:32
GI4LKG	19:13	LU1DVT	00:58	9H4B	18:48

---

countries has topped the 100 mark, and packet-radio DXCC *is* possible.

With the assistance of HF propagation, it is now possible to make packet-radio contacts with stations in all 50 states. To recognize this achievement, the ARRL now offers the Worked-All-States (WAS) award with a packet endorsement to any operator who can submit written confirmation of packet-radio contacts with stations in all 50 states (the District of Columbia counts as Maryland). The proof of contact (usually a QSL card) must state that the mode used to make the contact was packet radio and that two-way communication was established. Contacts made through repeater or network devices do not count. Anyone interested in applying for the packet-radio WAS should send an SASE to ARRL/WAS, 225 Main Street, Newington, CT 06111 to obtain a WAS application form.

Mail Forwarding

Besides DX contacts, another significant HF packet-radio activity is the mail-forwarding function performed by various PBBS stations throughout the United States. The mail-forwarding function is the means by which messages uploaded to local PBBSs are transferred from one area of the country to another. Much mail-forwarding takes place on VHF and UHF, but long-distance forwarding usually involves some use of HF. Forwarding long-distance mail on HF is quicker (fewer hops), and in some cases it is the only way that the message can be transferred.

For example, to forward a message from one coast to the other coast, it would take many VHF and UHF mail-forwarding stations to relay that message to its destination. On HF, however, two mail-forwarding stations (one on each coast) can perform the same task. There may also be some gaps in the VHF and UHF path needed to relay the message from coast-to-coast. HF relays can fill these gaps. Refer to Figure 9.2 for a comparison of HF and VHF long-distance mail forwarding.

At this time, the HF network of mail-forwarding relay stations is fairly stable. Each mail-forwarding station has a list of all other mail-forwarding

Figure 9.1—A typical VHF-to-HF mail-forwarding gateway PBBS.

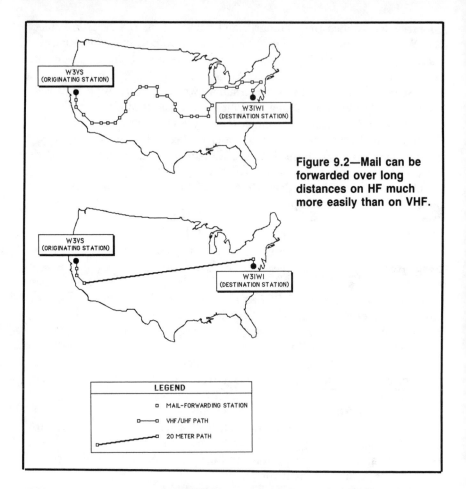

Figure 9.2—Mail can be forwarded over long distances on HF much more easily than on VHF.

LEGEND

□ MAIL-FORWARDING STATION

□——□ VHF/UHF PATH

□————□ 20 METER PATH

stations, and is usually configured to connect with these stations only. If you attempt to make a connection with a mail-forwarding station, you will be summarily disconnected. These stations are similar to dedicated digipeater or node stations. Their only purpose is to relay messages to other mail-forwarding stations; they cannot be used by other stations for other purposes.

Most of the mail-forwarding stations are located on the same frequencies (refer to Table 9.1). To promote the unimpeded flow of the mail-forwarding process, you should not transmit on the mail-forwarding channels.

Good Operating Procedures

As we mentioned in the chapter on VHF and UHF operating, packet-radio operation requires a knowledge of good operating practices, just like any other Amateur Radio communications mode. It's important to learn the procedures before you transmit.

Table 9.1

Suggested Frequencies for Packet-Radio Activity

The following frequencies are recommended for HF packet-radio operation by the ARRL Digital Committee (specified frequencies are channel centers). Use of RTTY subbands for packet-radio operations (especially normal QSOs) is encouraged. 1200-baud operation (with FCC approval) should be possible using the spectrally efficient emission mode of minimum-shift keying (MSK). With a view toward eventual adoption of such systems, 2-kHz channel spacing is assumed.

1800-1830 kHz	: United States RTTY subband
1802.3	: automatic message-forwarding (subject to propagation)
1830-1840	: United States RTTY subband for intercontinental usage
3594.3 kHz	: intercontinental message forwarding*
3605-3645	: United States RTTY subband
3607.3	: North American message forwarding
7038.3	: intercontinental message forwarding*
7080-7100 kHz	: United States RTTY subband
7091.3	: North American message forwarding
10140-10150 kHz	: United States RTTY subband
10145.2	: intercontinental message forwarding
10147.3	: North American message forwarding
14070-14099.5 kHz	: United States RTTY subband
14102.3	: intercontinental message forwarding*
14108.3	: intracontinental message forwarding*
18100-18110 kHz	: United States RTTY subband
18106.3	: automatic message-forwarding (subject to propagation)
18108.3	: automatic message-forwarding (subject to propagation)
21070-21100 kHz	: United States RTTY subband
21096.3	: automatic message-forwarding (subject to propagation)
21098.3	: automatic message-forwarding (subject to propagation)
24920-24930 kHz	: United States RTTY subband
24926.3	: automatic message-forwarding (subject to propagation)
24928.3	: automatic message-forwarding (subject to propagation)
28070-28150 kHz	: United States RTTY subband
28102.3	: automatic message-forwarding (subject to propagation)
28104.3	: automatic message-forwarding (subject to propagation)

20-meter frequencies should be considered experimental in nature. 30-meter frequency use is subject to noninterference to fixed stations outside the United States. 10-meter frequencies are chosen as potential network entry points for Novices and Technicians.

*Frequency is an exception to the RTTY subband rule to provide usable automatic message-forwarding channels.

Suggested Operating Frequencies

Over the years, various parts of the HF Amateur Radio bands have become the home for different modes of communications. RTTY, SSTV, DX, traffic nets, beacons and other amateur operations all have a place they can call home on the HF bands. Most amateurs respect these "gentlemen's agreements" and do not operate a different mode in those portions of the bands that are dedicated to other modes of operation. Although packet radio is the new kid on the block, it has already settled on some HF frequencies that are recognized by others as intended for packet radio only.

At this time, 20 meters is the most active HF packet-radio band. Originally, 20-meter packet-radio operators chose 14.103 MHz as the frequency for their activity because it was just above another digital mode of communications, 20-meter RTTY activity between 14.070 and 14.099 MHz (in these references, the specified frequency is the center frequency).

As it turned out, 14.103 MHz was too close to the 20-meter DX beacons operating on 14.100 MHz. Although the beacons generally did not hamper packet-radio operations, the packet-radio activity did interfere with the DX beacons under certain circumstances. If the packet-radio operators were right on 14.103 and the DX operators used narrow CW filters, there was no interference. If the packet-radio operators drifted down towards the beacons or the DX operators were using wider SSB filters, however, it was possible for interference to occur.

After a hue and cry was sounded by DXers around the world, many packet-radio stations moved off 14.103 MHz. Other stations, unaware of the problem, remained on 14.103 MHz, and it is still one of the most active HF packet-radio frequencies. A realignment of packet-radio activity is expected, however, in light of the ARRL Board of Directors' approval of the packet-radio band plans recommended by the ARRL Digital Committee (see Table 9.1).

The growth of packet radio on 20 meters paralleled the growth of packet radio on 2 meters. As packet-radio activity overwhelmed 145.010 MHz, the activity spread out onto the channels surrounding 145.010 MHz (down to 144.910 and up to 145.090 MHz). Similarly, as activity outgrew 14.103 MHz, and with DX beacons and RTTY below 14.100 MHz, packet-radio operators had only one direction to go; they moved up the band to 14.105, 14.107 and 14.109 MHz.

The most popular HF packet-radio channel, 14.103 MHz, became the calling frequency on 20 meters, while 14.107 and 14.109 MHz became populated with PBBSs. On 14.105 MHz, a transition frequency, there were some PBBS operations, as well as some casual contacts that moved up to 14.105 MHz after initially connecting on the 14.103-MHz calling frequency. 14.105 MHz was also used as the calling frequency for those stations that had abandoned 14.103 MHz in deference to the beacon stations.

In general, the PBBSs on 14.107 MHz were open to all users. Here you could upload and download messages and files to and from a PBBS on the other side of the country just as you would upload and download to and from a 2-meter PBBS on the other side of town. On the other hand, the PBBSs on 14.109 MHz are closed to most users. Most, if not all, of the PBBS operations on 14.109 MHz are strictly involved with mail-forwarding operations, as discussed earlier in this chapter. If you attempt to connect with one of these mail-forwarding PBBSs, your connect request will be rejected. It is interesting to monitor 14.109 MHz and watch the mail-forwarding operation in action, but you should not transmit on 14.109 MHz, because you will succeed only in slowing down the mail-forwarding process.

After 20 meters, the most active packet-radio HF bands are 40 and 10 meters. On 40, 7.093 MHz and 7.097 MHz are the most active packet-radio channels, with 7.097 MHz acting as a general-usage frequency and 7.093 MHz used by PBBSs that only perform mail-forwarding operations (the 40-meter equivalent of 14.109 MHz). Mail forwarding on 14.109 MHz is a daytime and early evening operation for long-haul message relay, while mail forwarding on 7.093 MHz is a nighttime operation for short-distance message relay. On 10 meters, 28.103 and 28.105 MHz are the most active 300-baud channels, while 28.195 and 28.205 MHz are the most active 1200-baud channels. The other most-active HF packet-radio frequencies are found on 30 and 80 meters. Refer to Table 9.1 for a list of the packet-radio subbands on each HF band.

Relief From Congestion

If you use an HF calling frequency to establish a connection, it is good operating practice to move the contact to another, less-active frequency. The HF calling frequencies are often very congested. There is a high potential for packet collisions, and with the constant changes in HF propagation, these crowded channels get very confusing. As the propagation shifts, connected stations can no longer hear each other and the frequency becomes full of repeated packets seeking acknowledgments that will never be sent. It is hard enough to contend with other connected transmissions without adding these unacknowledged packets to the congestion, so it is best to move to a quieter frequency after making a connection on the calling frequency.

CQs And Beacons

The general rules concerning packet-radio CQs and beacons that were discussed in Chapter 7 also apply to HF packet-radio operations.

Calling CQ plays a more important role on HF than it does on VHF and UHF. Every hour of the day a different part of the world may be available on HF. You never know who is monitoring the frequency, and calling CQ may be the only way to flush out a contact. Beacons can also be used to flush out a DX contact, but calling CQ is preferred. The CQ call gets the job done, and it is usually shorter than a beacon. Unless you have a good reason to transmit a beacon (if you are operating a contest, for example ["CQ Field Day"], or a special-event station ["CQ from the World's Fair]), stick with the traditional CQ.

Conclusion

This chapter described the fundamental operating procedures for HF packet-radio communications. With a TNC connected to a low-band transceiver, you are now ready to chase DX digital-style. Well over 100 nations now permit amateur packet radio, so there are a lot of potential international connections out there. Good luck and good DX!

CHAPTER TEN

Time-Shifting Communications

Time-shifting packet radio was not invented by H. G. Wells. Actually, it was invented by Hank Oredson, WØRLI, back in 1984. Since that time, time shifting has taken on various shapes and sizes to be one of the driving forces that has made packet radio grow so quickly.

What Are We Talking About?

Time-shifting communication sounds space-aged and very complicated, but it is actually fairly simple to define. In fact, it is not even new. RTTY operators have been using time-shifting communications for a long time. Simply defined, time-shifting communications is the function of transferring information between two people who may not be present on the air at the same time. In other words, using time-shifting communications permits me to send information to you while you are involved in some other activity, yet I can be reasonably assured that you will receive the information (sooner or later). The packet-radio bulletin board system (PBBS) is used to time-shift packet-radio communications.

Bulletin Boards and Mailboxes

During the personal-computer age, the telephone-line *bulletin board system* (*BBS*) has become very common. Simply connect a modem between your computer and your telephone line and you can dial up thousands of different BBSs around the world. Using a BBS, you can read messages stored on the BBS by other users and you can store messages addressed to the other users. You can also download public-domain computer programs that are stored on a BBS to run on your computer.

The PBBS works essentially the same way as a BBS. The only difference is that instead of connecting a modem to your computer and your telephone line as you would to access a BBS, you connect a TNC to your computer and your transceiver to access a PBBS (refer to Figure 10.1). Another difference is that to access a BBS, you must purchase the telephone service from your local telephone company; to access a PBBS, you need a valid Amateur Radio license (which is free).

A PBBS is a packet-radio station that is interfaced to a computer that runs software to perform BBS functions over the airwaves.

Another means of time-shifting communications is provided by the

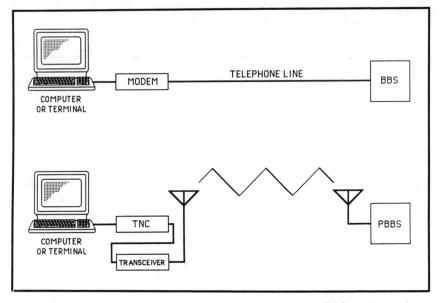

Figure 10.1—The differences between a telephone-line BBS and a packet-radio BBS.

packet-radio mailbox. A packet-radio mailbox is similar to a PBBS, but the term "mailbox" is generally accepted to mean a message receiving and sending system for one station, rather than a bulletin board for all stations. My packet-radio mailbox allows me to store messages to other stations who might check into my mailbox. It also permits other stations to send messages to me via my mailbox. Unlike a PBBS, however, my mailbox does not provide a means for amateurs to send messages to other stations.

Whether a PBBS or a mailbox is used, time-shifting packet-radio communication is a very powerful communications tool of the computer age. Let's find out how it got started.

One Person's Trash Is Another's Treasure

The Xerox 820-1 was a computer, introduced around 1980, that used a Zilog Z80 central processing unit (CPU) and ran the CP/M operating system. It featured 64 kbytes of RAM, two 8-bit parallel ports, two serial ports, a disk controller and an 80-column by 24-line video-display driver, all on a single printed-circuit board (refer to Figure 10.2).

In the early 1980s, Xerox discontinued selling the 820 and sold off the remainder that they had on hand (both new and returned units) as surplus. Their warehouse in Texas was the source for the surplus computer, which could be had for as little as $50 per board!

Hank Oredson, WØRLI, wrote a software package for the 820 that

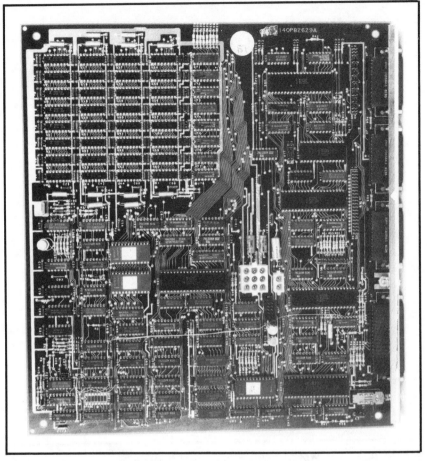

Figure 10.2—The Xerox 820-1 computer PC board.

permitted it to function as a PBBS (and more). Besides the normal functions that you would expect to find in any BBS, such as the ability to send and receive messages and files, Hank added two features that made his BBS even more powerful.

One feature took advantage of the two serial ports provided by the 820. With a TNC connected to each port, Hank's software permitted a user connected to the TNC on one port to communicate through the TNC connected on the other port. Assuming that each TNC was connected to radio equipment operating on different frequencies, this system provided a gateway from one frequency to the other (refer to Figure 10.3 for an illustration of the gateway function). For example, if the TNC on one port was connected to a 2-meter transceiver and the TNC on the other port was connected to

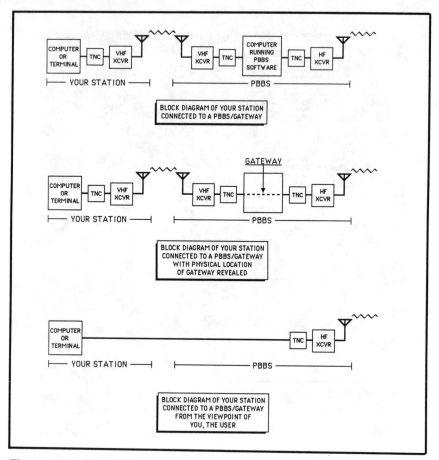

Figure 10.3—The WØRLI Mailbox gateway function.

an HF transceiver, a PBBS user on 2 meters could use the gateway to make packet-radio connections on HF.

Another feature created a rudimentary packet-radio network for the automatic forwarding of messages between PBBSs. This mail-forwarding function allows PBBS users to send mail to the users of other PBBSs.

When addressing the mail, the user includes the call sign of the other PBBS in addition to the call sign of the intended recipient of the mail. Whenever the PBBS has mail to send to another PBBS, it consults a routing table that lists the path to the destination PBBS. When a path is found, the

PBBS automatically sends the message to the first PBBS in the path. Each PBBS hands the message off to the next PBBS in the path, and eventually the message is delivered to the destination PBBS.

Beyond The 820

The WØRLI PBBS spread throughout packet radio. Wherever there was a pocket of packet-radio activity, there was likely to be a WØRLI PBBS in operation. The 820 computer was inexpensive and the software was free. Hank not only gave his software away, he also continued to improve it. As each new version appeared, more and more WØRLI PBBSs hit the air. There was only one problem: the source of surplus 820 boards began to dry up. By mid-1985, the little warehouse in Texas was unable to supply enough "new" surplus boards to meet the demand.

More operators wanted to set up PBBSs, so Jeff Jacobsen, WA7MBL, decided to meet this demand by writing PBBS software for the IBM PC. WA7MBL's PBBS was compatible with WØRLI's version, and as IBM PC compatibles got cheaper and cheaper, WA7MBL's PBBS became a more viable alternative to the WØRLI version. Admittedly, the most inexpensive PC clone was still more expensive than a surplus 820, but at least the PC compatibles were readily available (and expandable). The PC clone also provided the ability to store a lot more information than was possible with the 820. Anyone who runs a PBBS will tell you that there is never too much storage capacity on the PBBS computer, so the WA7MBL PBBS was a blessing in this regard.

Having run out of computer once, WØRLI decided to embark on a new PBBS project that would not be tied to any one computer. With the help of David Toth, VE3GYQ, Hank wrote a new version of the PBBS in the computer language called C. Programs written in C are said to be very "portable"; they may be run with only minor modifications on any computer for which the C programming language is available. Hank and David finished their C PBBS in late 1986, and it ran on the ever-present IBM PCs and PC compatibles.

Meanwhile, folks throughout packet radioland were not letting the grass grow under their feet. Instead, they were busy writing PBBS and mailbox software for their own personal computers. The end result was a variety of PBBS and mailbox software for various popular computers, including the Commodore 64, the IBM PC, the Radio Shack Color Computer, the Radio Shack TRS-80 Models I and III and even the portable Radio Shack TRS-80 Model 100! Some of these programs were compatible with the WØRLI/WA7MBL PBBSs and some were not. The accompanying sidebar, "PBBS and Mailbox Software," details what is available.

PBBS And Mailbox Software

A variety of PBBS and mailbox software is available for a number of popular personal computers. Here is a list of the software available as of the publication date of this book.

Atari 520ST/1040ST

Atari ST Mailbox—Thor Andersen, LA2DAA, wrote a WØRLI-type mailbox program for the Atari 520ST and 1040ST computers. To obtain a copy of the software, contact Thor at Riddersporen 6, N-3032 Drammen, Norway.

PBBS—Mike Curtis, WD6EHR, has ported the WØRLI PBBS software to the Atari 520ST and 1040ST computers. The program has most of the features of the original program and is available by sending Mike a blank 3½-inch diskette and postpaid diskette mailer. Contact Mike at 7921 Wilkinson Ave, N Hollywood, CA 91605

Commodore Amiga

AmigaBBS—Randal Lilly, N3ET, wrote this PBBS software to run with the Kantronics KPC-1, KPC-2, KPC-4 and KAM TNCs. The software is available on the Amiga Amateur Radio Public Domain Disk #5, which is distributed by Kathy Wehr, WB3KRN, RD#1, Box 193, Watsontown, PA 17777. To obtain a copy of the disk, send Kathy a blank formatted disk, a sturdy return envelope, a label printed with your name and address and sufficient return postage.

CONNplex—Mike Staines, WA1PTC, has written a multiple-connect PBBS program for the Amiga that may be obtained from him at 10 Sorrento Rd, Wallingford, CT 06492.

Commodore C-64

C64 Packet Talker—This unique mailbox system for the C-64 stores messages for up to 300 users and converts all packet-radio messages to voice. It is available from Engineering Consulting, 583 Candlewood St, Brea, CA 92621.

Packet Radio BBS—This C-64 program was written in BASIC by Verne Buland, W9ZGS. It may be downloaded from CompuServe's HamNet.

WB4APR PBBS—Bob Bruninga, WB4APR, wrote Commodore C-64 software that emulates many of the features of the WØRLI PBBS. The features include message storage, limited file storage and automatic message forwarding. This BASIC program may be obtained by sending a formatted diskette and $5 to Bob at 59 Southgate Ave, Annapolis, MD 21401.

IBM PC

APLink—Vic Poor, W5SMM, wrote this AMTOR mailbox and WØRLI/WA7MBL-compatible PBBS software for the IBM PC and compatibles. It is available by sending a formatted, blank diskette, a self-addressed mailing label and return postage to Paul Newland, AD7I, PO Box 205, Holmdel, NJ 07733. It is also available from the Tucson

Amateur Packet Radio Corporation (TAPR), PO Box 12925, Tucson, AZ 85732.

ARES/Data—ARES/Data is a multiple-connection, multiport database and conference bridge designed specifically for tracking victims and emergency personnel in a disaster. It was written by William Moerner, WN6I, and David Palmer, N6KL, and may be downloaded from CompuServe's HamNet.

BB—The BB program for the IBM PC and compatibles is a multiple-connection PBBS that was written by Roy Engehausen, AA4RE. It may be downloaded from CompuServe's HamNet, or from the WA6RDH BBS at 916-678-1535. It is also available on disk from the Tucson Amateur Packet Radio Corporation (TAPR), PO Box 12925, Tucson, AZ 85732.

CBBS Mailbox System—CBBS was written for the IBM PC and compatibles by Ed Picchetti, K3RLI, and Joe Lagermasini, AG3F. It may be downloaded from CompuServe's HamNet and is also available on disk from the Tucson Amateur Packet Radio Corporation (TAPR), PO Box 12925, Tucson, AZ 85732.

MPC—This multiport AMTOR and packet-radio BBS for the IBM PC and compatibles was written by Lacy McCall, AC4X. It may be downloaded from CompuServe's HamNet.

MSYS—MSYS is a multiple-user, multiport PBBS that runs on the IBM PC and compatibles (it requires a hard disk). MSYS supports gateway, KA-Node and TCP/IP operations and was written by Mike Pechura, WA8BXN. It may be downloaded from CompuServe's HamNet.

Pavillion Software Packet Conference Board System—Pavillion Software produced this packet-radio conference-board system for the IBM PC/XT and compatibles. Besides traditional message functions, including message forwarding, the system serves up to 26 users concurrently, provides multi-user conferencing, a user-to-user talk function, DX-spotting announcements, DX logging and general announcement functions. For information concerning the availability of this software, write to Pavillion Software, PO Box 803, Amherst, NH 03031.

ROSErver/Packet Radio MailBox System (*PRMBS*)—This multiple-user PBBS/packet server for the IBM PC and compatibles attempts to eliminate some of the SYSOP maintenance that other systems require. Written by Brian Riley, KA2BQE, and Dave Trulli, NN2Z, it may be downloaded from the RATS BBS at 201-387-8898 and is available on disk from the Tucson Amateur Packet Radio Corporation (TAPR), PO Box 12925, Tucson, AZ 85732

WØRLI Mailbox—This is the original PBBS software re-written in C by Hank Oredson, WØRLI, and David Toth, VE3GYQ. The current version is intended for the IBM PC and compatibles and may be downloaded from CompuServe's HamNet, the WA6RDH BBS (916-678-1535), the VE3GYQ BBS (active at 519-660-1442 when a new version is out) and the VE4UB BBS (204-785-8518), and is also available on disk from the Tucson Amateur Packet Radio Corporation (TAPR), PO Box 12925, Tucson, AZ 85732.

WA7MBL PBBS—This is the Jeff Jacobsen, WA7MBL, implementation of the original WØRLI PBBS for the IBM PC and compatibles. It is fully compatible with WØRLI systems. The WA7MBL PBBS software may be downloaded from CompuServe's HamNet and is available on disk from the Tucson Amateur Packet Radio Corporation (TAPR), PO Box 12925, Tucson, AZ 85732.

Wake Digital Communications Group (WDCG) PBBS—The WDCG's PBBS runs on the IBM PC and compatibles. It supports file transfers using ASCII, XMODEM and "XPACKET" protocols. The system includes a fully developed message bulletin board, but does not support mail forwarding. The software may be downloaded from CompuServe's HamNet or may be obtained from the WDCG, c/o Randy Ray, WA5SZL, 9401 Taurus Ct, Raleigh, NC 27612.

Tandy Color Computer

WJ5W CoCo/PBBS—Monty W. Haley, WJ5W, produced a partial implementation of the WØRLI PBBS for the Radio Shack/Tandy Color Computer. The program is written in BASIC and may be obtained directly from Monty at Rte 1, Box 210-B, Evening Shade, AR 72532.

Tandy TRS-80 Model 100

N1AED Mailbox—Dick Roux, N1AED, wrote this mailbox program for the Radio Shack/Tandy TRS-80 Model 100 portable computer. The program allows stations connected to the mailbox to send and receive messages to and from the operator of the mailbox. Dick's mailbox software may be downloaded from BBSs, PBBSs or CompuServe's HamNet, or may be obtained directly from the author by sending a blank audio cassette and a self-addressed, stamped cassette mailer to 25 Greenfield Dr, Merrimack, NH 03054.

N1AED Mini-PBBS—Dick Roux, N1AED, also wrote this PBBS for the Radio Shack/Tandy TRS-80 Model 100 portable computer. The system is able to automatically receive forwarded messages from WØRLI and WA7MBL PBBSs, but is unable to automatically send messages for forwarding (the limited computer memory precludes storing the large forwarding list required for automatic forwarding). The Mini-PBBS comes in different flavors for Model 100s with or without disk storage. N1AED's programs may be downloaded from BBSs, PBBSs or CompuServe's HamNet, or the program may be obtained directly from the author by sending a blank audio cassette and a self-addressed, stamped cassette mailer to 25 Greenfield Dr, Merrimack, NH 03054.

Tandy TRS-80 Models I and III

KC8JN PBBS—This is a single-port implementation of the WØRLI PBBS written in BASIC for the Radio Shack/Tandy TRS-80 Models I and III by Greg Day, KC8JN. It is available for $5 directly from the author at 109 Meadow Rd, Wintersville, OH 43952.

Xerox 820

PBBS—Although WØRLI transferred his PBBS software efforts from the Xerox 820 computer to the IBM PC and its ilk a number of years ago, John Bennett, N4XI, picked up the torch and continued to keep the 820 PBBS software up to date. If you would like a copy, send two 8-inch single-sided disks and a self-addressed mailer with sufficient return postage to John at 5805 Whitethorne Dr, Evansville, IN 47710.

Hands-On Time-Shifting

Currently, the WØRLI and WA7MBL PBBSs are the ones you are most likely to encounter. The two PBBSs are compatible and the commands that you use to control each PBBS are similar. The accompanying sidebars list the commands that are available with each PBBS, and the following paragraphs describe how to use the PBBS commands to access and use the various features of the PBBS.

WØRLI Mailbox Command Set

The following commands are available with version 10.11 of the WØRLI MailBox public-domain software, written in C by Hank Oredson, WØRLI, and David Toth, VE3GYQ.

General commands

B—Log off the PBBS
Jx—Display call signs of stations recently heard or connected on TNC port x
N x—Enter your name (x) in system (12 characters maximum)
NH x—Enter the call sign (x) of the PBBS where you normally send and receive mail
NQ x—Enter your location (x)
NZ n—Enter your ZIP Code (n)
P x—Display information concerning station whose call sign is x
S—Display status of PBBS
T—Ring bell at the SYSOP's terminal for one minute

Help commands

? *—Display description of all PBBS commands
?—Display summary of all PBBS commands
? x—Display summary of command x
H *—Display description of all PBBS commands
H—Display summary of all PBBS commands
H x—Display description of command x
I—Display information about PBBS
I x—Display information about station whose call sign is x
IL—Display list of local users of the PBBS
IZ n—List users at ZIP Code n
NE—Toggle between short and extended command menu
V—Display PBBS software version

Message commands

K n—Kill message numbered n
KM—Kill all messages addressed to you that you have read
KT n—Kill NTS traffic numbered n
L—List all messages entered since you last logged in

L *n*—List message numbered n and messages numbered higher than *n*

L< *x*—List messages from station whose call sign is *x*

L> *x*—List messages addressed to station whose call sign is *x*

L@ *x*—List messages addressed for forwarding to PBBS whose call sign is *x*

L *n1* *n2*—List messages numbered *n1* through *n2*

LA *n*—List the first *n* messages stored on PBBS

LB—List all bulletin messages

LF—List all messages that have been forwarded

LL *n*—List the last *n* messages stored on PBBS

LM—List all messages addressed to you

LT—List all NTS traffic

R *n*—Read message numbered *n*

RH *n*—Read message numbered *n* with full message header displayed

RM—Read all messages addressed to you that you have not read

S *x*—Send message to station whose call sign is *x*

S *x* @ *y*—Send a message to station whose call sign is *x* at PBBS whose call sign is *y*

SB *x*—Send a bulletin message to *x*

SB *x* @ *y*—Send a bulletin message to *x* at PBBS whose call sign is *y*

SP *x*—Send a private messate to station whose call sign is *x*

SP *x* @ *y*—Send a private message to station whose call sign is *x* at PBBS whose call sign is *y*

SR—Send a message in response to a message you have just read

ST *x*—Send an NTS message to station whose call sign is *X*

ST *x* @ *y*—Send an NTS message to station whose call sign is *x* at PBBS whose call sign is *y*

File transfer commands

D*x* *y* — From directory named *x*, download file named *y*

U *x*—Upload file named *x*

W—List what directories are available

W*x*—List what files are available in directory named *x*

W*x* *y*—List files in directory named *x* whose file name matches *y*

Port commands

C *x*—Send data via port *x*

C *x* *y*—Via port *x*, send connect request to station whose call sign is *y*

CM *x* *y*—Send message numbered *x* to station whose call sign is *y*

CM *x* *y* @ *z*—Send message numbered *x* to station whose call sign is *y* at PBBS whose call sign is *z*

M *x*—Monitor port *x*

Roundtable commands

RT—Initiate roundtable function.

<ESC> D *x*—Allows roundtable control station to disconnect station

whose call sign is x from roundtable
<ESC> H—Obtain assistance
<ESC> P—Display ports available to roundtable
<ESC> N x—Enter your name (x)
<ESC> Q x—Enter your location (x)
<ESC> U—Display list of stations in roundtable

WA7MBL PBBS Command Set

The following commands are available with version 5.12 of "The WA7MBL Packet Bulletin Board System" public-domain software written by Jeff Jacobsen, WA7MBL.

General commands

    B—Log off the PBBS
    J—Display call signs of stations recently heard or connected to as many as six TNCs
    JK—Display call signs of stations recently connected
    Jx—Display call signs of stations recently heard or connected on TNC port x
    N x—Enter your name (x) in system (12 characters maximum)
    T—Ring the bell at the SYSOP's terminal for one minute
    V—Display PBBS software version, date of software release, copyright notice, number of active messages, and next message number

Help commands

    H—Display description of all PBBS commands
    I—Display information about PBBS
    X—Toggle between short and extended command menu
    ?—Display description of all PBBS commands
    ? x—Display description of command x

Message commands

    K—Kill a message sent to or by you
    KM—Kills all messages addressed to you that you have read
    K n—Kill message numbered n
    L—List all messages entered since you last used the L command
    LB—List all bulletin messages
    LL n—List the last n messages stored on PBBS
    LM—List all messages addressed to you
    LN—List all unread messages addressed to you
    LT—List all NTS traffic
    L> x—List all messages addressed to station whose call sign is x
    L< x—List all messages from station whose call sign is x
    L n—List messages numbered higher than message numbered n
    L n1 n2—List messages numbered n1 through n2
    L@ x—List messages addressed to PBBS whose call sign is x
    R—Read a message

RM—Read all messages addressed to you
RN—Read all unread messages addressed to you
R *n*—Read message numbered *n*
R *n1 n2. . .n6*—Read messages numbered *n1, n2, n3, n4, n5* and *n6* (one to six messages may be read using this command)
S—Send a message
S *x*—Send a message to station whose call sign is *x*
S *x @ y*—Send a message to station whose call sign is *x* at PBBS whose call sign is *y*
SB *x*—Send a bulletin message to *x*
SB *x @ y*—Send a bulletin message to *x* at PBBS whose call sign is *y*
SP *x*—Send a private message to station whose call sign is *x*
SP *x @ y*—Send a private message to station whose call sign is *x* at PBBS whose call sign is *y*
ST NTS*x*—Send an NTS message to state abbreviated as *x*
VM—Read all messages addressed to you with full message header displayed
VN—Read all unread messages addressed to you with full message header displayed
V *n*—Read message numbered *n* with full message header displayed
V *n1 n2. . .n6*—Read messages numbered *n1, n2, n3, n4, n5* and *n6* with full message header displayed (one to six messages may be read using this command)

File transfer commands

D—Download a file from the PBBS
D *x*—Download file named *x*
D *x|y*—Download file named *x* from directory named *y*
D *x n*—From file named *x*, download *n* number of lines
D *x n1 n2*—From file named *x*, download lines numbered *n1* through *n2*
U—Upload a file to the PBBS
U *x*—Upload file named *x*
U *x|y*—To directory *x*, upload file named *y*
W—List what files are available
WN—List new files uploaded since you last logged on
W *x*—List files in directory named *x*

YAPP Binary File Transfer commands (only available for MS-DOS computers running YAPP terminal program)

Y—Display description of YAPP Binary File Transfer
YD—Start downloading a file using YAPP Binary File Transfer
YN—List new binary files uploaded since you last logged on
YU—Start uploading a file using YAPP Binary File Transfer
YW—List what binary files are available

Logging On

Before you can use a PBBS, you must *log on* in order to inform the PBBS that you wish to begin using the system. Logging on to a PBBS is a simple matter of making a connection with the PBBS. (Since the PBBS serves only one function, the only reason you would make a connection with it is to use it as a PBBS, so connecting is logging on.) To log on to the W1AW-4 PBBS, for example, at the command prompt type:

cmd: Connect W1AW-4 <CR>

Once you are connected/logged-on to a PBBS, the PBBS sends you a preamble, followed by a list of commands and a command prompt, which is the greater-than sign (>). For example, after you log on to PBBS W1AW-4, it sends:

CENCT:W1AW {-5} Connected to W1AW-4
This is the ARRL Hq BBS/Mailport
[MBL-5.12-$]
Hello Stan, W1AW-4 PBBS is QRV!
New messages from 12792 - 12860, total number of active messages 207.
W1AW BBS (B,D,H,I,J,K,L,N,R,S,T,U,V,W,X,Y,?) >

In this example, the preamble indicates the alias and call sign of the digipeater or network node (CENCT:W1AW-5), if any, that was used to access the PBBS, the call sign of the PBBS (W1AW-4), the PBBS software being used (WA7MBL version 5.12), the messages added to the PBBS since you last logged on (12792-12860), the number of messages stored on the PBBS (207), and a list of available commands (B, D, H, I, J, K, L, N, R, S, T, U, V, W, X, Y, ?).

The PBBS is now ready for your command. To send a command, you simply type the letter representing the desired command, along with any qualifiers related to the command, and follow your typing with a carriage return (<CR>). The carriage return causes your TNC to send the command to the PBBS. If the command is a legitimate command used in the proper way, the PBBS responds accordingly. The PBBS sends you a quizzical **What?** or ***** Invalid Command** if you use an illegal command, or if you use a legal command incorrectly.

Some PBBS commands consist of only one letter. For example, to request that the PBBS computer sound a bell to alert the *system operator* or *SYSOP*, you invoke a one-letter command (the letter "T" for talk to SYSOP).

Many PBBS commands use qualifiers to make the commands more specific. For example, the one-letter "L" (for list) command causes the PBBS to send you a list of all messages stored on the PBBS since the last time you logged on. If you add the qualifier "M" (for mine) to the "L" command, the resulting "LM" command performs a more specific task. Instead of listing all of the messages stored on the PBBS since you last logged on, it lists only the messages stored on the PBBS that are addressed to you. The accompanying sidebars that list the WØRLI and WA7MBL PBBS commands also list the command qualifiers.

After you log on to a PBBS for the first time, you can personalize future communications with the PBBS by storing your name in the system. This is accomplished using the "N" (for name) command. For example, if your name is Laurie, type:

N Laurie < CR >

Logging Off

When you are finished using a PBBS, you must *log off* to inform the PBBS that you are finished using it. To log off, send the PBBS the "B" (for bye) command. The PBBS will send you a departing message and then disconnect you. For example, after you log off PBBS W1AW-4, it disconnects and *** **DISCONNECTED** is displayed at your terminal.

If the system does not receive a packet from you within a few minutes, the PBBS automatically logs you off and disconnects. This automatic-disconnect function prevents the PBBS from being tied up if conditions have deteriorated and your packets can no longer be received, or if you simply forget to log off a PBBS you are connected to.

A Directory of Messages

When you log on to a PBBS, it will inform you if there are any new messages for you (messages addressed to you that have been stored on the system since the last time you logged on). If you want to find out what other messages have been stored on the PBBS, you may obtain a directory of the stored messages by invoking the "L" (for list messages) command. Figure 10.4 illustrates a typical message directory that was produced by a PBBS after the "L" command was used.

The directory provides the following information concerning each message stored on the PBBS:

Msg#: the message number, a sequential number assigned by this PBBS.

T: the type of message, if any, assigned by the station originating the message, typically, B for bulletin, F for forward-and-keep, T for traffic, P for private, S for service, and so on.

S: the status of the message; N indicates that the intended recipient of the message has not read it, Y indicates that the intended recipient has received it, F indicates that the message has been forwarded, $ indicates that the message is a bulletin.

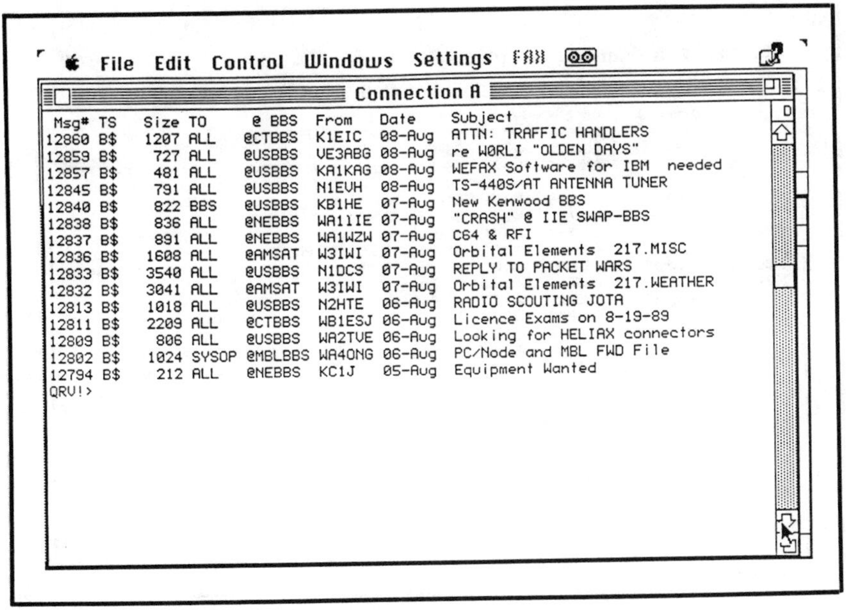

```
   File   Edit   Control   Windows   Settings  [AN]  [OO]

================================= Connection A =================================
Msg# TS   Size  TO     @ BBS   From    Date    Subject
12860 B$  1207  ALL    @CTBBS  K1EIC   08-Aug  ATTN: TRAFFIC HANDLERS
12859 B$   727  ALL    @USBBS  VE3ABG  08-Aug  re W0RLI "OLDEN DAYS"
12857 B$   481  ALL    @USBBS  KA1KAG  08-Aug  WEFAX Software for IBM   needed
12845 B$   791  ALL    @USBBS  N1EVH   08-Aug  TS-440S/AT ANTENNA TUNER
12840 B$   822  BBS    @USBBS  KB1HE   07-Aug  New Kenwood BBS
12838 B$   836  ALL    @NEBBS  WA1IIE  07-Aug  "CRASH" @ IIE SWAP-BBS
12837 B$   891  ALL    @NEBBS  WA1WZW  07-Aug  C64 & RFI
12836 B$  1608  ALL    @AMSAT  W3IWI   07-Aug  Orbital Elements   217.MISC
12833 B$  3540  ALL    @USBBS  N1DCS   07-Aug  REPLY TO PACKET WARS
12832 B$  3041  ALL    @AMSAT  W3IWI   07-Aug  Orbital Elements   217.WEATHER
12813 B$  1018  ALL    @USBBS  N2HTE   06-Aug  RADIO SCOUTING JOTA
12811 B$  2209  ALL    @CTBBS  WB1ESJ  06-Aug  Licence Exams on 8-19-89
12809 B$   806  ALL    @USBBS  WA2TVE  06-Aug  Looking for HELIAX connectors
12802 B$  1024  SYSOP  @MBLBBS WA4ONG  06-Aug  PC/Node and MBL FWD File
12794 B$   212  ALL    @NEBBS  KC1J    05-Aug  Equipment Wanted
QRV!>
```

Figure 10.4—A PBBS's response to the "L" command.

Size: the size of the message in bytes.

To: the intended recipient of the message.

@ BBS: the intended destination PBBS of the message, if any.

From: the station that originated the message.

Date: the date (in day-month format) that the message was stored on this PBBS.

Title: the subject of the message.

The "L" command lists messages that may be of no interest to you (see Figure 10.4). To limit the messages that are listed, you may add a qualifier to the "L" command. For example, to obtain a directory of only those messages addressed to "all" users of the PBBS, you type:

L> ALL <CR>

The PBBS's response to this command is illustrated in Figure 10.5; notice the difference between the PBBS's response to the "L > ALL" command and the all-inclusive "L" command, as shown in Figure 10.4.

Reading The Mail

Once you have determined that there are messages stored on the PBBS that you are interested in reading, you may use the "RM" (for read mine) command to read only those messages addressed to you. You may also use the "R" (for read message) command followed by the message's number

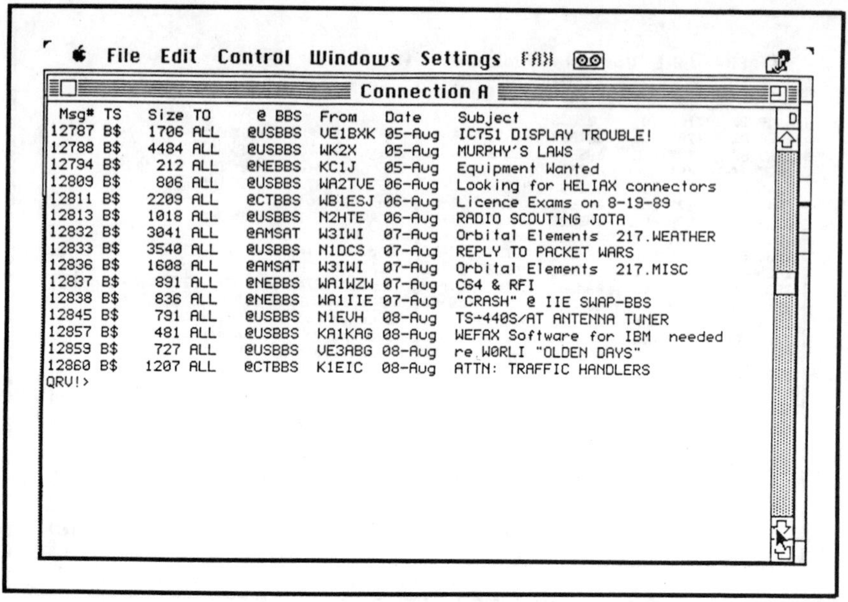

Figure 10.5—A PBBS's response to the "L> ALL" command.

to read a particular message. In either case, after you invoke the command, the PBBS retrieves the requested message from its storage and sends it to you for your reading pleasure.

The *message header* is displayed before the actual contents of the requested message.

Usually, the message header contains some of the same information concerning the message that is displayed when you invoke the "L" command. The header contains the message number, type, status, intended recipient, etc. If the message has been forwarded from one or more other PBBSs, the call sign of each PBBS that has relayed the message is listed under the "Path:" portion of the header. Here is an example of the header of a forwarded message:

[12852] PY
Path: W1AW!W1OPS!N1DKF!WB1DSW!W9ZRX!K9IU
Date: 08 Aug 89 12:06:36 Z
From: N9GMU@K9IU
To: WA1LOU
Subject: KUDOS FOR BOOK

In this example, the Path information indicates that the message was originated at PBBS K9IU and relayed through PBBSs W9ZRX, WB1DSW, N1DKF and W1OPS, and finally to its destination PBBS, W1AW.

The text of the message is displayed after the header. When you have read any messages that are addressed only to you, you should delete them to free some space in the PBBS's storage. You can delete a specific message by invoking the "K" (for kill message) command followed by the number of the message you wish to delete. For example, to delete message number 3773, type:

K 3773 <CR>

Qualifiers may also be used with the "K" command. The most commonly used K-command qualifier is "M" (for mine). The resulting "KM" (for kill mine) command deletes all messages addressed to you which you have already read.

Sending Mail

Sending mail by means of a PBBS is accomplished by using the "S" (for send message) command. Simply invoke the "S" command, followed by the intended recipient of your message. If the intended recipient is another Amateur Radio operator, you type the letter S followed by the ham's call sign; for example,

S WA4SWF <CR>

The intended recipient does not have to be an individual Amateur Radio operator. For example, you can address the message to "ALL" in cases where your message is a bulletin or contains information of general interest. You can also address the message to a specific group (to "NYHAMS," for example).

If you are sending the message to a ham at another PBBS, your message must be forwarded automatically to the other PBBS. In this case, you use the "S" command followed by the call sign of the intended recipient, the at-sign (@) and the call sign of the destination PBBS. For example, to send a message to WA4SWF at PBBS KA4ROS, you type:

S WA4SWF @ KA4ROS <CR>

The PBBS can handle private messages (messages that are not intended for general consumption). To send a private message, use the "S" command followed by the qualifier "P" (for private) and the call sign of the intended recipient of the message. After a private message is stored on a PBBS, only the station that sent the private message and the intended recipient of the private message (or the SYSOP) can list, read or kill the message.

After you have invoked the "S" command, the PBBS will ask you for the title of your message. Type a brief title that represents the general content of the message and follow it with a <CR>. The PBBS will now prompt you to send your message. You may type your message manually, or you may upload the message from memory or storage (disk or tape) if your terminal or computer has this capability. In either case, be sure to insert a <CR> at the end of each line of your message (each line should be less than 80 characters in length, including spaces). The line-ending <CR>s are required because some systems can only handle lines of a finite length. Lines that are too long get truncated. After the content of your message is sent to the PBBS, type a <CTRL-Z> followed by a <CR> to indicate to the PBBS that the end of the message has been sent. When the PBBS receives the <CTRL-Z>, it stores your message for later retrieval or for mail-forwarding.

To speed up the process of sending a message, you can create it off-line with a word-processor or text editor using the following format:

S *name/call sign of recipient plus PBBS, if any* <CR>
***title of message* <CR>**
***line 1 of message text* <CR>**
***line 2 of message text* <CR>**
***line 3 of message text* <CR>**

***last line of message text* <CR>**
<CTRL-Z> <CR>

You supply the information in italics, then save it all in ASCII format under an appropriate file name (perhaps the call sign of the intended recipient).

When you log on to your local PBBS, send the file and it will be interpreted as another message being sent using the "S" command (for private messages, use "SP" instead of "S" in the first line of the file). The PBBS will still prompt you for the title and text of your message. These prompts should be ignored because that information has already been sent in your file. (The reason that you see these prompts is that when the PBBS detects the "S" command in the first line of the file, it sends you a message title prompt before it reads the second line of your file. Similarly, when the PBBS reads the title of your message in the second line of your file, it sends you a message text prompt before it reads the third line of your file.)

File Manipulation

Most PBBSs have files stored in their computer system. These files may consist of digipeater, network and PBBS maps, packet-radio news, public-domain software, Amateur Radio newsletters or almost anything of interest to the amateur packet-radio operator.

To find out what files are stored on a PBBS, use the "W" (for what files) command. Often, the PBBS's file storage is subdivided into two or more subdirectories. If this is the case, the PBBS will respond to the "W" command by asking you to be more specific and to append a qualifier to the "W" command. For example, your local PBBS may have four subdirectories named "A" through "D." To find out what is stored under subdirectory "C," you type:

WC <CR>

The PBBS responds by sending you a list of the names of all of the files stored under subdirectory C. The "W" command also shows how much free space is available for new files on the PBBS disk(s).

If you wish to receive a file from the PBBS (download a file), you use the "D" (for download file) command, followed by the name of the desired file. The name of the file you request must be entered exactly as it appeared when you invoked the "W" command. The PBBS will not be able to find the file if you do not specify the name correctly. If the file is stored in a subdirectory, the subdirectory qualifier must be appended to the "D" command.

The WØRLI and WA7MBL PBBSs require slightly different formats when you use the "D" command with a subdirectory qualifier. WØRLI PBBSs require that the "D" command be immediately followed by the subdirectory qualifier, a space and the file name. WA7MBL PBBSs require that the "D" command be followed by a space, the subdirectory qualifier, a slash (/) and the file name. For example, using a WØRLI PBBS to download a file named "TNC.DOC" from subdirectory "B," you type:

DB TNC.DOC <CR>

Using a WA7MBL PBBS to download a file named "NOCA.MAP" from subdirectory "MAPS," you type:

D MAPS/NOCA.MAP <CR>

The PBBS responds to your use of the "D" command by finding the requested file and sending it to you. (If your terminal is actually a computer emulating a terminal, you may be able to save the received file to disk or tape for later reading, printing or uploading. If this is the case and you wish to save the file, you should enable the terminal's file-save function immediately after you invoke the "D" command.)

If you wish to store a file at the PBBS, (upload a file), you use the "U" (for upload file) command. If subdirectories exist on the PBBS, the "U" command requires the same subdirectory qualifier as the "D" command (with the same differences between the WØRLI and WA7MBL systems).

Most systems can only handle file names containing a maximum of eight characters, followed by a period and a three-letter extension. An extension is used to identify the file. For example, "ANTDSGN.BAS" may be a file containing an antenna-design program written in BASIC, while "ANTDSGN.DOC" may be a file containing information or documentation on how to use the "ANTDSGN.BAS" program. Do not embed spaces within a file name. Spaces may cause the PBBS to truncate the file name at the space and save the file using a name that was not intended. For example, instead of "ANT DSGN.BAS," you end up with a file named "ANT" or an error message from the PBBS.

After you have informed the PBBS that you wish to upload a file, the PBBS will prompt you to begin sending the file. Unless the file is very short, do not manually enter the file at your terminal keyboard. This is very inefficient and time-consuming. Rather, you should use a computer running terminal-emulation software that has the capability to upload files from memory, tape or disk storage. When the file transfer is complete, send the PBBS a <CTRL-Z> and a <CR> to inform the system that the end of the file has been sent. When the PBBS receives the end-of-file indication, it closes and stores the file.

You do not want to be informed that you have used up all the available storage space in the middle of a file transfer. Unless the "W" command shows that there is plenty of disk space available, you should ask the PBBS SYSOP if there is enough storage space available for your file before you upload it. Use the "T" (for talk to SYSOP) command to elicit an immediate response (if the SYSOP is available), or use the "S" command to send the SYSOP a message.

PBBS Assistance

A number of PBBS commands provide assistance to users in the form of specific information that can be provided by the PBBS on request. Two commands that provide general assistance are the "H" (for help) command, which provides a short description of each PBBS command, and the "I" (for information) command, which provides a short description of the PBBS itself. The W1AW-4 PBBS's response to the "I" command is typical:

Welcome to the ARRL Hq Packet BBS! The system is comprised of:
Micronic CPU (IBM Clone)
Seagate 20 Meg hard drive
WA7MBL 5.12 PBBS software
MFJ 1270 and 1270B TNCs
Heath 121 RS-232 switching
Heathkit HW-2036A 2 meter transceiver - 145.01 Mc user port
Midland 13-506 220 Mc transceiver - 221.11 Mc BBS only port
AEA 2M Isopole @ 65 feet
Cushcraft 220 Mc 7 element Yagi @ 55 feet
Astron RS-7A power supply
Mail autoforward time is at minute 50 every hour. Until the multi-tasker system is debugged, users are requested to avoid using the BBS during the mail forwarding times.

Comments may be left by sending a private message to WA1MBK. Thanks and enjoy the system! 73, Jeff WA1MBK Sysop W1AW PBBS

The "J" (for just heard or just connected) command assists the user by providing information concerning packet-radio activity and how to get at it. The "J" command lists the call signs of the stations most recently heard by the PBBS, or the call signs of the stations most recently connected to the PBBS. For example, if you send PBBS W1AW-4 the "J" command followed by the qualifier "A" (for the TNC connected to the PBBS's port A), the PBBS lists the call signs of the stations most recently heard by and connected to the TNC monitoring 145.01 MHz, with the monitored time and date noted, as follows:

Monitored on 145.01 MHz

NF1E	1233 05-Jun
W1NY	1134 05-Jun
NR1L	1106 05-Jun
K1MEA-11	1032 05-Jun
N1API-9	0800 05-Jun
WM2D	0741 05-Jun
K1MEA-4	0542 05-Jun
K1HEJ-15	0423 05-Jun
N1API-6	0342 05-Jun
WA1NLD	0250 05-Jun

If you send PBBS W1AW-4 the "J" command followed by the qualifier "L" (for list connected stations), the PBBS lists only the call signs of the stations most recently connected to the PBBS, with the monitored time and date noted, as follows:

Connected:

NF1E	1235 05-Jun A
W1NY	1140 05-Jun A
KC1J	1133 05-Jun A
N1API	0802 05-Jun A
W1NY	0638 05-Jun A
W1NY	0443 05-Jun A
K1HEJ	0426 05-Jun A
WA1NLD	0252 05-Jun A
WA1NLD	0042 05-Jun A
W1HUE	0038 05-Jun A

(Note that the "L" qualifier is WØRLI PBBS software-specific. With WA7MBL PBBS software, the "K" qualifier performs the same function.)

The "P" (for path) command provides a list of the digipeaters and network nodes that a specific station used to connect to the PBBS. For example, if you send the following command to the W1AW-4 PBBS:

P WA1OCK <CR>

the PBBS responds with the following information, which can help you determine the path to another station:

WA1OCK connected to W1AW via K1IKE,W1NY-1

Finally, there is the "T" (for talk to SYSOP) command that allows you to obtain information right from the horse's mouth. When you send the "T" command, the bell at the SYSOP's terminal rings for one minute to get the SYSOP's attention. If the SYSOP responds, you may converse with him directly. If the SYSOP does not respond, you will be informed of that fact and be offered an alternative:

SYSOP did not answer, you might leave a message in the MailBox

Good Operating Procedures

PBBS operations are very popular. When you use a PBBS, there are likely to be other stations waiting in line to use the PBBS as soon as you are through. For this reason, you should be sure that you use the system in the most time-efficient manner. By following a few simple PBBS operating procedures, you will be able to log on to the PBBS, check the latest messages and log off as quickly as possible.

Patience is a virtue whenever you send a command to the PBBS. Most of the time the PBBS responds quickly, but sometimes the response may be delayed. Delays are usually caused by packet collisions during high levels of channel activity. Whatever the cause, if the PBBS does not respond to your command quickly, be patient and do not send the command again. If the link between your station and the PBBS is any good and you repeat a command, the PBBS will eventually receive the command twice. This means that the PBBS will respond to the command twice. If the response to a repeated command is time consuming, that time is now doubled! When you send a command, once is enough.

If you are going to send more than one command to the PBBS, you can save time by sending more than one command at a time. Since each PBBS command must be followed by a <CR>, it would seem impossible to send more than one command, because that same <CR> also forces the TNC to send a packet. To send more than one command at a time, the <CR> must be disguised so that the TNC does not recognize it as the Sendpac (send packet) character. This is accomplished by using the "Pass" character, which causes the TNC to ignore whatever character immediately follows it (by default, the pass character is <CTRL-V>). Whenever you want the TNC to ignore a <CR>, precede the <CR> with a <CTRL-V>. For example, to send the "L," "RM," "KM" and "J" commands in one packet, you would type:

L <CTRL-V> <CR> RM <CTRL-V> <CR> KM <CTRL-V> <CR> J <CR>

In order to send this packet, the TNC must recognize a <CR> at the end of the string of commands, so a <CTRL-V> must not precede the final <CR> in the string.

Finally, do not perform time-consuming tasks during the prime-time operating periods. Prime time is not the time to upload or download long files or to list all of the messages stored on the system. During prime time, the level of activity is high and the resulting packet collisions cause the time-consuming tasks to consume even more time. Other stations are probably waiting to use the PBBS, so save the time-consuming tasks for later.

Specialized Systems

Besides the classic WØRLI and WA7MBL PBBS operations, a number of specialized PBBS operations are now appearing as amateurs put their creative talents to use and discover new ways to implement the PBBS concept. The National Traffic System (NTS) is now using the PBBS network to relay traffic cross-country. For a full discussion of NTS on packet radio, refer to Chapter 13—Applications.

On-line data bases are another PBBS function appearing on the air. These PBBSs allow users to store information on the system and search or cross-reference that stored information. On the West Coast, Eric Williams, WD6CMU, created the White Pages data base that allowed users to query and update a compilation of information concerning the users of WØRLI-compatible mailboxes and their home PBBSs. On the East Coast, Jim Robinton, N1CRZ, maintained the Common Interest Cross Reference BBS that permits users to store their interests on the system and search for other users with similar interests.

PBBSs that support multi-user conferencing are now being used to allow amateur packet-radio operators to conduct traditional roundtable conversations (conversations between more than two hams). Until now, packet-radio roundtables were difficult to maintain because packet-radio protocols only support point-to-point communications. The "unproto" mode can be used to conduct a roundtable, but in the unproto mode, no receiving station checks the packet for accurate reception and there is no assurance that everyone in a roundtable is able to receive everyone else at all times. Multi-user conferencing PBBS software has eliminated this problem. Many stations can be connected to the PBBS simultaneously and can converse with each other. Popular uses for multi-user conferencing include DX spotting and holding club get-togethers on the air.

Amateur packet radio is still in its youth. As this communications mode matures, more and more specialized PBBS operations will surely be heard on the packet-radio channels.

Running Your Own PBBS

After they get a taste of PBBS operations, many amateurs get the urge to place their own system on the air. Monitoring the packet-radio channels shows clear evidence of this as more and more PBBS operations appear on the air every day. As many new PBBSs appear, many also disappear. The reason for this is that running a PBBS requires more time and effort than many operators realize at first.

To understand this better, let's look at what it takes to run a PBBS. For starters, consider the outlay of equipment that must be dedicated to the cause. To run a PBBS requires a complete packet-radio station (TNC, radio and antenna) and a computer to run the PBBS software. Unless you plan to run your PBBS on a part-time basis, you must dedicate this equipment to PBBS operation full-time. (A part-time PBBS seems to be a good solution, but it really isn't, because the time you are likely to want to use your equipment is the same time that others are likely to want to use your PBBS.)

Besides dedicating some equipment, running a PBBS requires dedicating some of your free time. A PBBS does not run without maintenance. Besides maintaining equipment, the operator must maintain the PBBS software. Depending on the software and the amount of usage that your PBBS experiences, there are chores that must be performed in order to keep the software running properly.

If you believe that you have enough dedication to run a PBBS, the next step is to decide where to put your PBBS: HF, VHF or UHF. In many areas, PBBSs proliferate on 2 meters. If there is a 2-meter PBBS next door, why put another PBBS on that band? Why not choose a packet-radio channel that has a need for a PBBS? Besides 2 meters, the other VHF and UHF bands are good choices. The Novice 220-MHz band is a prime area for a PBBS. Or how about a PBBS on 6 or 15 meters, where there are very few PBBS operations? With the sunspot cycle now swung favorably toward those bands, 6- and 15-meter PBBSs will be very much in demand. Note that if you plan on putting a PBBS on any VHF or UHF band, you should contact your area frequency coordinator (as listed in the *ARRL Repeater Directory*) and find out what requirements, if any, exist for PBBS operations. There may be a plan in effect that confines PBBS operations to certain frequencies. Better to check first and avoid being sorry later.

After you determine where your PBBS will operate, you must obtain the required equipment. Radio equipment (transmitter, receiver, antenna and peripherals) for the selected frequency must be procured. A TNC is a necessity. A computer must be selected to run the PBBS software. Unless you plan to write your own PBBS software, make sure that the computer you select is one that already has PBBS software available by referring to the sidebar "PBBS And Mailbox Software." (If you are able to obtain the "classic" PBBS computer, the Xerox 820-1, an invaluable series of articles, "Xerox 820-1 Compendium," written by AMRAD's Andre Kesteloot, N4ICK, and Dave Borden, K8MMO, was published in six parts in *QEX* between June 1986 and January 1987.)

Finally, you must obtain the PBBS software (again, refer to the sidebar). The software documentation will describe how to set up the PBBS equipment. The selection of certain TNC parameters is critical for PBBS operation, so make sure that you check the documentation for the specifics.

Running a PBBS requires a lot of dedication, but it is also a satisfying experience, because you are providing a service to others. The bottom line is that it is also a lot of fun.

Conclusion

For ages, man has been intrigued by the possibility of controlling time. With PBBS and mailbox operation, hams have achieved some limited control of time.

CHAPTER ELEVEN

Network Communications

The packet-radio network is a complex evolutionary system of packet-radio stations that has been organized to transfer packets between points A and B. Depending on the locations of these points, the packets being transferred between them may travel through a simple network consisting of one station operating on one frequency or through a variety of networks consisting of tens of stations operating in the HF, VHF and UHF radio spectrum.

No LAN Is An Island

In the past, if you wanted to connect to another packet-radio station, you had to know the exact path through the network that was required to make the connection. If one or more stations were in that path, you had to know each station's call sign and use them when you invoked the "Connect" command. Imagine that every time you mailed a letter, you had to know the name of each intermediary post office that would handle the letter and had to include each post office in the address on the front of the letter's envelope. If you left out a post office, your letter would not get delivered. Similarly, if you left out a call sign of one station in the path, your connection would not be completed.

Luckily, the post office does not require that you be familiar with its vast network to mail a letter. Similarly, in many parts of the global packet-radio network, you do not have to be familiar with the packet-radio network to make a connection with another station. If you have used the PBBS automatic message-forwarding system, you have had a taste of how this aspect of the packet-radio network works.

Sending a message via the PBBS automatic message-forwarding system is similar to sending a letter via the postal system. In either case, you do not have to know who will be handling your mail before it is delivered. All you need to know is the identity of the intended recipient and the address where the intended recipient picks up his mail. For example, to send mail via the postal system, you address the envelope with the intended recipient's identification (the recipient's name) followed by the address where the recipient picks up his mail. To send mail via the PBBS automatic message-forwarding system, you address the mail with the intended recipient's Amateur Radio identification (the recipient's call sign), followed by the at-sign (@) and the address where the recipient picks up his packet-radio mail. Packet-radio operators usually pick up their mail at their local PBBS, so the address for a packet message is simply the destination PBBS's call sign. Once you have properly addressed your mail, the system (either postal or PBBS) does the rest, automatically forwarding your mail to its destination.

Today, some packet-radio communications follow this format; in the future, all packet-radio communications will follow this format. You will only need to know the call sign of the station you wish to contact and the station's address. Someday, you will not have to know the station's address.

Let's look at the network today and how its future is already being implemented.

Digital Repeaters

Only a few years ago, packet-radio networking was completely dependent on digital repeaters (digipeaters). Digipeating is a function built into every AX.25-compatible TNC that permits the TNC to receive, temporarily store and then retransmit (repeat) the packet-radio transmissions of other stations. A digipeater only repeats transmissions that are specifically addressed for routing through that digipeater, as opposed to a typical voice repeater, which retransmits everything it receives.

In light of the other packet-radio networking operations that are available today, digipeating is a rudimentary form of networking. Only eight digipeater stations can be used between any two points that are attempting to transfer packets and, in order to use the digipeaters, the call sign of each must be known and specified when invoking the initial "Connect" command. Even though digipeating is rudimentary in comparison to what is available today, it served a purpose when it was the only type of networking available, and it still serves a purpose today when an intermediary station or two is needed in a pinch to complete a connection.

Even a very modest packet-radio station can be used to send messages over great distances using the capabilities of a digipeater. For example, up in the northland, K1WJ is running his packet-radio station around a one-watt, hand-held, 2-meter transceiver and an indoor antenna. He wants to contact AB1U in the midland, but with his very modest station, he is unable to connect directly to AB1U. K1WJ is able to connect with KC1MK, however, and KC1MK is able to connect with AB1U, so K1WJ commands his TNC to connect with AB1U via KC1MK. KC1MK acts as a digipeater and passes transmissions between K1WJ and AB1U to establish a connection and conduct a conversation.

If one digipeater does not suffice, additional repeaters (theoretically, as many as eight, but fewer in actual practice) may be used to complete the path between any two stations desiring to complete a packet-radio connection. In the preceding example, if K1WJ wants to connect with WA1UFC in the southland and he knows that WA1UFC is able to connect with AB1U, but not with K1WJ or KC1MK, K1WJ can command his TNC to connect with WA1UFC via KC1MK and AB1U. Both KC1MK and AB1U act as digipeaters to pass packets between K1WJ and WA1UFC. K1WJ sends packets to KC1MK, KC1MK sends K1WJ's packets to AB1U, and AB1U sends K1WJ's packets to WA1UFC; WA1UFC's packets make the journey back to K1WJ by means of the same path in reverse.

There are two types of digipeaters. Those used most often are dedicated to digipeater operation. These dedicated digipeaters are similar to voice repeaters in that they serve no other function except to act as a repeater. Like voice repeaters, they are often located in high places to provide the best coverage for the area they serve.

The second type of digipeater is a station that normally serves as someone's personal packet-radio station. Such a station is used by its owner to contact other packet-radio stations and is not a dedicated digipeater. As we mentioned earlier, however, any TNC is capable of acting as a digipeater; if someone's home station is in a better location than yours, you may occasionally call upon the better-located station to act as a digipeater.

The two types of digipeaters are nearly identical. They both use the same equipment (a TNC, a transceiver and an antenna) and you use the same TNC command to use the services of either type of digipeater. The only difference is that a dedicated digipeater is always available to serve you (barring power outages or equipment malfunctions), whereas the home packet-radio station is not always available for your use. The owner may be operating on a different frequency or in a different mode, or the station may be off the air.

On rare occasions, you may be able to receive a packet-radio station loud and clear on the desired frequency, but you still may be unable to use that station as a digipeater because the TNC's digipeater function is disabled. The TNC's digipeater function is controlled by the means of the "Digipeat" command and is enabled by default. In the spirit of cooperation among packet-radio stations, nearly every VHF/UHF packet-radio operator leaves the digipeater capability enabled. If you need to change the status of this function for some reason, at the command prompt type:

cmd: DIGIpeat x <CR>

where x is ON to enable the digipeater function or OFF to disable it.

If point-to-point communications are possible without using a digipeater, then don't use a digipeater. In fact, it's best to use an unoccupied frequency when possible. Packets are transferred between stations more quickly when the stations are communicating directly with each other; at the same time, the digipeater is freed up to serve stations that cannot communicate point-to-point. This is analogous to using FM voice simplex operation rather than a voice repeater whenever possible.

If point-to-point VHF/UHF communications are not possible, then go ahead and use a digipeater. To attempt to make a connection with another station using digipeaters, you use the same "Connect" command that is used to make a connection without a digipeater. You simply add the optional "Via" sub-command to indicate the digipeater(s) to be used. For example, at the command prompt type:

cmd: Connect WA1LOU Via WA1UTQ <CR>

where WA1LOU is the call sign of the station you wish to contact and WA1UTQ is the call sign of the digipeater station you wish to use to contact WA1LOU.

If more than one digipeater is needed to make the connection, "Connect" and "Via" are used, at the command prompt, by typing:

cmd: Connect WA1LOU Via WA1UTQ,K1IKE,W1AW-5 <CR>

where WA1LOU is the call sign of the station you wish to contact and WA1UTQ, K1IKE and W1AW-5 are the call signs of the digipeater stations you wish to use to contact WA1LOU. Note that commas (,) separate the digipeater station call signs and that SSIDs must be included if the station's SSID is anything other than 0. Also, note that the order of digipeater call signs is critical. The first digipeater call sign must be the digipeater station that is the first to receive and retransmit your transmissions, while the last digipeater call sign is the last to receive and repeat your transmissions. Another way to put it is the first digipeater call sign is the digipeater closest to your station, while the last digipeater call sign is the digipeater closest to the station that you are trying to contact. (Refer to Figure 11.1 for an illustration of how to address digipeater stations properly using the "Connect" command and "Via" sub-command.)

Traffic Jams and Collisions

You should always use the minimum number of digipeaters required to complete a connection. As a rule, a maximum of three digipeater stations should be used in the average VHF and UHF packet-radio environment. (The "average" packet-radio environment is a frequency where there are a number of other stations in operation.)

Whenever you transmit a packet on a frequency where there is other activity, there is a chance that another station will transmit a packet at the same time you do. This should occur only rarely, because a TNC does not transmit when it hears another packet-radio station transmitting. The TNC waits for the other station to stop transmitting before it begins transmitting.

The packet environment is not ideal, however. Since the reception area of each station is different, the originating TNC may not hear all of the sta-

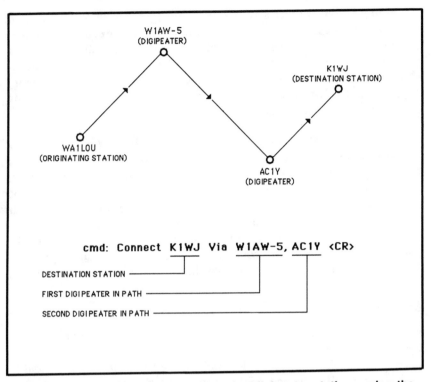

Figure 11.1—The proper way of addressing digipeater stations using the "Connect" command and "Via" sub-command.

tions that the destination TNC can hear. As a result, your TNC may transmit a packet while another station is transmitting because it cannot hear that station. The destination station (especially if it is a wide-coverage digipeater) may be able to hear both stations; the resulting unintelligible interference between the two packet transmissions is called a collision between packets. When a collision occurs, the transmitted packet never reaches its destination, no acknowledgment of receipt is sent by the destination station and the originating station must retransmit the packet.

If you are sending a packet to a digipeater, a collision is more likely to occur. Most dedicated digipeaters are in very good radio locations, and they can hear many stations at once. The more stations the digipeater can hear that cannot hear each other, the greater the chance that the digipeater station will experience packet collisions.

Your station's packet may collide with a packet from another station far out of your own station's reception area, but within the digipeater's reception area. The potential for such a collision exists at each digipeater, so if you use more than one digipeater to send a packet, the problem is compounded and the chance that a collision will occur increases. As you use more digipeaters, it is less likely that your transmitted packet will be received by the intended destination station.

The Remedy for Bad Paths: Try a Different Path!

If you are connected to another station and you find that each packet that is sent must be retransmitted a number of times before it is acknowledged, then the path between the connected stations is poor. The problem may be caused by collisions with other packets or because the stations are too far apart and reception is marginal. Whatever the problem, there is a remedy provided by the TNC's "Reconnect" command. When you discover that the path you have selected for the connection is a poor one, you can change paths in the middle of a contact by entering the Command Mode and typing at the command prompt:

cmd: RECOnnect WA1LOU Via N1ID <CR>

where WA1LOU is the call sign of the station you are already connected with and N1ID is the call sign of the digipeater station you wish to use to reconnect to WA1LOU. The same rules apply to the "Reconnect" command as to the "Connect" command: SSIDs are required when the SSID is other than 0, commas separate the call signs of more than one (and not more than eight) digipeaters, the order of the call signs of digipeaters is critical, and the use of digipeaters, and thus "Via," are optional.

Locating Digipeaters

Your TNC has the ability to use digipeaters to send your packets beyond the ordinary range of your station's equipment. In order to use a digipeater, however, you have to know what's out there. In other words, you need a "road map" from your station to the station you want to connect to. There are a number of ways to find out what is available in your area.

The ARRL Repeater Directory lists dedicated packet-radio digipeaters by state and province (refer to Figure 11.2). Simply look up the listings for your state or province in the directory and find what dedicated digipeaters are located in your area. The only drawback to using the directory for digipeater listings is that the directory is published once a year and the state of dedicated digipeaters changes daily. What is true one day can be very different one month later.

Various individuals and groups provide network maps for their local geographical area (usually for a state or province) on an irregular schedule (Figure 11.3 provides an example of such a map). These maps illustrate the

PACKET
MONTANA—NEW JERSEY

Location	Output	Input	Call	Notes	Sponsor
MONTANA					
Ashton	145.01		WA7MFJ-1	M	
Billings	145.01		K7PO-1	D	
Bozeman	145.01		W7YB	D	W7YB
Butte	145.01		WA7KZF-1	D	
Deer Lodge	145.01		W7VNE-1	D	
Glendive	145.01		KC7AA-1	D	
Great Falls	145.01		WB7ETT-1	D	
Havre	145.01		KA7RRR-1	D	
Kalispell	145.01		W7ZKA-1	D	
NEBRASKA					
Beaver Crssng	145.01		WBØTAJ-1	D	LARC
Kearney	145.01		WAØIVW-1	D	
Mead	145.01		WBØTAJ-2	D	LARC
Omaha	145.01		KØBOY-1	D	
Tekamah	145.01		NFØN	D	NFØN
NEVADA					
Ely	145.01		WB7WTS-1	D	ENARS
Hawthorne	145.01		WA6TLW-2	D	
Las Vegas	145.01		K7WS-1	D	K7WS
Las Vegas	145.01		K7WS-2	D	K7WS
Las Vegas	145.01		WA7HXO-1	D	WA7HXO
Peavine Pk	145.05		WA7DIA-1	D	
Slide Mt	145.01		WA6TLW-1	D	
NEW JERSEY					
Alpine	145.03		K2LSX-1	D N	Dgplx/MAMARC
Bayonne	145.07		W2ODV	D	BayonneEM
Bayonne	145.07		W2ODV-0	D	BEMARC
Belmar	145.05		KA2RAF-2	D N	Dgplx/RATS
Belmar	221.11		KA2RAF-2	D N	Dgplx/RATS
Bergenfield	145.07		N2DSY-4	M	Dgplx/RATS
Bergenfield	221.11		N2DSY-4	G	Dgplx/RATS

Figure 11.2—A page from *The ARRL Repeater Directory* listing packet-radio operations by their location. In the "Notes" column, "D" stands for digipeater, "G" for gateway, "M" for message storage (PBBS) and "N" for network (high-level protocol).

paths between digipeaters and packet-radio bulletin-board systems (PBBS) and are available from various sources: landline bulletin boards, club newsletters, packet-radio publications, and so on. The most easily accessible source for a local network map is your local PBBS. If a network map exists for your area, it is most likely to be stored as a file on the local PBBS for your downloading pleasure.

Once you obtain a network map, you use it as you would a road map. Find a digipeater that is located near you, find a digipeater that is located near the station you intend to contact, and trace the route on the map between the two digipeaters. The network map may be more current than the *Repeater Directory*, but the maps become out of date just as quickly. Don't be too surprised if you can't use a digipeater that is shown on your latest network map, or if everyone else is using a digipeater you've never heard of!

The best way to find out about the dedicated digipeaters in your area is through on-the-air monitoring. Your TNC provides a self-contained digipeater-location service. The previous chapter describes the various monitoring commands that are available in a TNC. Among these commands is the "Mrpt" command, which allows you to obtain a list of the digipeaters used for passing packets in your area. To enable this function, both the "Monitor" and "Mrpt" functions must be on (**cmd: Monitor ON <CR>**

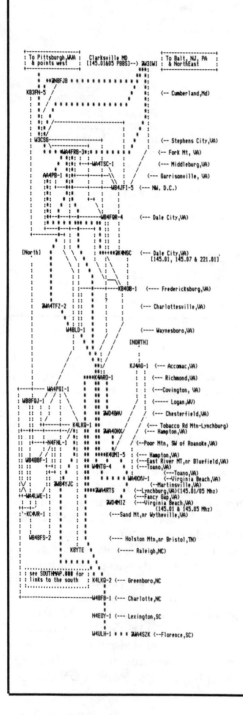

Figure 11.3—A typical packet-radio network map, this one illustrating the network in Virginia. It was assembled by K4NGC and shows the primary routes used for mail forwarding [indicated by asterisks (*)] and the secondary routes [indicated by colons (:), hyphens (-), and slant bars (/ or \ )]. PBBS call signs are prefixed with the at-sign (@).

and **cmd: MRpt ON** <CR>). Once enabled, monitored packets are displayed in the following format:

KB1MW>KZ1Z,N1API-2,K1KI*: Do you have any info from Bridgeport?

where KB1MW is the call sign of the station originating the packet, KZ1Z is the call sign of the destination station for the packet, and N1API-2 and K1KI are the call signs of the stations digitally repeating the packets between KB1MW and KZ1Z. The asterisk (*) after K1KI indicates that K1KI is the station that is actually being received by your station.

From this one monitored packet, you can deduce that:

1) K1KI is a digipeater within the reception area of your station,

2) If you wish to contact KB1MW, the correct path is "Via K1KI,N1API-2"

3) If you wish to contact KZ1Z, the correct path is "Via K1KI."

Figure 11.4 shows some of the information you can deduce from a monitored packet. All of that information is obtained from only one monitored packet. If you monitor additional packets, you can find out a lot of useful information concerning the paths in your area. The best part is that the information obtained path finding with the Mrpt function is always current.

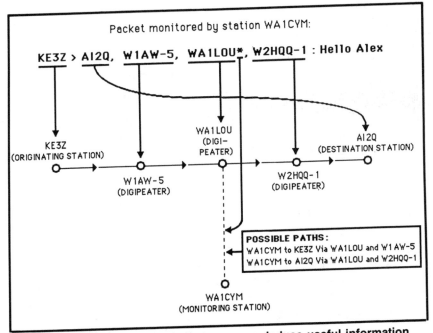

Figure 11.4—With "Mrpt" enabled, you can deduce useful information from a monitored packet.

Voice Repeater Packeting

Packet repeating is not limited to digipeaters; voice repeaters may be used for packet repeating if necessary. The differences between repeating packets using digipeaters and voice repeaters are important.

When a digipeater receives a packet for repeating, it holds the packet while it waits for the channel to clear before it retransmits the packet. A voice repeater retransmits immediately. As soon as the carrier of the packet transmission is detected by the repeater's receiver, the repeater keys its transmitter and retransmits whatever information (if any) is contained on the carrier. When the carrier is no longer detected, the repeater waits a short time (the "squelch tail" or "hang time") for a carrier to return. If no carrier is detected within the hang time, the repeater stops transmitting.

When you use a digipeater to retransmit a packet, you must specifically address the digipeater when invoking the "Connect" command. For example, to initiate a connection with station WA1LOU by means of digipeater K1XA-5, at the command prompt you type:

cmd: Connect WA1LOU Via K1XA-5 <CR>

The call sign or signs of the digipeater or digipeaters must be included in the command.

When you use a voice repeater, you don't address the voice repeater when invoking the "Connect" command. For example, to initiate a connection with station WA1LOU by means of voice repeater WA1NQP, at the command prompt type:

cmd: Connect WA1LOU <CR>

The call sign of the voice repeater must not be included in the command. If you want the packet to be retransmitted by one or more digipeaters after it is repeated by a voice repeater, however, the call signs of digipeaters must be included. For example, to initiate a connection with station WA1LOU using voice repeater WA1NQP and then using digipeaters K1XA-5 and K1JCL-1, at the command prompt type:

cmd: Connect WA1LOU Via K1XA-5,K1JCL-1 <CR>

The call sign of the voice repeater must not be included in the command, but the call sign(s) of the digipeater(s) must be included. (Refer to Figure 11.5 for an illustration of how to address digipeater stations properly through a voice repeater.)

One other difference between digital and voice repeater operation is that digipeaters receive and transmit on one frequency, whereas voice repeaters receive and transmit on different frequencies. The repeater's receive frequency is called the input frequency (input to the repeater) and its transmit frequency is called the output frequency (output from the repeater).

The single-frequency operation of a digipeater conserves radio spectrum

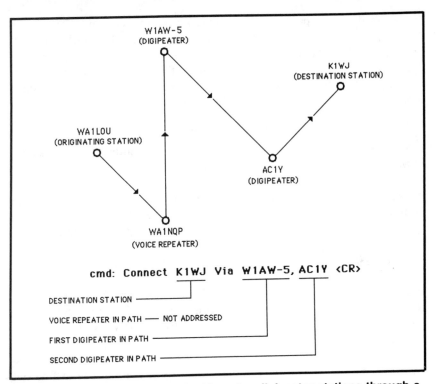

Figure 11.5—The proper way of addressing digipeater stations through a voice repeater.

space when compared with the dual-frequency operation of a voice repeater. When a voice repeater is used for repeating packets, however, it offers an advantage over digipeaters because it alleviates the collision problem. There are no collisions when each packet-radio station can hear every other packet-radio station, and a voice repeater provides each station with that ability. When any one station transmits a packet, that transmission is instantaneously repeated by the voice repeater for all other stations to hear and all of the other stations will wait until the transmission is completed. As a result, collisions are minimized.

When using a voice repeater to repeat packets, some Amateur Radio etiquette comes into play. It is not a good idea to start sending packets through any voice repeater just because it is on the air. The owner or operator of the repeater may not be as open-minded as you are about new communication tools and may shut the repeater down in mid-packet. It is a good idea to consult with the voice repeater's keeper and get his blessing before sending packets through his machine.

In addition, you should never interrupt a voice conversation on a repeater to start sending your packets. Although packet transmissions are short enough to be squeezed between the breaks in a voice conversation, such transmissions probably will annoy the voice operators. In short order, you may find that your packets are no longer welcome on the repeater. The voice operators on the repeater may need to be convinced that your packet transmissions will not interfere with their communications.

Hank's Handiwork

Hank Oredson's WØRLI automatic message-forwarding system has been in operation for a number of years. The system has become more effective as more network operations and PBBSs have come on the air to make the network more complete. Today, there are fewer gaps in the network than yesterday and, as a result, a message entering the WØRLI system is more likely to reach its intended destination today than yesterday (and it will get there more quickly!).

The WØRLI system works like this. Messages are entered into the system with addresses that include the call sign of the message's intended recipient and the call sign of the recipient's local WØRLI-compatible PBBS (where the recipient picks up his mail). The format of the address is "call sign of recipient" @ "call sign of recipient's local PBBS" ("W4RI @ W1AW," for example).

Every hour or so, the PBBS checks to see if it has any outgoing messages. If any exist, the PBBS reads the address of the message to find out where the message is going. Next, it consults a table that lists which PBBS is next in line to relay messages to the destination PBBS. Finally, the PBBS initiates a connection with the next-in-line PBBS and, if a connection is made, the PBBS sends the message to that next-in-line PBBS.

The next-in-line PBBS follows the same procedure and relays the message to the next PBBS in the chain. Sooner or later, the message is relayed to the end-of-the-line PBBS where the intended recipient picks up his mail.

Note that just as the postal system uses different media to deliver its mail (by truck, by plane and by mail carrier), the WØRLI system also uses different media. A packet-radio message may be relayed by PBBSs that are connected on HF, VHF, UHF and even satellite links. In any case, the medium is transparent to its users.

Initially, message forwarding was conducted on the same packet-radio channels used by everyone else. As more and more packet-radio stations came on the air, however, the competition between message-forwarding PBBSs and other packet-radio stations was causing a breakdown of the network. To help alleviate this problem, message forwarding is often being conducted on channels that are devoted exclusively to such operations.

On VHF, instead of trying to forward messages on the jam-packed 2-meter packet-radio frequencies, many message-forwarding PBBSs have moved their operations to less-active 220-MHz packet-radio channels. These

PBBSs still have 2-meter operations which accept and deliver messages, but they also have ports on 220 MHz that are used for the actual message forwarding. The 220-MHz ports serve only for the message-forwarding function; a packet-radio station that attempts to connect with a message-forwarding PBBS on 220 MHz will be rejected. Similarly, exclusive HF message-forwarding channels are being used on 20 and 40 meters. Attempting to connect with an HF message-forwarding PBBS will also result in a connect rejection.

SKIPNET

SKIPNET is a full-time HF message-forwarding system, operating under an FCC special temporary authorization (STA). The STA is required for full-time operation because FCC rules do not permit unattended automatic operation of Amateur Radio stations below 50 MHz. Under the STA, approximately 50 message-forwarding PBBSs throughout the United States are operating 24 hours-a-day on 20 through 80 meters. These stations provide the long-distance links required for effective packet-radio message-relay capabilities. The reliable long-distance links greatly enhance Amateur Radio's emergency-communications capabilities.

Before the STA, HF message forwarding could be performed only when a control operator was present at the message-forwarding station. The problem with the live control operator requirement is that stations may be off the air (because no control operator is present) when they are required for message forwarding. With unattended HF automatic message forwarding, all message-forwarding stations are available at all times to relay messages from other message-forwarding stations.

The purpose of the STA is to prove to the FCC that unattended HF automatic message forwarding can be conducted without harmful interference to other Amateur Radio operations. The FCC has been concerned that the malfunction of automatically controlled forwarding station transmitters could deny other amateurs the use of the operating frequency. Another concern is that improper communications might be automatically relayed without timely action. If the experiment is successful, the FCC may grant a permanent rule change to permit unattended automatic control of packet-radio operations below 50 MHz.

Note that the only function of the stations that comprise SKIPNET is to forward messages. If any station other than a SKIPNET station attempts to make a connection with a SKIPNET station, that connection will be rejected. Therefore, it is highly recommended that such connection attempts be avoided because all they do is gum up the workings of SKIPNET.

Worms In Space

In 1987, an experimental satellite link between packet-radio network nodes located in California and Maryland provided a temporary one-hop

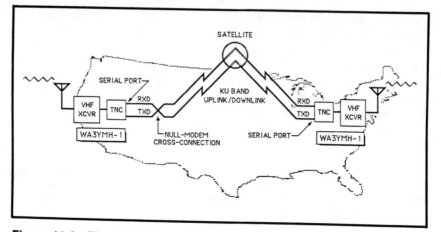

Figure 11.6—The WA3YMH-1 wormhole acted as a digipeater with a coverage area that encompassed parts of the East and West Coasts of the United States.

connection between packet-radio stations on the United States East and West Coasts. Mike Bach, WB6FFC, is co-founder of the Vitalink Communications Corporation, and it was Vitalink's commercial geosynchronous satellite that provided the transcontinental wormhole. The satellite provided the interconnection between the serial ports of the TNCs on each coast (Figure 11.6 shows an illustration of the wormhole operation). The call sign of the operation was WA3YMH-1.

To the user, the wormhole appeared to be a single digipeater with coverage that encompassed areas of Maryland and California. For example, if East Coast packet-radio station K1HTV wished to connect to west-coast packet-radio station WB6ASR by means of the wormhole, K1HTV used the command "Connect WB6ASR Via WA3YMH-1" at his station.

The WA3YMH-1/Vitalink wormhole is no longer in operation, but new satellite wormholes have been activated since its demise. Today, wormholes between Ottawa, Ontario and Calgary, Alberta and between Maryland and Minnesota are in operation and others may come on the air at any time.

The wormhole experiments are a precursor of the incorporation of Amateur Radio satellites into the future packet-radio network. At times, it seems that the future is already here!

The Network of Tomorrow is Here Today

There is a lot of discussion about the future of the packet-radio network. Everyone generally agrees as to where the network is going, but there is some contention as to how it is going to get there.

Where is the network going? The future packet-radio network will be easy to use and transparent to its users; you will simply command the network to connect your station to some other station and the network will do the rest.

How is the network going to get there? Ask different people and you will get different answers. We seem to be at a point where people will have to put up or shut up as a number of implementations of the future network are now in operation.

As the various implementations are tried and tested, one system may come out on top and be used throughout the network. It is also possible that compatible implementations may be used in different parts of the network. We will have to wait and see what happens. In the meantime, there is an interesting selection of network implementations for us to use and enjoy; a description of each follows.

NET/ROM

Ron Raikes, WA8DED, and Mike Busch, W6IXU, developed new firmware for the TNC 2 (and TNC-2 clones) that supports Levels 3 and 4, the Network and Transport layers of the packet-radio network. NET/ROM replaces the TNC-2 EPROM (that contains the TAPR TNC-2 firmware) and converts the TNC into a *network node controller* (*NNC*) for use at wide- and medium-coverage digipeater sites. Since it is so easy to convert an off-the-shelf TNC into an NNC via the NET/ROM route, NET/ROM has become the most popular network implementation in the packet-radio world and has been installed at most dedicated digipeater stations, thus propelling the standard AX.25 digipeater into packet-radio history.

The popularity of NET/ROM has its up side and its down side. The up side is that NET/ROM is installed everywhere and, as a result, it does not have to interface with other incompatible network implementations in order to complete a connection. This makes for a seamless, yet far-reaching packet-radio network.

The down side of NET/ROM's popularity is that it has become so popular that it has been stolen (NET/ROM is a commercial product; it is not free). Stolen NET/ROM code has been passed around among amateurs and installed in TNCs throughout the world unabashedly. This blatant activity would lead you to believe that NET/ROM was in the public domain! Although such theft hurts the NET/ROM developers directly, we will all suffer ultimately because other codesmiths will now think twice about developing any future Amateur Radio software-based products, and that is a loss for all of Amateur Radio.

How NET/ROM Works

The NET/ROM network user no longer has to be concerned with the digipeater path required to get from one point to another. All the user needs to know is the local node of the station he wishes to contact. NET/ROM knows what path is required, and if one path is not working or breaks down for some reason, NET/ROM will switch to an alternative path if one exists. The user can be assured that NET/ROM is on top of things, because each NET/ROM node automatically updates its node list periodically, and whenever a new node comes on the air, the other NET/ROM nodes become aware of the new node's existence automatically. In addition to automatic route updating, routing information may also be updated manually by means of a terminal keyboard or remotely using a packet-radio connection.

Once you are connected to another station via the NET/ROM network, most of your packets get through because *node-to-node packet acknowledgment* is used rather than *end-to-end acknowledgment*. When a user sends a packet from one point to another via the AX.25 digipeater network, his packet is simply handed off from one digipeater to another. If the intended destination station receives the packet without error, it sends an acknowledgment back along the same hand-to-hand path. Anywhere along the path, the packet or acknowledgment may collide with another packet and be lost. If the packet is lost, the originating station does not receive an acknowledgment of receipt from the destination station, so it resends the packet along the entire path again.

When a user sends a packet through a NET/ROM network, things are done differently. Each time the packet is transferred to a new node, that new node sends an acknowledgment of receipt back to the previous node. If a packet or acknowledgment is lost, only the unacknowledged node has to resend the packet (to the next node). The originating station does not have to send the packet through the entire path. Figure 11.7 illustrates the difference between end-to-end and node-to-node acknowledgment.

Besides offering node-to-node acknowledgment, NET/ROM also allows you to build cross-frequency or cross-band multiport nodes. This is done by installing NET/ROM in two TNCs and connecting their serial ports together (NET/ROM was used in the WA3YMH-1 wormhole TNCs discussed earlier in this chapter with the serial ports connected via the satellite). In addition to providing these sophisticated NNC functions, NET/ROM also provides the standard AX.25 digipeater function.

NET/ROM uses AX.25 for links between neighboring nodes and links with its local users. In addition, NET/ROM uses a Transport-layer *sliding window protocol* that provides end-to-end error control to counteract lost, duplicate or out-of-sequence packet frames that result from node failures and path changes. The sliding window protocol also provides end-to-end flow control to assure that one particular path is not disproportionately loaded with traffic. Since NET/ROM strictly separates the Network and Transport layers and provides a datagram-network service at *Level 3*, it is possible that NET/ROM can be used as a subnetwork for TCP/IP and other higher-level network systems.

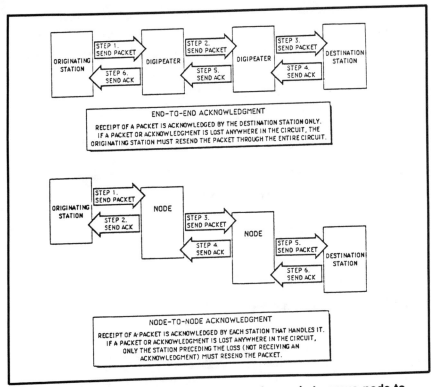

Figure 11.7—End-to-end acknowledgment of a packet versus node-to-node acknowledgment.

How To Use NET/ROM

Consider the following scenario: you wish to contact another station some distance away via packet radio, but you have no idea what path is required to make the contact. No problem!

You connect with the local NET/ROM node by typing:

cmd: Connect W1AW-5 <CR>

where W1AW-5 is the call sign of the NET/ROM node. Your terminal will display:

*** CONNECTED to W1AW-5

Next, you ask the local node for a list of all the other nodes that it can contact via one path or another by typing:

NODES <CR>

The local node looks up a list and your terminal displays:

CENCT:W1AW-5} Nodes:
SCCT:K1IKE-1　ENY:WB2KMY-1　VNH:WA1TLN-1　SPRFLD:W1NY-1
PUT:KG1O-9

On the list you find a distant node (WB2KMY-1) that is near the station you wish to contact, so you command the local node to connect with that distant node by typing:

Connect WB2KMY-1 <CR>

The local node fulfills your wish and your terminal displays:

CENCT:W1AW-5} Connected to WB2KMY-1

You now command the distant node to connect with WB2COY by typing:

Connect WB2COY <CR>

The distant node obliges and your terminal displays:

ENY:WB2KMY-1} Connected to WB2COY

Note that when the distant node makes a connection with the distant station, it uses your call sign with an SSID different from that of your TNC. If WA1LOU had initiated the NET/ROM connection in the example above, WB2COY's terminal would indicate that his station was connected to WA1LOU-15, not WA1LOU-0. The SSID used by the network node is determined by subtracting your SSID from 15; in this case, $15 - 0 = 15$.

Also note that NET/ROM has an inactivity timer that will summarily disconnect you if you have not sent anything to the node within the time set in the inactivity timer (the default setting is 15 minutes). When you wish to disconnect, you must first switch your TNC to the command mode (via <CTRL-C>) and invoke the "Disconnect" command.

As shown in the above scenario, a user can connect with a local node, obtain a list of other known nodes, establish a communication circuit with a distant node and connect to another station that is local to the distant node (all of the NET/ROM user commands are listed and described in the accompanying sidebar "NET/ROM User Commands"). Long gone are the days of deciphering complicated and out-of-date digipeater maps. The hard work is now done for you.

KA-Node

KA-Node is Kantronics implementation of a node-to-node acknowledgment protocol. It is available in every Kantronics TNC, except the original KPC-1, and in the Kantronics All Mode (KAM) controller. As explained in the description of NET/ROM above, node-to-node acknowledgment pro-

NET/ROM User Commands

There are six NET/ROM user commands: "Connect," "CQ," "Ident," "Nodes," "Parms" and "Users." All except "CQ" may be invoked by using the first letter of the command: C, I, N, P and U respectively. A description of each command follows. Note that these commands are used only after you have connected with a NET/ROM node (using your TNC's "Connect" command).

Connect x—Causes a node to initiate a connection with another node whose call sign is x or another user whose call sign is x.

Connect x via y1 y2...y8—Causes a node to initiate a connection with another user whose call sign is x via one to eight digipeaters whose call signs are y1 through y8.

CQ x—Causes a node to send "CQ" followed by text whose contents is x (CQ is only available with NET/ROM Version 1.3 and higher).

Ident—Causes a node to identify itself.

Nodes—Causes a node to display its routing table, that is, a list of all nodes that are connectable from the local node, except for hidden nodes [hidden nodes are those whose node identifier starts with the number sign (#)].

Nodes *—Causes a node to display its routing table, including hidden nodes [hidden nodes are those whose node identifier starts with the number sign (#)].

Nodes x—Causes a node to display one to three routes to the node whose call sign or node identifier is x.

Parms—Causes a node to display the following 24 node parameters:
1. Maximum destination list entries (1-400, default: 50)
2. Worst quality for auto-updates (0-255, default: 1)
3. Channel 0 (HDLC) quality (0-255, default: 192)
4. Channel 1 (RS-232) quality (0-255, default: 255)
5. Obsolescence count initializer (0-255, default: 6)
6. Obsolescence count minimum to be broadcast (1-255, default: 5)
7. Auto-update broadcast interval (0-65535 sec, default: 3600)
8. Network "time-to-live" initializer (0-255, default: 64)
9. Transport time-out (5-600 sec, default: 60)
10. Transport maximum tries (2-127, default: 3)
11. Transport acknowledge delay (1-60 sec, default: 3)
12. Transport busy delay (1-1000 sec, default: 180)
13. Transport requested window size (1-127 frames, default: 4)
14. Congestion control threshold (1-127 frames, default: 4)
15. No-activity time-out (0-65535 sec, default: 900)
16. Link digipeater wait "Dwait" (0-127 × 10 ms, default: 16)
17. Link T1 time-out "Frack" (1-15 sec, default: 4)
18. Link tx window size "Maxframe" (1-7 frames, default: 7)
19. Link maximum tries (0-127, default: 10)
20. Link T2 time-out (0-65535 × 10 ms, default: 100)
21. Link T3 time-out (0-65535 × 10 ms, default: 18000)
22. AX.25 digipeating (0-1, default: 1 = enabled)
23. Validate call signs (0-1, default: 1 = enabled)
24. Station ID beacons (0-1, default: 1 = enabled)

Users—Causes a node to display a list of stations that are using the node.

vides improved throughput over the standard AX.25 end-to-end acknowledgment. Besides node-to-node acknowledgment, KA-Node allows you to gateway from one port to another when you are connected to a dual-port KA-Node, which is available in the Kantronics KAM and KPC-4.

While KA-Node and NET/ROM are similar in that they both offer node-to-node acknowledgment, they are dissimilar in other ways. The most important difference is that KA-Node does not perform automatic routing as does NET/ROM. The user must command the KA-Node as to the desired path to another node or station. In this way, KA-Node is more like an AX.25 digipeater than a NET/ROM node. Although KA-Node does not achieve the same functionality as NET/ROM, it is still an improvement over digipeating, and as a result it is a popular packet-radio tool.

How To Use KA-Node

From the user's perspective, using a KA-Node is similar to using a NET/ROM node. The first thing you do is make a connection to your local KA-Node by typing:

cmd: Connect NORM <CR>

where NORM is the KA-Node identifier of the KA-Node. Your terminal will display:

*** CONNECTED to NORM
CONNECTED TO NODE NORM (W2JUP) CHANNEL A
ENTER COMMAND B,C,J,N,X, OR HELP
?

You are now connected to a KA-Node and it is awaiting your command. To make a connection to another station that is in the operating range of NORM, you type:

Connect AI2Q <CR>

where AI2Q is the call sign of the other station.

To make a connection to another KA-Node that is in the operating range of NORM, you type:

Connect STAN <CR>

where STAN is the KA-Node identifier of the other KA-Node. In either case, NORM will attempt to establish a connection and, if it is successful, your terminal displays:

###LINK MADE

You may now communicate with the other station.

If the connection has been made to another KA-Node, your terminal will also display:

**CONNECTED TO NODE STAN (WA1LOU) CHANNEL A
ENTER COMMAND B,C,J,N,X, OR HELP
?**

To make a connection to another station that is in the operating range of STAN, you type:

Connect N1ED <CR>

where N1ED is the call sign of the other station. STAN will attempt to make a connection with N1ED, and if it is successful, the ###LINK MADE message will be displayed at your terminal and you can commence communications with N1ED.

You can also make a connection to another KA-Node that is in the operating range of STAN by typing:

Connect BILL <CR>

where BILL is the KA-Node identifier of the other KA-Node. Here is where the difference between a KA-Node and a NET/ROM node is conspicuous. If you were using NET/ROM nodes in this example, rather than KA-Nodes, the NET/ROM node may have been able to make the connection between NORM and BILL automatically; you may have been able to command NORM to connect with BILL and have avoided the intermediary connection to STAN. (NORM may in fact use STAN as an intermediary to connect to BILL, but that would be transparent to the user.) The automatic-routing feature of NET/ROM makes this possible.

Without automatic routing, the KA-Node user must do the routing manually. KA-Node does provide some assistance in this regard, however. By invoking the "Nodes" command, KA-Node will provide you with a list of both KA-Node and NET/ROM nodes that the local KA-Node has heard along with the date and times of such monitoring. The "Nodes" command is similar to the "MHeard" command in your TNC and may be used in a similar way. Just as you use the "MHeard" command to inform you as to what stations are connectable from your station, you can use the "Nodes" command to inform you what nodes are connectable from the local KA-Node.

KA-Node also allows the user to obtain a list of everything that it has heard (individual stations, PBBSs and digipeaters, as well as nodes) by invoking the "Jheard" command. In effect, the "Jheard" command causes the KA-Node to dump its MHeard log to you. This can be useful if you need to know if another station in range of the local KA-Node has been recently active, or to find out what PBBSs and digipeaters are connectable from the local KA-Node. (All of the KA-Node user commands are listed and described in the accompanying sidebar "KA-Node User Commands.")

KA-Node User Commands

There are seven KA-Node user commands: "Abort," "Bye," "Connect," "Help," "Jheard," "Nodes," and "XConnect." A description of each command follows. Note that these commands are used only after you have connected with a KA-Node (using your TNC's "Connect" command).

Abort—Causes a node to stop attempting a Connect or XConnect request. To abort, no other data must be sent between invoking the "Connect" or "XConnect" command and the "Abort" command.

Bye—Causes a node to initiate a disconnection.

Connect x—Causes a node to initiate a connection with another node whose call sign or node identifier is x or another user whose call sign is x.

Connect x via y1 y2...y8—Causes a node to initiate a connection with another user whose call sign is x via one to eight digipeaters whose call signs are y1 through y8.

Help—Causes a node to list and briefly describe its command set.

JHeard—Causes a node to display its MHeard log, that is, a list of the call signs or node identifiers of packet-radio stations it has recently heard on frequency along with the date and time of monitoring.

JHeard S—Causes a node to display its MHeard log without the date and time of monitoring.

JHeard L—Causes a node to display its MHeard log along with the destination stations worked and the digipeaters used, if any.

Nodes—Causes a node to display a list of other KA-Nodes and NET/ROM nodes it has heard recently along with the date and time of monitoring.

XConnect x—Causes a KAM or KPC-4-equipped node to initiate a connection on its other port with another node whose call sign or node identifier is x or another user whose call sign is x.

TexNet

The Texas Packet Radio Society (TPRS) has been developing a higher-level packet-radio network called TexNet, which is composed of dual-port network-control processors (NCP) that provide AX.25-compatible 1200-baud user access on 2 meters and node-to-node linking at 9600 bauds on 70 cm. TexNet firmware can support 256 nodes within one network, and each node can provide several user services, including access to TexNet, a bulletin board, digipeaters, weather information and a conference bridge that provides connected-mode round-table service.

How TexNet Works

Each NCP contains a Z80 microprocessor with 24 kbytes of ROM to contain the firmware, 40 kbytes of RAM, a timer circuit and input/output ports. Each NCP is battery powered for emergency communications and has provisions for the addition of a hard-disk controller for more versatility. The firmware provides a Level 3 Network layer that uses datagrams with node-to-node acknowledgments (refer to the description of NET/ROM earlier in this chapter for a discussion of node-to-node versus end-to-end packet acknowledgment).

How To Use TexNet

Access to any TexNet service is accomplished by connecting to a local node using the node's call sign and a specific SSID. An SSID of 0 accesses a digipeater, an SSID of 2 accesses the first conference bridge, SSID 3 accesses the second conference bridge and SSID 4 accesses the network. Use of the various services can occur simultaneously on the same node, with a maximum of 20 users.

Connecting to TexNet (SSID -4) presents the user with the opportunity to use a set of TexNet network commands whenever the network command prompt (NETWORK CMD?) appears (refer to the accompanying sidebar "TexNet User Commands" for a list and description of all the commands). The "Connect" command allows you to make connections with other users in the network by specifying the user's call sign and the user's local TexNet node. For example, typing:

Connect WD5IVD @ DALLAS <CR>

causes TexNet to attempt to establish a connection between your station and station WD5IVD at the Dallas TexNet node.

The "Message" command allows you to access the Packet Message System (PMS), which is essentially a multiconnect PBBS mailbox that uses a subset of the W0RLI Mailbox command set. There is only one PMS for the whole network. All users access the same PMS, which provides better message-handling reliability because there is no message-forwarding on the network. The "Locations" command provides you with a list of the names of the nodes in the network. The "Weather" command connects you to the weather server module of the PMS, which provides up-to-the-minute weather information.

The prime movers of TexNet are George Baker, W5YR, Tom McDermott, N5EG, and Tom Aschenbrenner, WB5PUC. TexNet presently interconnects the Texas communities of Austin, Corpus Christi, Dallas, Houston, Midland, Murphy, Plano, Rockport, San Antonio and Waco with 9600-baud radio and landline links. It is also being used in Oklahoma and Michigan. The longest path of the Texas TexNet installation is the 240-mile trip between Murphy and Rockport. The round trip delay from Murphy to Rockport to Murphy is a mere six seconds!

TexNet User Commands

The TexNet user commands are listed and described as follows. Most of the commands may be invoked by entering only the first letter of the command, for example, "B" for the "Bye" command. Note that these commands are used only after you have connected with a TexNet node (using your TNC's "Connect" command).

?—Causes a node to list the user commands.

Bye—Causes a node to disconnect the user from network.

Connect *x* @ *y*—Causes a node to initiate a connection with a user whose call sign is *x* at a node whose name is *y*.

Connect *x* v *y1* *y2* @ *z*—Causes a node to initiate a connection with a user whose call sign is *x* via one or two digipeaters whose call signs are *y1* and *y2* at a node whose name is *z*.

Connect *x* @ *y*, *n*—Causes a node to initiate a connection with a user whose call sign is *x* via port *n* at a node whose name is *y*.

Connect CQ @ *x*—Causes a node whose name is *x* to send "CQ."

Help—Causes a node to list user commands.

Locations—Causes a node to list the 7-character names of all of the network nodes.

Message—Causes a node to initiate a connection to the Packet Message System (PMS). (The PMS uses a subset of the WØRLI Mailbox command set.)

Message @ *x*—Causes a node to initiate a connection to the Packet Message System (PMS) at a node whose name is *x*. (The PMS uses a subset of the WØRLI Mailbox command set.)

Statistics @ *x*—Causes a node whose name is *x* to list the following statistics that have been accumulated since midnight:
Frame buffers available
Frame buffers in use
Maximum frame buffers used
Total connects
Connects to Packet Message System

TCP/IP

An early proposal for higher-level packet-radio networking was presented by Phil Karn, KA9Q, at the Fourth ARRL Amateur Radio Computer Networking Conference in March 1985. Phil proposed that Amateur Radio adopt the Defense Advanced Research Projects Agency (DARPA) Internet Protocol (IP) and Transmission Control Protocol (TCP) as the standard Level 3 (Network layer) and Level 4 (Transport layer) protocols for amateur packet radio.

The KA9Q Internet Protocol Package is software written by Phil that embodies his proposal for higher-level packet-radio networking. He wrote

Connects to bridge
Connects to network
Network circuits active
Maximum network circuits up
Frame buffers TX ($\times$ 10), PCHAN0
Frame buffers TX ($\times$ 10), PCHAN1
Frame buffers TX ($\times$ 10), PCHAN2
Frame buffers RX ($\times$ 10), PCHAN0
Frame buffers RX ($\times$ 10), PCHAN1
Frame buffers RX ($\times$ 10), PCHAN2
Frame buffers resent-TX D ($\times$ 10), PCHAN0
Frame buffers resent-TX D ($\times$ 10), PCHAN1
Frame buffers resent-TX D ($\times$ 10), PCHAN2

Statistics Y @ x—Causes a node whose name is x to list the following statistics that had been accumulated the previous day:
Frame buffers available
Frame buffers in use
Maximum frame buffers used
Total connects
Connects to Packet Message System
Connects to bridge
Connects to network
Network circuits active
Maximum network circuits up
Frame buffers TX ($\times$ 10), PCHAN0
Frame buffers TX ($\times$ 10), PCHAN1
Frame buffers TX ($\times$ 10), PCHAN2
Frame buffers RX ($\times$ 10), PCHAN0
Frame buffers RX ($\times$ 10), PCHAN1
Frame buffers RX ($\times$ 10), PCHAN2
Frame buffers resent-TX D ($\times$ 10), PCHAN0
Frame buffers resent-TX D ($\times$ 10), PCHAN1
Frame buffers resent-TX D ($\times$ 10), PCHAN2

Weather—Causes a node to initiate a connection to the weather server module of the Packet Message System (PMS).

the software for the IBM PC and compatible computers and it has been ported to the Apple Macintosh and Commodore Amiga computers. The KA9Q package consists of a collection or "suite" of protocols and applications that are intended to transfer information between computers.

How TCP/IP Works

The TCP/IP protocol is based on the datagram concept (as are all of the networking protocols discussed thus far in this chapter). A datagram is a self-contained message that includes the complete source and destination addresses of the message, as well as control information and the actual contents of the message. Each datagram is independent from other datagrams and, as a result, each must include all of the information needed to route it through the network.

Although the protocol name "TCP/IP" is an abbreviation for two protocols, the Transport Control Protocol (TCP) and the Internet Protocol (IP), the TCP/IP "protocol" used in the KA9Q package actually consists of a group of protocols including the Address Resolution Protocol (ARP), File Transfer Protocol (FTP), Serial Line Interface Protocol (SLIP), Simple Mail Transfer Protocol (SMTP), Telnet protocol and the User Datagram Protocol (UDP), as well as TCP and IP. Figure 11.8 illustrates the relationship of the various protocols contained in the KA9Q package and how they fit into the ISO Open Systems Interconnection Reference Model (OSI-RM) described in Chapter 3—Theory of Operation.

IP (Internet Protocol) is a Level 3 or Network-layer protocol. It routes packets of data (datagrams) by use of addresses that are 32-bit binary numbers. Each network node, that is, each computer at each packet-radio station in the TCP/IP network, has a unique *IP address* that has been assigned by the local IP address coordinator. ARPANET assigned the address block starting with the digits 44 to amateur packet radio (as well as naming the amateur TCP/IP packet-radio network *AMPRNET*). As a result, the first two digits of all amateur packet-radio IP addresses are 44 (for example, the IP address of WA1LOU is 44.88.0.14).

IP datagrams sent via packet radio are normally contained in the I field of an AX.25 UI frame. To send the AX.25 frame, the computer must learn the call sign of the station to which the datagram is being sent. The Address Resolution Protocol (ARP) performs this function by broadcasting a "who is 44.88.0.14" request, which would be answered, in this example, by WA1LOU's TCP/IP system.

TCP (Transport Control Protocol) is a Level 4 or Transport-layer protocol that provides data integrity between the data's points of origination and destination, whenever such integrity is required. It assembles data for transmission into packets and disassembles received packets into received data, while checking for errors and managing packet transmissions on the network. When TCP is not required, *UDP (User Datagram Protocol)* is available at Level 4 to perform other functions. For example, UDP is used by messages to determine which applications, within a destination computer, the messages are intended for.

SLIP (Serial Line Interface Protocol) is a Level 2 or Link-layer protocol that provides a simple serial-data transfer between the Network-layer protocols and the EIA-232 interface of the Physical layer. KISS, for "Keep It Simple, Stupid," is a Link-layer non-protocol for serial input and output that was written by Mike Chepponis, K3MC. KISS is a firmware replace-

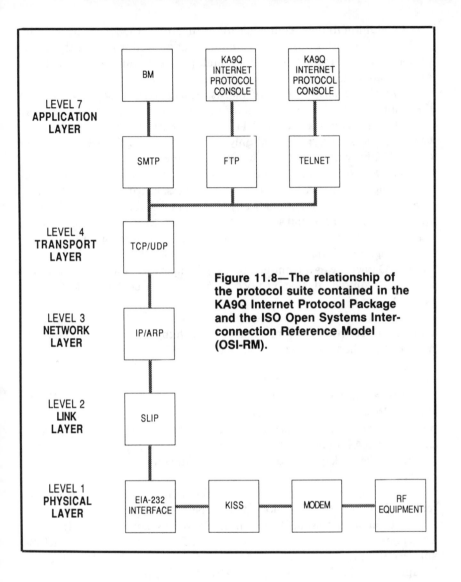

Figure 11.8—The relationship of the protocol suite contained in the KA9Q Internet Protocol Package and the ISO Open Systems Interconnection Reference Model (OSI-RM).

ment for TAPR TNCs (and TAPR TNC clones) that supports SLIP rather than the Link-layer connections of AX.25. As a result, no AX.25 connection is established with the other end of the circuit. Instead, KISS accepts serial data from the computer and sends it as AX.25 unconnected information (UI) packet frames (the packet-radio equivalent of the datagram). Received datagrams are transferred directly to the computer for disassembly by TCP. In effect, the KA9Q package performs much of the work that, up to now, has been performed by our TNCs.

In addition to these communications functions, the KA9Q package includes applications for use during communication sessions. Since the KA9Q package has the capability to perform multiple tasks simultaneously, several of these applications can be used at the same time.

FTP (File Transfer Protocol) allows the user to transfer files to or from the computer at another node. Since the data is transparent to TCP, any kind of data may be transferred. FTP provides password protection and three levels of file security: (1) read-only, (2) read-only, write new files, and (3) read-only, write new files, overwrite old files.

SMTP (Simple Mail Transfer Protocol) provides an automatic message-forwarding function. After the user enters a message for another station and saves it on disk, SMTP automatically attempts to establish communications with that other station and sends the message once communication is established. The drawback with using SMTP is that it requires specific message formatting. To alleviate this drawback, *Bdale's Mailer (BM)* is included in the KA9Q package as a front-end to SMTP to perform the specific formatting task required by that protocol. BM was written by Bdale Garbee, N3EUA.

Finally, *Telnet* is a terminal-emulation protocol that provides a user-to-user "chat" function for communications with the live operator of another node (rather than with the station's computer).

How to Use TCP/IP

Before you can use TCP/IP, you need a computer that will run the KA9Q Internet Protocol Package (an IBM PC or clone, an Apple Macintosh or a Commodore Amiga). Once you have a KA9Q-able computer, you need the correct KA9Q package for that computer. Each computer has its own version of the package; the packages are not interchangeable between computers.

You also need a TNC that supports the KISS non-protocol. Most current TNCs support the KISS mode. Older TNCs that do not support the mode may be brought up to snuff by purchasing new KISSable firmware from the TNC manufacturer. If the KISSless TNC is a TNC 2 or TNC-2 clone, KISSable firmware is available from TAPR. TNC 1s can also be made KISSable by upgrading the TNC 1 with the TAPR TNC-2 upgrade kit.

Once your TNC is KISSable, you enable the KISS mode at the command mode by typing:

cmd: KISS ON <CR>

Note that you must use a terminal or a computer running terminal-emulation software to enable the KISS mode; you cannot use the KA9Q package to enable the KISS mode. Next, toggle the TNC's power off and on. If KISS is enabled, the STA and CON front panel indicators will blink on three times as the TNC is initialized.

TCP/IP User Commands

A list and description of the KA9Q TCP/IP user commands follows. They are based on the KA9Q Internet Protocol Package, Version 871225.32 Alpha 4, Macintosh Version 1.0. Most of the commands may be invoked by entering only the first one or two letters of the full command name, for example, "D" for the "Disconnect" command and "AR" for the "ARP" command.

?—Displays list of TCP/IP commands.

ARP x—Displays ARP table.

Attach x—Configures and selects a hardware interface for use by the TCP/IP system.

AX25 x—Sets the following AX.25 parameters: Digipeat, Maxframe, Mycall, Paclen, Reset, Retry, Status, Window.

CD—Displays computer's current directory.

CD x—Changes to computer directory named x.

Close—Ends an AX.25, FTP, or Telnet session.

Connect x—Initiates an AX.25 connection with a station whose call sign or IP address is x.

Connect x y1...y8—Initiates an AX.25 connection with a station whose call sign or IP address is x via one to eight digipeaters whose call signs are y1 through y8.

Dir—Displays contents of computer's current directory.

Disconnect—Ends an AX.25 session.

Echo x—Accepts or refuses remote node's offer to echo local node keyboard entry during a Telnet session (x = accept or refuse).

EOL x—Controls how carriage returns are interpreted when local keyboard entry is echoed by a remote node during a Telnet session. (If x = standard, carriage returns are interpreted as carriage returns. If x = unix, than carriage returns are interpreted as line feeds.)

Escape—Displays hexadecimal value of command-mode escape character.

Escape n—Selects command mode escape character with a hexadecimal value equal to n.

Exit—Quits KA9Q software and returns the control of the computer to the computer's operating system.

Finger @ x—Requests information about users of the node whose call sign or IP address is x.

FTP x—Initiates an FTP session with a remote node whose call sign or IP address is x.

Help—Displays list of TCP/IP commands.

Hostname—Displays host name of local node.

Hostname x—Sets host name of local node to x.

IP Address—Displays IP Address of local node.

IP Address n—Sets IP Address of local node to a value equal to n.

IP Status—Displays IP and ICMP (Internet Control Message Protocol) statistics.

IP TTL—Displays the time-to-live (TTL) parameter. (TTL is the maximum number of hops a packet is permitted to use.)

IP TTL n—Sets the time-to-live parameter to a value equal to n. (TTL is the maximum number of hops a packet is permitted to use.)

Kick—Causes a server to resume operation after timing-out.

Log—Indicates whether server sessions are being logged.

Log x—Stops or starts the logging of server sessions (x = *stop* or the name of the file that will contain the log).

Mbox x—Controls mailbox function and displays status of NET/ROM support software (x = *off* or *on*).

Mode x y—For hardware interface x, selects the datagram or virtual-circuit mode (y = *datagram* or *vc*).

NETROM x—Controls the interface to the NET/ROM support software.

Param x y—For the TNC connected to hardware interface x, sets parameters y.

Ping x—Packet Internet Groper; tests communication channel between stations by requesting the route time between the local node and a remote node whose call sign or IP address is x.

PWD—Displays computer's current directory.

PWD x—Changes to computer directory named x.

Record x—Adds all of the data received during a current Telnet session to the file whose name is x. (If x = *off*, file will be closed.)

Reset—Causes a local reset of the current session.

Reset x—Causes a local reset of the current x-type session [x = *AXCB* (AX.25) or *TCB* (TCP Control Block)].

Route—Displays IP routing table.

Route x—Changes IP routing table to x.

Session—Displays current session(s).

Session n—Causes local node to enter converse mode with session that is numbered n.

SMTP Maxclients—Displays maximum number of outgoing SMTP sessions (default = 10).

SMTP Maxclients n—Sets maximum number of outgoing SMTP sessions to a value of n (default = 10).

SMTP Timer—Displays interval (in seconds) between each transmission of outgoing mail.

SMTP Timer n—Sets interval (in seconds) between each transmission of outgoing mail to a value of n.

Start FTP x—Starts Internet server x.

Stop FTP x—Stops Internet server x.

TCP Kick x—Causes any data in TCB x queue to be sent immediately.

TCP Status—Displays TCP statistics.

Telnet x—Initiates a Telnet session with the node whose call sign or IP address is x.

Trace x n—Causes tracing of data on the hardware interface whose value is x according to the following option selections: if n = 000, tracing is disabled; if n = 111, tracing of all input and output containing ASCII characters is enabled; if n = 011, tracing of input and output headers is enabled.

Tzone x n—Sets local time zone to x and the difference, in hours, between the local time zone and UTC/GMT to a value of n.

UDP Status—Displays status of UDP queues.

Upload x—During a current AX.25 or Telnet session, sends the file whose name is x.

There are two additional requirements before you can start TCP/IPing. First, you must obtain an IP address from your local IP address coordinator. Ask other TCP/IPers who the local coordinator is or contact Brian Kantor, WB6CYT, the national IP address coordinator. After you have obtained an IP address, you must modify files in the KA9Q package to contain your IP address and other information. Also, the placement of files within computer directories and sub-directories is critical (and varies with computer), so refer to the KA9Q documentation on how to modify, set up and locate the necessary files.

Once you are all set up to TCP/IP, you can start using the commands in the sidebar "TCP/IP User Commands." One of the most common TCP/IP operations that you are likely to use is file transfer. The following example illustrates how easy it is.

I want to download a copy of the local IP addresses from KA1SMW's computer. First, I wish to test the path between my station and KA1SMW, so I invoke the PING command at the command prompt, by typing:

net> ping ka1smw <CR>

(Note that the command prompt for the KA9Q package is "net>" followed by a space.) My system pings KA1SMW's system and my terminal displays:

44.88.0.24: echo reply id 0 seq 61531, 7000 ms

KA1SMW's IP address is 44.88.0.24 and 7000 ms is the amount of time it took to send the ping from my station to KA1SMW. Now that I know that KA1SMW is on the air, I will initiate an FTP session, at the command prompt, by typing:

net> ftp ka1smw <CR>

As my system establishes an FTP session with KA1SMW, my terminal displays:

SYN sent
Established
220 ka1smw.ampr.org FTP version 890421.1e ready at Sat Aug 26
18:22:26 19

KA1SMW's system is now waiting for me to log in. To do so, at the command prompt I type:

user anonymous <CR>

and my terminal displays KA1SMW's response:

331 Enter PASS command

I respond to the password request by typing:

pass wa1lou <CR>

Most systems are set up to allow "anonymous" users to log in using their call sign as a password; these users are usually granted a read-only file-security privilege. My terminal now displays:

230 Logged in

Now that I am logged in to KA1SMW's system, I want to obtain a list of the files that are available for downloading. To do this, I type:

dir <CR>

and my terminal displays:

200 Port command okay
150 Opening data connection for LIST \public
net_1e.agn   0 17:37 8/18/89
net_1e.arc   433
10:10 8/17/89
net_1e.old   69,121 19:57 8/10/89
ip_adrs.ct   36,505
07:32   8/11/89
unknown.doc   37,501 00:47   8/14/89
5 files.   13,617,152 bytes free. Disk size 33,400,832 bytes.
Get complete, 266 bytes received.

The file I want to download is "ip_adrs.ct." To do so, I type:

get ip_adrs.ct <CR>

and my terminal displays:

200 Port command okay
150 Opening data connection for RETR ip_adrs.ct

During the next few minutes, my terminal displays nothing. My transmitter is turning off and on, however, and my disk drive is whirring, which indicates that I am likely receiving the file requested from KA1SMW. Finally, my terminal displays:

Get complete, 36,505 bytes received
226 File sent ok

The file transfer was a success. Now I end the FTP session, at the command prompt, by typing:

net> close

and my terminal displays:

FIN wait 1
net> FIN wait 2
Time wait
Closed (Normal)

and I am logged off KA1SMW's system. The file transfer was easy and while the actual transfer was occurring, I could have opened another session to perform other tasks simultaneously.

The KA9Q Internet Protocol Package is becoming very popular throughout the world, and it is probably the second-most-popular networking protocol currently in use in amateur packet radio (NET/ROM is number one). If you own an IBM PC or clone, an Apple Macintosh or a Commodore Amiga, you owe it to yourself to at least try out the KA9Q package. The package is available free for non-commercial use and may be obtained for a very nominal fee (the cost of the blank disks). Give it a try!

RATS Open System Environment (ROSE)

The RATS Open System Environment (ROSE) was developed over a number of years by The Radio Amateur Telecommunications Society (RATS) of New Jersey. It is a firmware replacement for the TNC-2 class of TNCs that causes the TNC to act as a packet switch.

How ROSE Works

Like the other networking protocols discussed so far, ROSE's function is to let the network do the work when trying to establish a packet-radio communications circuit. The network, not the user, performs the task of determining the path between stations. And like the other protocols, ROSE uses node-to-node rather than end-to-end packet acknowledgment. Unlike the other networking protocols, however, ROSE uses the virtual circuit or *connection protocol* to do the job, rather than the datagram or *connectionless protocol*.

Terry Fox, WB4JFI, presented one of the first proposals for higher-level packet radio at the Third ARRL Amateur Radio Computer Networking Conference in April 1984. His proposal for a virtual-circuit network was based on the CCITT X.25 protocol.

A virtual circuit gives the appearance of providing a direct connection between you and another packet-radio station. Before communications commence, a "call setup" packet is sent through the network to set up a fixed path to the other station. Once the path is established, data packets may be sent through the circuit. These data packets are not burdened by a header containing the full address of the desired path (like AX.25 packets that include digipeater-routing information) because the network attempts to maintain the path for the duration of the communications. When communications are completed, the virtual circuit is cleared by removing the information about the path from the memory of each device along the communication path.

Tom Moulton, W2VY, wrote the ROSE code, which permits you to contact another station in the network as long as you know the other station's call sign and the ROSE node number used by the other station; you do not have to specify the network path between you and the other station.

To specify a network node, ROSE uses the CCITT X.121 country-code numbering system; in North America, the system is based on the telephone numbering system (area codes and local dialing prefixes in the United States and Canada). The ROSE node number consists of the three-digit area code followed by the three-digit local dialing prefix of the node, for a total of six digits. For example, "203879" would represent the area code for Connecticut (203) and the local dialing prefix for downtown Wolcott (879).

How To Use ROSE

Using ROSE is fairly straightforward; you do not have to learn any special commands, as the standard "Connect" command unlocks the key to ROSE. For example, if WA4SWF wished to make a connection with W1AW, he would type:

Connect W1AW Via KA4ROS-3, 203666 <CR>

where W1AW is the call sign of the intended station to be contacted, KA4ROS-3 is the call sign of the ROSE switch nearest WA4SWF and 203666 is the ROSE node number of the ROSE switch nearest W1AW. (Note that the SSID of a ROSE switch is usually -3.) To end the contact with W1AW, WA4SWF simply invokes the "Disconnect" command.

ROSE allows you to use digipeaters when necessary to complete a path between you and the nearest ROSE switch, or between the ROSE switch nearest the station intended for contact and that station. The following two examples illustrate this feature.

Connect W1AW Via KA4ROS,W4RI-3,203666 <CR>

In this example, the intended station to be contacted is W1AW and the

ROSE node number of the ROSE switch nearest W1AW is 203666. The ROSE switch closest to the station initiating this connection is W4RI-3, but in order to "reach" W4RI-3, KA4ROS must be called upon to act as a digipeater between the initiating station and W4RI-3.

Connect W1AW Via W4RI-3,203666,K8CH <CR>

In this example, the intended station to be contacted is W1AW and the ROSE node number of the ROSE switch nearest W1AW is 203666, but in order to reach W1AW, K8CH is called upon to act as a digipeater between W1AW and switch 203666. (The ROSE switch closest to the station initiating this connection is W4RI-3.)

Besides using digipeaters to complete a connection, ROSE switches themselves may be used as digipeaters. The only limit is that only one ROSE switch may be used as a digipeater at any one time, unlike standard AX.25 digipeaters, which permit the use of up to eight digipeaters to complete a path. To use a ROSE switch for local digipeating, simply subtract one from the SSID of the switch and use the "Connect" command as follows:

Connect W1AW Via W4RI-2 <CR>

where W1AW is the call sign of the intended station to be contacted and W4RI-2 is the call sign of the ROSE switch (W4RI-3 minus 1 = W4RI-2) that is being used as a digipeater.

Besides the switch, RATS has also developed the WØRLI-compatible ROSErver/Packet-Radio Mailbox System (PRMBS) Message Handling System that supports remote file and database requests and remote execution of applications besides the usual PBBS functions.

Conclusion

The success of amateur packet radio lies in a packet-radio network that is a well-oiled machine. If the network machinery runs poorly, packet radio will come to a grinding halt. This is why the work of the various groups and individuals described in this chapter needs the support and cooperation of every Amateur Radio packeteer. They are the ones oiling the network machinery. Packet radio's existence depends on them!

Network Hardware

Most of the discussion of network communications revolves around software and firmware, but what about the hardware that is an integral part of making the networks work? The following list of network switches, controllers and high-speed modems represents the hardware end of the packet-radio network.

Switches/Controllers

PacComm DR-100 Switch—a single-port digipeater or ROSE switch.

PacComm DR-200 Switch—a dual-port ROSE switch.

SANDPAC PS-186—a high-speed multiport packet switch that may operate at data rates as high as 1 Mbit/s; designed by members of the San Diego Packet Radio Association, the PS-186 has been licensed for manufacture and sale by AEA.

TexNet NCP—a dual-port network-control processor (NCP) that provides AX.25-compatible user access and node-to-node linking.

High-Speed Modems

AEA RFM-220 Radio Modem—a 19,200-baud FSK 220-MHz transceiver with a 25-watt output; it may also be used for FM voice communications.

DRSI 2400-Baud Modem—a 2400-bit/s DPSK (differential phase-shift keying) modem designed for use with the DRSI PC*Packet Adapter Type 1; the 2400-bit/s signal rate is derived from a dibit (a group of two bits) data stream operating at 1200 bauds.

G3RUH 9600-Baud Modem—a 9600-baud modem intended for use with amateur narrow-band FM voice radios; it was designed by James Miller, G3RUH.

GLB Netlink 220 Data Transceiver—a 19,200-baud FSK 220-MHz digital transceiver with an output of 2 watts.

Hamtronics 9600-Baud Digital RF Links—a 9600-baud 220- or 450- MHz transceiver with selectable 50- or 15-watt output.

HAPN 4800-Bit/S Modem—a 4800-baud modem designed by the Hamilton (Ontario) Area Packet Network.

Heatherington 56-kB RF Modem—a 56,000-baud, MSK (minimum-shift keying), 28-MHz transceiver intended for use with 220, 430, 902 or 1296-MHz linear transverters; it was designed by Dale Heatherington, WA4DSY, and is distributed by Georgia Radio Amateur Packet Enthusiast Society (GRAPES).

K9NG 9600-Baud Modem—Steve Goode, K9NG, designed this 9600-bit/s FSK modem.

Kantronics 2400 Modem—a 2400-bit/s DPSK modem designed for installation in the Kantronics KPC-4 and KAM controllers; the 2400-bit/s signal rate is derived from a dibit (a group of two bits) data stream operating at 1200 bauds.

Kantronics 2400-TNC Modem—a 1200-baud BPSK (binary phase-shift keying) and 2400-baud QPSK (quadrature phase-shift keying) modem designed for installation in TNC 1s, TNC 2s and clones.

Kantronics MSK Modem—a 300/1200-baud MSK modem designed for installation in the Kantronics KPC-4 and KAM controllers.

Kantronics QPSK Modem—a 1200-baud BPSK and 2400-baud QPSK modem designed for installation in the Kantronics KPC-4 and KAM controllers.

Kantronics TNC-2400 2400-Bit/S Modem—a 2400-bit/s DPSK modem designed for installation in TNC 1s, TNC 2s and clones; the 2400-bit/s signal rate is derived from a dibit (a group of two bits) data stream operating at 1200 bauds.

PacComm NB-96 Digital Transceiver—a 2- to 5-watt single-band digital transceiver for 144, 220, 440, or 920 MHz that uses the G3RUH 9600-baud modem.

PacComm NB-96 External Modem—the G3RUH 9600-baud modem in a standalone enclosure.

PacComm NB-96 Modem Card—the G3RUH 9600-baud modem on a PC card that is intended for piggyback installation in the TNC 2, its clones and all PacComm TNCs.

PRUG 9600-Bit/S Modem—a 9600-bit/s modem based on the CCITT V.29 protocol; it was designed by the Packet Radio User's Group (PRUG) in Tokyo.

TAPR packetRADIO—an inexpensive 25-watt, 1200-baud AFSK and 9600-baud FSK 144-MHz digital transceiver with five crystal-controlled channels; its prototype was the hit of the 1989 Dayton HamVention.

CHAPTER TWELVE

Space Communications

O rbiting Satellite Carrying Amateur Radio Number 1, better known as OSCAR I, was launched on December 12, 1961. On that date, Amateur Radio entered the space age. The development of the technology that put man (and OSCAR) in space required advances in electronics, advances that resulted in today's computer technology. Since the computer age is a result of the space program, and packet radio is a child of the computer age, it is only fitting that the circle be completed as packet radio enters space on board Amateur-Radio satellites.

Packet-radio communications via satellite fall into two broad categories: real-time communications and store-and-forward communications. In real-time satellite communications, a satellite relays packets immediately from one station to another—acting like a digipeater on a very, very high hill. In store-and-forward communications, the satellite acts like an orbiting PBBS, storing messages as it passes over one station and relaying them later as it passes over another part of the earth. During real-time communications, all stations that want to exchange packets must be able to "see" the satellite at once, so satellites in high orbits are used. For store-and-forward communications, the satellite can be in a low earth orbit, and the earth's rotation will take the on-board PBBS within range of anywhere on the earth at least once a day. Both kinds of satellite packet-radio communications have been tested in the Amateur Satellite Service, and each type will play a role in future packet-radio networks.

The Early Right Stuff

Some plans for future packet-radio networks place heavy emphasis on orbiting packet-radio transponders. Before these plans could be implemented, experiments had to be conducted to determine if they were practical.

The practicality of packet-radio space communications was tested and proven on March 11, 1984, when AMSAT OSCAR 10 was successfully used as a repeater to connect packet-radio stations on the East and West Coasts of the United States. Tom Clark, W3IWI, in Maryland and Ron McMurdy, WA0OJS, in California made the first contact. Later that year (on October 28), packet-radio stations in various parts of North America (Bill Jordan, W4DAQ, in Alabama, Randall Smith, VE1PAC/VE6, in Alberta, Wes Morris, K7PYK, in Arizona, and Bob Diersing, N5AHD, in Texas) used

Figure 12.1—AMSAT-OSCAR-10 is shown here being loaded with propellant.

OSCAR 10 to access the W3IWI PBBS located in Maryland. During a 60-minute period of this experiment, K7PYK successfully downloaded 50 kbytes of data from the W3IWI PBBS via the satellite!

Another step towards a space-based packet-radio network was completed on January 16, 1985, when the Digital Communications Experiment (DCE) aboard UoSAT-OSCAR 11 was first used. The DCE was built to show that low-earth-orbiting satellites can be used to store and forward packet-radio messages. In January 1985, messages were sent and received by stations in Hawaii, California and England using OSCAR 11. This was a joint operation by Rick Dittmer, WH6AMX, Larry Kayser, WA3ZIA, and Hugh Pett, VE3FLL, in Hawaii, Harold Price, NK6K, in California and Martin Sweeting, G3YJO, in England. These experiments led to a number of packet-radio space operations that are currently in the works or on the air (UoSAT-OSCAR 11 and Fuji-OSCAR 12 are currently in orbit around the earth, while other spacecraft are still in the works. Descriptions of these projects follow).

The scope of this book is limited to packet-radio operations, therefore, the following descriptions only include the packet-radio aspects of each project. More information on assembling and operating an Amateur Radio satellite ground station can be found in the ARRL book, *The Satellite Experimenter's Handbook*, by Martin R. Davidoff, K2UBC.

UoSAT-OSCAR 11

Since the successful store-and-forward experiment using UoSAT-OSCAR 11 (UO-11) was conducted in 1985, new software has been developed for the DCE allowing it to serve as a reliable store-and-forward message system. The software is called MSG2 and it can store 128 messages with a maximum size of 16,000 characters per message and a total message capacity of 96,000 characters. MSG2 was developed by NK6K and Jeff Ward, K8KA.

Because UoSAT-OSCAR-11 (UO-11) has only a single 1200-bit/s uplink and downlink channel that must be shared by many on-board experiments, direct access to the DCE is limited. To allow all packet-radio stations to take advantage of the DCE store-and-forward system, UoSAT and AMSAT have established a network of gateway or teleport stations. These stations are special PBBS systems that accept mail just like other PBBS sta-

Figure 12.2—Satellites bring Amateur Radio into the space age. Here, UoSAT-OSCAR-11 is being assembled. This satellite carries a packet-radio store-and-forward system.

Figure 12.3—The UoSAT ground station at the University of Surrey.

tions, but the gateway stations also have extra communications hardware and software that enables them to use the DCE. These gateway stations use the DCE to forward messages over long distances, just like some PBBS stations use the HF bands for long hauls. If you cannot connect directly to one of the DCE gateway stations, you can forward your messages to the nearest gateway using the standard PBBS mail-forwarding system.

DCE gateways are now active in Antarctica, Australia, England, New Zealand, South Africa, the Soviet Union and the United States, and the network is growing. If you want to send long-distance packet-radio messages to one of the countries served by the DCE, you should first contact the SYSOP of the gateway nearest you. The SYSOP will tell you how to address your messages and what kind of service you can expect. Remember to check the international traffic regulations that might apply to your messages.

Fuji-OSCAR 12

The Fuji-OSCAR 12 (FO-12) satellite, known before launch as JAS-1, was developed by Japan AMSAT (JAMSAT) and was successfully launched on August 12, 1986. Aboard the satellite is a Mode-JD packet-radio store-and-forward transponder (Mode J indicates the uplink and downlink frequencies in typical amateur-satellite fashion and D is the abbreviation for digital). This transponder functions as a multi-user PBBS. Four 1200-bit/s PBBS uplink channels operate on 145.85, 145.87, 145.89 and 145.91 MHz using Manchester-coded FM. One downlink channel on 435.91 MHz oper-

Satellite Transponders

Designation	Uplink*	Downlink*
Mode A	146 MHz	29 MHz
Mode B	435 MHz	146 MHz
Mode J	146 MHz	435 MHz
Mode L	1269 MHz	436 MHz
Mode S	435 MHz	2304 MHz

*All frequencies are approximate. (Source: *The Satellite Experimenter's Handbook* by Martin R. Davidoff, K2UBC, ARRL, Newington, CT, 1984, p 3-4)

ates at 1200 bit/s using nonreturn-to-zero-inverted (NRZI) phase-shift keying (PSK). Four uplink channels are provided because many ground stations may attempt to access the satellite at once. Only the satellite transmits on the downlink frequency, so one channel is sufficient. The mode JD transponder has 1 Mbyte of memory.

The PBBS is completely compatible with the AX.25 Version 2.0 protocol. Any AX.25 TNC may be used to format packets for transmission to the satellite and to extract information from received packets. An external modem is required to provide the Manchester-coded FM uplink signal and to demodulate the PSK downlink signal. There are several sources for FO-12 modems: an article by Fujio Yamashita, JS1UKR, on building a PSK demodulator for FO-12 use appeared in the August 1986 issue of *QEX*, pages 3-7; a blank PC board for an FO-12 Mode JD modem, designed by James Miller, G3RUH, is available from AMSAT-UK, London E12 5EQ, England; and an FO-12 Mode JD modem kit of electronic components and printed-circuit boards is available from Tucson Amateur Packet Radio Corporation (TAPR), PO Box 12925, Tucson, AZ 85732.

JAS-1B, a follow-up mission to Fuji-OSCAR 12, is scheduled for launch in early 1990. Plans for JAS-1B include an improved design for its power system, which, until now, has been the one major fault with the operation of Fuji-OSCAR 12.

Mode JD Operating Procedures

To use FO-12 Mode JD, your packet-radio station must be properly equipped. A Mode-JD modem must be connected to your TNC and to a 2-meter FM transmitter and a 70-cm SSB receiver.

Once your station is properly equipped, you must set the TNC parameters to values that are compatible with Mode JD. AX.25 Version 2 must be used. If you use a TNC 2, the AX25L2V2 parameter must be ON; if you use a TNC 1, you must install WA8DED code and invoke the V2 command, or modify the TNC 1 with the TAPR TNC-2 upgrade kit. The frame-acknowledgment timer must be set to 6 seconds or longer (with a WA8DED TNC 1, invoke the F6 command; with TNC-2 firmware, set Frack to 6).

FO-12 will not accept packets longer than 199 bytes, so you must set your TNC-2 Paclen parameter to 199 or less (a Paclen of 128 or 64 is recommended). You should also set your TNC-2 Maxframe or WA8DED O parameter low to keep the number of unacknowledged packets at a minimum (a Maxframe of 2 or 3 is recommended). FO-12 itself sends 128-byte packets and allows only one outstanding packet at a time. FO-12 also rejects digipeated packets; this means that you must send packets directly to the satellite.

FO-12 carries an analog (Mode JA) transponder in addition to its PBBS (Mode JD) transponder. These two systems must share the limited solar power available to the small satellite, so only one can be turned on at a time. You can find out if the satellite is in Mode JD by listening to the packet-radio downlink frequency (435.91 MHz). If Mode JD is turned on and no stations are connected to the PBBS, FO-12 will transmit packets once per minute. If stations are using the PBBS, you will hear continuous packets.

The call sign of the FO-12 Mode-JD PBBS is 8J1JAS. Accessing the Mode-JD PBBS is like accessing any other packet-radio station; you invoke the "Connect" command at the TNC command prompt by typing:

cmd: Connect 8J1JAS <CR>

When the satellite receives your packet on one of its 2-meter uplink frequencies, FO-12 transmits packets on 435.91 MHz. Once your station is connected to FO-12, the satellite sends a command prompt (JAS>). The sidebar "Fuji-OSCAR 12 Mode JD Command Set" describes all of the commands that can be used in Mode JD. These commands are similar to the commands used to control earthbound PBBSs, with some exceptions. For example, there is no command to log off the system; you simply disconnect from FO-12 when you are finished using the PBBS. Also note that whenever a command uses a qualifier, a space must be inserted between the command and the qualifier. For example, to read the message numbered 735, at the Mode-JD command prompt you type:

JAS> R 735 <CR>

The software that runs the Mode-JD PBBS is under constant development, so if you are interested in using the system, stay aware (by means of the Amateur Radio press) of changes that may affect the operation of the system.

PACSAT

Since 1982, AMSAT has been planning a more advanced store-and-forward satellite, called PACSAT. The designers of PACSAT hope to take advantage of the lessons learned from FO-12 and UO-11 in order to create

Fuji-OSCAR 12 Mode-JD Command Set

The following commands are available in Mode JD of Fuji-OSCAR 12 (FO-12).

JAS>—Command prompt from FO-12.

F—Lists last 10 messages stored on FO-12. Repeating the F command lists the next 10 messages.

F*—Lists all messages

H—Provides description of commands

K*n*—Deletes message numbered *n*

Log Off—Use TNC "Disconnect" command to log off FO-12

R*n*—Read message numbered *n*.

W—Send message

W command notes:
1. After you send the W command, FO-12 sends the subject prompt (Subj).
2. The subject may contain a maximum of 32 characters and must be followed by <CR>.
3. After you enter the subject, FO-12 sends the text prompt (Text:).
4. End each line of the text with <CR>.
5. End the message with a line that only contains a period (.) followed by <CR> or only <CTRL-Z> followed by <CR>.

---

a satellite that can be accessed by simple ground stations using low power and fixed antennas. Because so many stations will want to access PACSAT directly, several million characters of memory will have to be carried and communications links will have to be faster than 1200 bits/s. PACSAT will be a state-of-the-art store-and-forward satellite, and its development by amateur satellite designers will be a further demonstration that Amateur Radio plays an important role in communications engineering.

The first PACSAT is scheduled to be launched in early 1990 along with three other miniature Amateur Radio satellites that have been dubbed "MicroSats" and two UoSATs. Three of the MicroSats will have packet-radio capabilities: PACSAT, which is sponsored by the ARRL, AMSAT-NA and TAPR; WEBERSAT, which is sponsored by AMSAT-NA and Weber State College; and LUSAT, which is sponsored by AMSAT-NA and AMSAT-LU. UoSAT-D, which is sponsored by AMSAT-UK, University of Surrey and Volunteers in Technical Assistance (VITA), also will have packet capability.

LUSAT, PACSAT and WEBERSAT MicroSats

Three of the six MicroSats that are scheduled for an early 1990 launch from the Guiana Space Center in French Guiana have similar packet-radio functions. LUSAT, PACSAT and WEBERSAT will provide digital

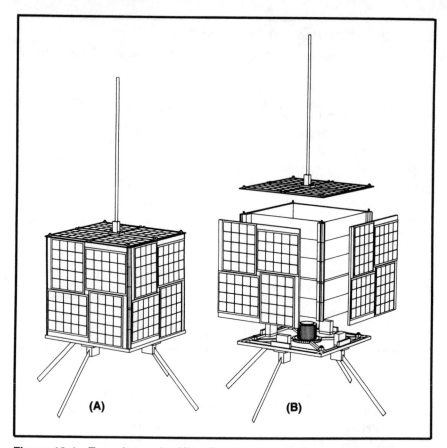

Figure 12.4—Two views of a MicroSat. Drawing A shows the satellite with its covers on; drawing B is an exploded view revealing the exterior solar panels and the five "trays" or internal modules that contain the satellite's circuitry and make it structurally sound. *(Drawings courtesy of Dick Jansson, WD4FAB)*

storing-and-forwarding operation in Mode JD with four 2-meter uplink channels and one 70-cm downlink channel. LUSAT's uplinks will be at 145.840, 145.860, 145.880 and 145.900 MHz and its downlink will be at 437.150 MHz. PACSAT's uplinks will be at 145.900, 145.920, 145.940 and 145.960 MHz and its downlink will be at 437.050 MHz. WEBERSAT's link frequencies are unknown at this time.

These three MicroSats will use the same modulation scheme as Fuji-OSCAR 12: Manchester-coded FM on the uplink channels and PSK on the downlink channels. Initially, these three MicroSats will operate at 1200 bit/s, but that data rate will be cranked up to 4800 bit/s after 4800-bit/s modems are designed and available to ground stations. A simple PBBS with the familiar WØRLI/WA7MBL user interface will be available on the satellites. Any standard TNC with the requisite external modems may be used to access these three MicroSats. The satellites will be in a sun-synchronous low earth orbit, which will permit users to access them at nearly the same time twice each day (tentatively at 10:30 AM and 10:30 PM local time).

UoSAT-D

UoSAT-D is also scheduled for the same early 1990 launch as LUSAT, PACSAT and WEBERSAT. It will carry an amateur packet-radio digital store-and-forward communications transponder that has been dubbed *Packet Communications Experiment* (*PCE*). PCE will be an orbiting packet-radio node with 4 Mbytes of message-storage space. It advances the work of the Digital Communications Experiment. The PCE system (hardware and software) has been developed under a contract from the VITA, which hopes to use store-and-forward communications in the future as a link with development workers in remote areas. The flight of the PCE on UoSAT-D and its use by radio amateurs will be funded by the University of Surrey and AMSAT-UK.

All packet-radio stations with appropriate equipment will have open access to the PCE via the AX.25 packet-radio protocol. The UoSAT-D PCE will use 9600-bits/s FSK uplinks and downlinks, which will be compatible with the K9NG-TAPR modem. The spacecraft will operate in Mode J, with the uplink in the 2-meter band and a downlink in the 70-cm band. RF communication links should be good enough to provide a consistent service to ground stations with modest non-steered antennas. A packet-radio experiment using a special polling protocol and an experimental high-power downlink mode for very small ground stations will also be included.

RUDAK

Although any OSCAR satellite with a linear transponder can be used to relay packets (this was done with AMSAT-OSCAR 10 in early tests), special satellite-borne digipeaters are now being developed. RUDAK (Regenerativer Umsetzer für Digitale Amateurfunk Kommunikation) is a digital repeater that was launched with the OSCAR 13 satellite on June 15, 1988 from the Guiana Space Center in French Guiana. Although the launch was successful, RUDAK failed. Plans call for the launch of RUDAK-2 in 1990 aboard the next Soviet Union Amateur Radio satellite organization's (ORBITA) Mode-B satellite, RS-14.

The AX.25 amateur packet-radio protocol will be incorporated into the RUDAK-2 software to permit AX.25-type digipeating. Also, a limited mailbox capability will be functional. Using the Manchester-coding technique and binary PSK (BPSK) modulation, the RUDAK-2 transponder will operate in Mode B with two separate receive channels for different baud rates: Channel

#1 for 1200 baud at 435.100 MHz and Channel #2 for 4800 baud at 435.150 MHz. The 2-meter downlink frequency will be 145.990 MHz. The nominal RF output of the 2-meter downlink transmitter will be 2 watts; however, it can be commanded by a ground station to an output of 12 watts.

Stations using RUDAK will need special equipment; both the uplink and the downlink use BPSK. The RUDAK team, part of AMSAT in the Federal Republic of Germany (AMSAT-DL), is developing a detailed ground station manual. The manual will help prospective users design and build RUDAK ground stations from readily available components.

SAREX

Amateur packet-radio experimentation is planned for future Shuttle Amateur Radio Experiments (SAREX) that will be conducted aboard the United States space shuttles. In October 1985, AMSAT and the ARRL began the groundwork for development of an experiment to be conducted by astronaut Ron Parise, WA4SIR, aboard space shuttle flight STS-61E, which was scheduled for launch on March 6, 1986. The experiment was planned to provide packet-radio robot operation aboard the shuttle. Preparation for the experiment was scuttled in the wake of the *Challenger* disaster in January 1986.

The experiment will be attempted again as an Amateur Radio station is tentatively scheduled to fly aboard the space shuttle flight STS-35 in 1990. Ron Parise, WA4SIR, a payload specialist for the ASTRO 1 payload to be carried on that flight, will operate the station in the orbiting shuttle and plans to communicate with Amateur Radio operators worldwide using voice and packet-radio communications. The orbit of the shuttle will permit amateurs located between approximately 46 degrees North and 46 degrees South latitude to communicate directly with the spacecraft. Also in 1990, Ken Cameron, KB5AWP, will pilot shuttle flight STS-37 and operate SAREX with voice, packet and video modes.

Natural Space Communications

In addition to the packet-radio satellite and shuttle experiments, amateur packet-radio operators have conducted experiments using natural space objects for packet-radio communication. Amateurs have bounced packets off the ionized trails of meteors entering the Earth's atmosphere and have bounced packets off our natural satellite, the moon.

Meteor Scatter

As space debris (meteors) enter the Earth's atmosphere, friction between the debris and the atmosphere causes the debris to burn up, leaving a very temporary ionized trail in their wake. This temporary ionized trail can reflect VHF and UHF signals back to Earth, extending the normal propagation limits of these signals.

Before packet radio, CW and voice modes were used for meteor-scatter communications. The ionized trails are short-lived, however, and very little data can be transferred using the relatively slow CW and voice modes. Several meteor trails must be used to pass enough data for a complete contact. The solution to this problem is to use a communications mode that transfers more data in a short time. Packet radio seems perfect for this application. On August 5, 1984, Ralph Wallio, WØRPK, in Iowa and Bob Carpenter, W3OTC, in Maryland used six meters to complete the first amateur packet-radio meteor-scatter contact (four nights earlier, Bob received 2 percent of Ralph's meteor-scattered packets). After that first contact, the two stations continued to make 50-MHz meteor scatter contacts on a routine basis. WØRPK used 250 watts into a five-element beam antenna and W3OTC used 150 watts into a six-element beam antenna. Packet lengths were limited to 30 to 40 characters and were transmitted at 1200 bauds using AFSK FM.

Later in August 1984, an organized effort was conducted using 1200-baud AFSK FM transmissions on 2 meters during the Perseids meteor shower. During this effort, several stations throughout the United States, including this author's station, successfully copied beacons and connect requests via meteor scatter. On August 12, during the peak of the shower, Rich Zwirko, K1HTV, in Maryland, and WØRPK completed the first 2-meter packet-radio meteor-scatter contact.

Meteors are constantly entering the Earth's atmosphere. As more packet-radio stations take advantage of this form of propagation, and as higher packet-radio data rates are achieved, meteor-scatter packet radio can become a reliable mode of communications.

Moonbounce (EME)

Earth-to-moon-to-Earth (*EME*) or *moonbounce* is a simple concept. If you send enough radio energy in the moon's direction, that old man moon will send some of it back to Mother Earth. This is high-transmitting-power and high-gain-antenna territory, a very specialized mode of VHF and UHF communications. As specialized as EME is, however, packet-radio EME experimentation has been conducted.

On June 29, 1986, W3IWI and Rich Strand, KL7RA, used an 85-foot antenna dish in Fairbanks, Alaska to transmit approximately 700-kW EIRP at the moon on 432 MHz. After a 2.2-second Earth-to-moon and back-to-Earth signal delay, they successfully copied their own packet-radio beacon. They also attempted to complete two-way contacts with stations in Mexico

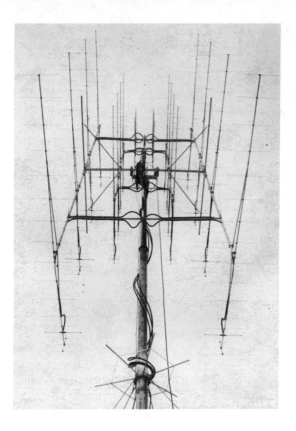

Figure 12.5—EME (moonbounce) work requires very high-gain antennas, like these at HB9CRQ.

and Vancouver, Canada, but signals were too weak and fluttery to establish packet-radio contacts. Further experimentation will have to be conducted to determine whether or not EME packet-radio communication is practical.

Conclusion

Packet radio is beginning its entry into space; the future of packet radio will be enhanced by successful use of space communications. Exciting times are in store for packet radio—it has the "right stuff."

CHAPTER THIRTEEN

Applications

I nitially, people were in awe when the first personal computers began showing up, but after the first impressions wore off, people asked, "But what can you do with it?" The same question can be asked with regard to amateur packet radio...it is an effective form of telecommunications, but what can you do with it? The answer to this question follows, as this chapter describes some actual examples of how packet radio is being used throughout the Amateur Radio world.

Amateur Television

A unique combination of packet radio and fast-scan television was assembled by the Big River Amateur Television System (BRATS) in the Davenport, Iowa area. The system consists of a standard 2-meter digipeater and a 420-MHz fast-scan amateur television repeater that are linked together to provide an ATV display of the 2-meter TNC output. This "ATV window" allows packet-radio users to peek at what the highly elevated digipeater is actually "seeing" in order to test their own packet-radio transmissions as they view their signals being received by the digipeater.

The digipeater, WBØBIZ-1, is located at the KWQC NBC TV Center and consists of a Kenwood TR-7950 50-watt transceiver, a Commodore C-64 computer, an AEA PK-64 TNC and a Hustler GP-6 omni-directional ground-plane antenna at 210 feet overlooking southeastern Iowa and the western Illinois Mississippi River Valley. Its coverage extends for approximately 100 miles; during enhanced band conditions, it is accessible from Indiana to Missouri.

Awards

The ARRL issued plaques to the first 10 stations to achieve packet-radio Worked All States (WAS) using direct (non-digipeater) contacts, and continues to issue packet-radio endorsements to the basic WAS award (packet-radio WAS is not a separately numbered award).

Call-Sign Directory

The WA4ONG PBBS/Buckmaster Publishing on-line CD-ROM call-sign directory is available for remote requests using a request format that is similar to the REQFIL (request file) format used by WA7MBL PBBSs. To use the directory, you send a message to SP REQQTH @ WA4ONG and at the "Enter subject..." prompt, enter the call sign whose QTH you seek, followed by @ and the call sign of your home PBBS.

For example, if you wish to obtain the mailing address of WØRLI and your home PBBS is W3IWI, you log on to W3IWI and at the command prompt type:

SP REQQTH @ WA4ONG <CR>

At the "Enter subject..." prompt, type:

WØRLI @ W3IWI <CR>

At the "Send message..." prompt, type:

<CRTL-Z> <CR>

Note that there is no text in the message.

Contests

Packet radio is now becoming a part of the Amateur Radio contest world. Two ARRL-sponsored contests now include packet radio, and more are sure to come as the popularity of the mode continues to grow.

Field Day

Since 1985, 100 bonus points can be earned by completing at least one packet-radio contact during the Field Day period. Digipeaters and network nodes can be used for the Field Day contact. Each year, more and more Field Day stations include a TNC in their equipment array.

RTTY Roundup

In 1989, the ARRL sponsored the first RTTY Roundup, a contest for the packet radio, Baudot, AMTOR and ASCII modes. The object of the contest is to work as many digital stations as you can worldwide. Your score equals the number of contest QSOs multiplied by the number of different US states, Canadian provinces and DXCC countries worked. Repeaters cannot be used to complete a contact.

The top scorer worldwide in 1989 was NG7P from Washington state, with 73,728 points (768 contacts and 96 multipliers). The contest was very popular and is expected to be an annual January event.

DOSgate

The DOSgate project was the brainchild of Rich Bono, NM1D. Instead of running a plain-vanilla PBBS, Rich decided to do something different, which became DOSgate. Essentially, DOSgate is software written by NM1D that allows remote packet-radio stations to use an MS-DOS computer. In other words, packet-radio stations, whose personal computer might consist of something as simple as a Commodore VIC-20, can access DOSgate and use the more powerful MS-DOS machine as if it were their own. Once you access DOSgate, you can play a game, track the orbits of the OSCAR satellites, look up a QTH with the on-line call-sign directory, write and compile programs, or send mail to another user (the system provides all of the usual PBBS functions in addition to providing a window into the MS-DOS world).

There are some technical limitations as to the kind of applications that can be run on the MS-DOS computer by the remote packet-radio operator, but DOSgate still has a lot to offer. For example, NM1D's personal DOSgate provides an Amateur Radio exam function, an OSCAR satellite tracking program, a great-circle-bearing program, a call-sign directory and a repeater database.

DX and Contest Spotting

Finding new stations and announcing their presence over the air is nothing new. Until recently, announcing the presence of stations that may represent a new country or contest multiplier was done almost exclusively on FM repeaters. Such systems have been successful in cranking up DXCC totals and contest scores, and many serious DX and contest clubs employ such systems. However, the FM-repeater spotting system does have some problems.

One problem is that spot announcements can be distracting while you are intently working another station. Typically, if a spot announcement blasts through in the middle of a contact, you quickly turn off the FM radio and attempt to work the station without the distraction. Maybe you will remember to turn the FM radio back on after the contact is completed, and maybe you won't. Another reason to turn off the FM radio (and forget to turn it back on) is that unless the repeater is dedicated to spotting operation, there is liable to be other non-spotting activity on the repeater to further distract you. In either case, while the FM radio is off, you know Murphy will strike and you'll miss an announcement for a new country or multiplier!

There are other problems, too. What you hear is not necessarily what was said. As a result, instead of chasing a new multiplier on 14.103, you end up chasing air on 14.301. Also, all spot announcements may not be important to you, yet you still have to listen to them all. If you are working a single band, announcements concerning activity on other bands are useless. Finally, by their nature, FM repeater coverage is limited and the club repeater may not encompass all of the territory where the club's members live.

Although spot announcements via FM repeaters are often helpful, things could be better, and new advances in packet radio have solved many of the problems inherent to spot announcements via FM repeaters.

Normally, one packet-radio station may communicate with only one other packet-radio station at a given time. Now, conference software is available for installation at key packet-radio stations or nodes to permit other packet-radio stations to communicate with more than one station at a time. When a station is connected to a conference node, it is able to communicate with all of the other stations connected with the same conference mode.

Software is also available to link conference nodes together so a station connected to one conference node can communicate with stations connected to other conference nodes (that are linked to the local conference node). The combination of conference software and node-to-node linking software can result in an enhanced DX- and contest-club spotting network that covers all of the members of the club.

Pavillion Software, whose *PacketCluster* software allows conference nodes to be linked together, also has *Packet Conference Board System* software which may be installed at a packet-radio station to provide a PBBS operation with multiple-user capability. Up to 26 stations may be connected to the system concurrently, and these stations may remain connected to the system and in constant communication with each other.

The Packet Conference Board System provides functions that are specifically designed for spotting announcements. To start the ball rolling, after you have connected to the system, you invoke the "CONFERENCE" command to enter the conference mode. Once you have entered the conference mode, the fun really begins. If you hear or work a station that may be of interest to other stations in the conference, you may use the DX command to make a spot announcement ("DX 14.152 1S1DX LISTENING UP 5," for example) and your announcement is displayed at the terminal or computer of every station connected to the conference. There is no chance of misinterpretation because the announcement is printed clearly for all to read and there is no chance of distraction because the announcement is printed silently for reading at the monitoring station's pleasure. And if the announcement scrolls off the display, it is not lost forever, because the system has a logging function.

The "SHOW DX" command displays the last five DX announcements. Appending a number to the "SHOW DX" command displays that number of previous DX announcements. If you are operating a single band and are not interested in activity on other bands, you can invoke the "SHOW DX" command followed by a specific band and the last five DX announcements on the specified band are displayed.

To run a packet-radio conference system requires an IBM PC/XT or compatible computer and a Kantronics KPC-2 TNC or compatible TNC (in addition to the conference software). A number of DX and contest clubs that are on the leading edge of contest technology are equipped with such systems. To stay competitive, other contest clubs can be expected to follow their lead.

Information Distribution

An efficient way of distributing information is by translating the information into a binary format. Binary files, however, can be difficult to transfer over the current amateur packet-radio network. To make binary file transfer easier, Greg Jones, WD5IVD, and Dhanapong Saengrussamee have written *R95*, a binary-to-data text-conversion program that runs on the IBM PC, its clones and the Apple Macintosh computer. R95 is shareware distributed by Texas Packet Software, PO Box 50106, Denton, TX 76206. (The following description originally appeared in the *Texas Packet Radio Society Quarterly Report*.)

R95 implements the Radix 95 binary-to-data text-conversion algorithm presented at the 7th ARRL Amateur Radio Computer Networking Conference in 1988. R95 implements R95 encoding and decoding, as well as the R95SPLIT format for splitting and combining data, as mentioned in the paper. The advantage of R95 over other conversion schemes is that it generates lower overhead. Radix 95 only generates 18% to 20% overhead on conversion, while using a 6- to 7-bit variable length encoding scheme.

R95 provides a way to convert data, such as compiled programs, graphic images or any other non-printable data, into printable ASCII characters and allow their transfer in the Converse Mode. A TNC can be configured in ways to allow the transfer of 8-bit data while in the Converse Mode (8bitconv ON, AWlen and Xflow OFF); alternatively, one can use the Transparent Mode. However, both methods are sometimes frustrating and time-consuming to the user. Having the ability to translate an 8-bit data file into printable ASCII characters offers great benefits.

8-bit to 7-bit conversion is fairly straightforward. The three steps involved are:

1. Translating a sequence of bits into printable ASCII code,
2. Transmitting the data, and
3. Converting the ASCII code back to its original form.

The problems facing the transmission of 8-bit data are how to transmit the eight (or more) binary digits, how to pass certain 7-bit sequences without having the sequence interpreted as a control character and how to avoid significant increase in file size (overhead).

Radix 95 offers a solution to these problems. It uses all printable ASCII characters (ASCII 32-126) to carry meaningful code, thus eliminating the transmission of eight or more bits and the transmission of control characters, while creating less overhead than most common conversion methods. By viewing the input file as a continuous string of bits, it is possible to break the file into segments of fixed or variable lengths, and as long as the segments are kept in the proper order during encoding and decoding, the transfer takes place correctly.

The R95 utility includes a number of bundled tools that makes the conversion task easier. The R95 tools provide R95 encoding, R95 decoding, R95 splitting and R95 combining. In addition, R95 allows the user to specify the input/output paths used and provides a DOS Gateway.

R95 creates two basic types of file formats: the R95 format file, which contains encoded data created by the R95 encoding function and read by the R95 decoding function, and the R95SPLIT format, which is used by the R95 splitting and R95 combining functions.

As an example, let's say John, W9DDD, wants to send a 32-kbyte binary TexNet image called DENTON.BIN to Greg, WD5IVD.

Depending on how far the file will travel, John will decide whether to send the file as is, or compress it with an archive program to reduce the file's size. Since he wants to make the transfer files as small as possible and create less impact on the network, he chooses to archive the file, creating DENTON.ARC. (ARC results in a 19-kbyte ARC file with approximately 59% compression.)

John now runs the R95 utility and selects encoding. He enters DENTON.ARC as the file to be encoded and R95 creates DENTON.R95 (indicating it is now in R95 format). (R95 encoding results in a 24-kbyte R95 format file with approximately 20% overhead.)

John must now determine if he needs to split the file or not. If Greg were a local connect or a mailbox upload area away, he could just send the whole file at once. If the file is to travel over Skipnet, he will keep the file split, sized less than 5 kbyte. Since John will be placing the files on the TexNet Dallas PMS, he will split the file into 7-kbyte segments. R95 now creates DENTON.001, .002, .003 and .004.

John then connects to TexNet and uploads the messages to the Dallas PMS. He sends SP WD5IVD because he does not want an unsuspecting person to read the messages by accident. He then enters DENTON.001 OF 004 as the message title to let Greg know what suffix to give each file as he captures it. John uploads DENTON.001. He repeats the preceding steps until he has sent all 4 messages.

Greg checks the Dallas PMS some time later and finds that he has four R95 files waiting for him. Greg then downloads each message and captures it to GREG.001, GREG.002... (Greg is able to use a different common file name).

Greg runs R95 and selects Combine. He enters GREG.001 as the file name with which to begin the R95 combining process. If there is an error in any of the split files, R95 will inform Greg that an error has occurred. If there is an error in one part, Greg will ask John to upload that one file again. Combine will reintegrate the file name contained in the R95SPLIT header to produce DENTON.R95 in this example.

Greg then selects Decode and enters DENTON.R95, which decodes DENTON.BIN (the name was contained in the R95 header). Hopefully this occurs without error.

The important thing to remember is that the packet-radio network is a fairly fragile environment, and when you want to transfer R95 files, you should attempt to be as low-impact as possible. That translates into using compression programs, as well as spacing the split files when you post and/or send them.

(Note that sending binary files that don't map to printable ASCII characters is okay above 50 MHz for contacts within the FCC's jurisdiction. One might run afoul of the FCC rules sending unreadable stuff on frequencies below 50 MHz, particularly if in QSO with a foreign station.)

Public Service Communications

Packet radio is the newcomer in Amateur Radio, but it has not taken long for packet's public-service applications to become obvious. In its short history, packet radio has provided communications in disasters, emergencies and for public events. Packet radio is also quickly becoming an integral cog in the National Traffic System machinery.

Emergency Communications

In 1984, the ARRL encouraged the use of packet radio by the Amateur Radio Emergency Service (ARES) when a 20-page chapter about packet-radio communications was published in the ARRL's *Emergency Coordinator's Manual* (Mike Riley, KX1B, editor). This book was distributed to Emergency Coordinators across the United States and Canada. The ARRL further encouraged the use of packet radio in emergency and disaster field operations by making a 100-point bonus available for Field Day stations that used packet radio during that annual event.

Since then, packet radio has been used to transfer traffic during the forest fires and floods that plague California. Packet radio was used to pass traffic during the 1985 Mexico City earthquake and during the January 1987 train wreck in Baltimore. Since packet-radio stations can be made very portable, they are often set up at the site of a disaster to transfer messages back to packet-radio stations set up at state and private emergency agency headquarters. (Refer to the accompanying sidebar concerning the portable packet-radio stations that were used during the 1988-89 Armenian earthquake relief effort.)

Government and private agencies involved with disasters and emergencies have been so impressed with the efficiency of amateur packet radio as a communications tool that they have provided funds for the purchase of packet-radio equipment for their agency headquarters and field operations.

Amateurs already have plenty of experience using packet radio under fire. Some lessons have been learned and, as a result, some guidelines have been established. A set of such packet-radio guidelines for emergencies and public-service events was compiled by Patty Winter, N6BIS, in 1986. An expanded version of these guidelines follows.

Planning

A thorough checklist should be prepared, including a list of the necessary TNC parameter settings for both the message-entry stations and portable digipeater stations (their parameters do differ).

Whenever possible, find out in advance what paths you will need to get traffic out of your operating location and what digipeaters will be needed to support these paths. The list of linked PBBS stations maintained by WØRLI can be very helpful in determining how to best move the traffic. When selecting a path, use as few digipeater hops as possible to increase data-transfer efficiency. If portable digipeaters are available, they may be placed on mountaintops to fill any gaps in the paths. If possible, test your paths with long files beforehand (long files tend to fail more often than short ones).

For a planned public-service event, all stations should be up and running at least one hour before the event begins. A realistic dry run one to two weeks beforehand is very helpful in determining if there are any problems in the packet-radio communications game plan.

Hardware Considerations

The packet-radio station should have storage capability for data entry. "Hard" storage on disk is preferable to storing all your messages in the computer's volatile memory. In an emergency, power sources are often unreliable; if the data is not on disk, it will vaporize whenever the power goes off. If possible, power the packet-radio station from an emergency power source

Figure 13.1—This portable packet-radio station, consisting of a TAPR TNC 2, a Radio Shack TRS-80 Model 100 laptop computer and a Tempo S1 2-meter handheld transceiver, is a versatile public-service communications tool. It can be operated at the site of an emergency or disaster and can be powered by either ac or dc.

to avoid commercial-power-line brownouts and blackouts. (The portable packet-radio station shown in Figure 13.1 uses a computer with volatile memory that is powered by rechargeable NiCd batteries. As a result, data stored in this computer's memory is safe under most circumstances.)

If possible, two compatible computers should be used at the message-entry stations. One computer is used to enter and edit the messages and the other is connected to a TNC and radio for the actual packet-radio transmission. The computers should be compatible so that disks containing the information from the message-entry computer can be transferred to the transmitting computer and used immediately (without requiring translation between incompatible computers).

A local PBBS can be very useful, if one is available or can be set up during the operation. The PBBS can be used to store and forward messages that are addressed out of the local area, or to store messages for stations that are not available when you need them. The object is to pass the traffic, and if you can pass it to a PBBS for later auto-forwarding, so much the better.

One packet-radio station in the emergency network should be connected to a printer to provide a written transcript of all of the traffic handled by the network. If more than one copy of the transcript is needed, use multiform (carbon) paper in the printer.

The use of standardized connectors provides flexibility when emergency equipment replacement is necessary. For example, many TNC-2-compatible TNCs use the same type of connector for the radio (a 5-pin DIN-type connector), terminal (a 25-pin D-subminiature connector) and power supply (a miniature phone plug). This means that most TNC-2-compatible TNCs are interchangeable (check the wiring of the 5-pin DIN-type radio connection for incompatibility between certain TNCs).

Backup software and hardware (both computer and radio) should be available to counteract Murphy's Law. As anyone who has operated during Field Day or an emergency can tell you, anything that can go wrong will!

Operating Procedures

There should be one packet-radio net-control station (NCS) if more than two packet-radio stations are involved in the effort. If voice communications are used, a voice NCS should be appointed also. If there are two net-control stations (one for packet radio and one for voice), they should be located near each other so that they will be able to coordinate the nets more effectively and avoid duplication of efforts.

The packet-radio NCS should establish the format, content and size of the packet-radio messages. If every station cannot hear every other station, the NCS should quickly establish and announce a routing list showing what digipeater paths each station should use to communicate with the other stations.

The packet-radio and voice NCSs should decide which mode will handle which traffic. Packet radio is best for large amounts of information, information requiring hard copy, complicated information with difficult spelling (names) or lots of numbers (addresses and telephone numbers) and information requiring some privacy or security. Voice communication is best for information that is tactical, uncomplicated and concise.

The message-entry station should be set up for speed. Preprinted message forms should be used to eliminate the entry of repetitive information. All stations that are originating messages should use the same standard message format for quick collation of the information by the receiving stations.

The size of transmitted files should be short enough (approximately 50 lines) to assure that the complete file will be sent before a disconnection occurs if the maximum number of retries is reached. The packets should be long enough, however, that each line of text does not force a new packet. If you send short (60- or 80-character) packets, you are wasting a lot of overhead (each packet's header and trailer).

Software for an Emergency

ARES/Data is a multiple-connect, multiport generalized database accessible via packet radio that also includes a full-featured conference bridge. The program is intended for use in a wide variety of emergency and public-service Amateur Radio situations.

The key idea behind ARES/Data is that it allows you to track any type of needed information that can be organized as four 20-character fields plus an 80-character message for each record. It may be used to track victims of a multiple-casualty incident, track ham manpower availability and assignments, record evacuees and shelter enrollment, track floats in a parade, provide a short-message database entry and record house-by-house damage assessments.

ARES/Data was written by William Moerner, WN6I, and Dave Palmer, N6KL, with the ideas and support of a committee of hams from the Santa Clara County ARES. It is a copyrighted, public-domain program, available without charge to anyone interested. It runs on an IBM PC or clone using DOS 3.2 with 400 kbytes of memory. To use the program via packet radio, the SYSOP needs at least a DRSI PC*PA packet-radio adapter or a serial port and a TNC with the Ron Raikes, WA8DED, firmware installed.

Traffic Handling

As far back as 1984, packet radio was being used to handle National Traffic System (NTS) traffic. At that time, NTS traffic was stored on various PBBSs in standard ARRL radiogram format along with other PBBS messages. Since the packet-radio network was not as extensive then as it is today, an operator could never be sure that the traffic would be forwarded and delivered to its intended destination. Back then, it was often recommended that a prayer be recited after an NTS message was stored on a PBBS.

Portable Packet-Radio Stations Sent to Assist USSR Earthquake Relief Effort

On December 9, 1988, the ARRL telexed the president of the Radio Sports Federation of the USSR (RSF), Yuri Zubarev, to express the League's condolences concerning the Armenian earthquake and to offer assistance. A direct reply was not immediately received, which was hardly surprising given the situation. On the following Monday, however, the ARRL learned from *QST* columnist Vern Riportella, WA2LQQ, that he had an electronic mail link through San Francisco-Moscow Teleport, Inc with Leonid Labutin, UA3CR, in Moscow, who was responsible for radio communications in support of the relief effort, under the aegis of the Young Communist League. Through Rip, Leo requested assistance in the form of portable packet-radio stations and technical experts who could help the Soviets develop their fledgling packet-radio network on a crash basis in response to the emergency.

Rip immediately set to work, maintaining close coordination with ARRL Headquarters at every step of the way. Donations of equipment were lined up from the Tandy Corporation (six Model 102 laptop computers), Yaesu USA (six FT-23R 2-meter transceivers) and AEA (six PK-88 TNCs, a PK-232 data controller and six HotRod antennas). The donations were shipped to ARRL Headquarters and the ARRL lab crew spent much of December 15-16 making up cables to integrate the donated equipment into six complete, separate packet-radio stations. A supply of batteries and some other accessories were added to the shipment.

On December 17, ARRL Executive Vice President Dave Sumner, K1ZZ, met Rip halfway between Newington, Connecticut and Kennedy Airport, New York to turn the gear over to him. It appeared that the gear might be carried to Moscow as checked baggage that afternoon by some Soviet scientists. That opportunity did not occur, however, until December 23, when it was put aboard Pan Am Flight 74.

The equipment arrived in Moscow the morning of Christmas Eve and was deployed immediately. Leo conveyed his heartfelt thanks to the ARRL and everyone involved.

In response to the request for packet-radio technical experts, the ARRL was able to identify two well-qualified volunteers who were willing to donate their time to make the trek and were young and healthy enough to endure whatever hardship might await them. However, as time went on (and as often happens in disaster situations), the apparent need for their assistance diminished and the League suspended its efforts to obtain visas for them. Through Leo, the ARRL assured the RSF that it would be pleased to send such a team to the USSR to assist with packet-radio development at their invitation in the future.

Telephone, telex and electronic mail communications had been available to both Moscow and Armenia throughout this period, and the League used these communications channels extensively. Rip's electronic mail connection was used for volumes of outbound traffic to concerned relatives in the US, and its delivery was handled by Armenian-American organizations (the NTS was available if required).

Today, if you store a properly addressed message on a PBBS, there is an excellent chance that it will reach its intended destination in a very short time. There are a number of reasons for this improvement in message handling. The packet-radio network is much more organized today, and it reaches into every populated nook and cranny of the United States and Canada. The major PBBS programs in use (WØRLI and WA7MBL) support NTS message handling. The NTS is also becoming more packet-radio oriented, while packet radio is becoming more NTS oriented.

Handling Traffic via a PBBS

The WØRLI/WA7MBL PBBSs have commands that support NTS message handling (refer to Chapter 10—Time-Shifting Communications), and an evolving packet-radio-based, NTS-traffic, auto-forwarding network is simplifying the forwarding of NTS traffic to its intended destination.

Sending NTS traffic via packet radio is easy. First, log on to your local PBBS and use the "ST" command in the following manner.

To send NTS traffic to another packet-radio station, you type:

ST WA1LOU @ W1AW <CR>

where WA1LOU is the call sign of the traffic's addressee and W1AW is the call sign of the addressee's home PBBS.

To send NTS traffic to another Amateur Radio station that is not active in packet radio, you type:

ST WA1TBP @ NTSCT <CR>

where WA1TBP is the call sign of the traffic's addressee and "NTSCT" is the result of combining the initials "NTS" with the two- or three-letter initials that represent the addressee's ARRL section, in this case "CT", for Connecticut.

To send NTS traffic to someone who is not an Amateur Radio operator, you type:

ST 06706 @ NTSCT <CR>

where 06706 is the ZIP code of the addressee's address and "NTSCT" is the result of combining the initials "NTS" with the two- or three-letter initials that represent the addressee's ARRL section, in this case "CT", for Connecticut.

After you invoke the "ST" command, the PBBS will prompt you for a subject. To facilitate the delivery of the traffic, enter the addressee's city, the two-letter abbreviation for the addressee's state or province, the addressee's telephone area code and the first three digits of the addressee's telephone number.

After you enter the title, the PBBS will prompt you for the text of the message. The text should be sent in standard ARRL radiogram format with a message number, precedence, handling instructions (optional), call sign of the station of origin, check, place of origin, time of filing (optional) and date, followed by the name, address and telephone number of the intended recipient of the message. The actual text of the message comes next, followed by the signature. (If precedence or check is Greek to you, please refer to any ARRL publication that deals with traffic handling. *The ARRL Operating Manual* is a good source for basic traffic-handling information.) When you are finished entering the message, send a <CTRL-Z> and <CR> to the PBBS and it will store the message for forwarding through the packet-radio network to its intended destination.

After a message is forwarded to a PBBS, how does it get transferred from the PBBS to its ultimate destination? Another operator at the destination end must take the traffic off the PBBS and deliver it, or relay it to a section or local NTS net for delivery.

If you wish to handle traffic, log on to your local PBBS and invoke the "LT" command. The PBBS will respond with a directory of all of the NTS traffic stored on the PBBS. Scan the titles of the listed messages to find any that you can handle (by relaying the message to an NTS local or section net or by delivering the message to its intended recipient via a telephone call). If you can handle a message, use the "R" command (R followed by the message's number) to receive a copy of the message. It's a good idea to use some kind of hard-copy device at this point; either send the message directly to a printer as the PBBS sends it to you, or open a disk-file buffer to save the message for printing at a later time. After you obtain a copy of the message, use the "K" command ("K" followed by the received message's number) to remove the message from the PBBS. The message is now in your hands for telephone delivery or further NTS relay.

QSL Manager Server

For those who are also interested in DXing, a "server" is on-line at the W1NY PBBS that keeps a database of DX stations, their QSL managers and information requests. You can submit a request to the server for a particular station's QSL manager. If the server has the information, you will get the information back immediately. If the server does not have the information you request, it will store your request and send you a message when that information becomes available. You can also use the server to find out what QSL routes are being requested and update the database.

Weather Service

Bill Hutchins, KB6CYS, probably had the first amateur packet-radio weather station on the air. When you connect to his Cypress, California station, it automatically sends you the current weather forecast, information concerning storm systems, the present temperature, dew point, barometric pressure, rate-of-change of pressure, wind direction and speed, maximum wind gust for the day, temperature minimum and maximum for the day and precipitation totals for the day, month and year.

Bill wrote a BASIC program for his Apple IIe computer that gathered data from a Heath ID-4001 weather computer and a Texas Electronics "rain bucket" via a home-brew interface card. His station relays weather forecasts from the National Weather Service (NWS), but Bill has been known to change the NWS forecast whenever he feels that conditions warrant such a change.

Hurricane Hunter Project Flies

HHAPP, the Hurricane Hunter Aircraft Packet Project, is in full swing. On August 6 and 7, 1987, NOAA's P3 Orion, carrying the KI4T-1 digipeater, flew into a weather formation near the Island of Hispanola, and Miami packet-radio stations digipeated through the aircraft as it left from and returned to Miami.

When the aircraft is flying at 15,000 to 18,000 feet, its radio horizon is approximately 200 miles, allowing a total communications path through the aircraft digipeater of 400 miles. This distance closely corresponds with the effective area of a hurricane. Since the aircraft digipeater beacons every 4 minutes, any station within receiving range of the beacon should send weather data from its location either through the aircraft to a PBBS or by some other route to the PBBS.

The packet-radio weather data sent during an approaching hurricane should be addressed to W4EHW @ W4NVU. W4EHW is the station at the National Hurricane Center in Coral Gables, Florida. US stations along the Gulf are asked to send weather information through W5XO PBBS in Gause, Texas, or WA5DVV PBBS in Gulfport, Mississippi. Eastern Seaboard stations may relay information down the coast in the most expedient manner. Efforts are being made to enlist participation from Caribbean countries, including Cuba, which sits strategically on the Florida Straits in the path of most hurricanes entering the Gulf of Mexico.

Timeliness of the weather data is of paramount importance. The success of the project will be in direct proportion to participation from amateur packet-radio stations with weather-measuring instruments.

White Pages

You may have noticed messages on your local PBBS addressed to or from WP, which stands for White Pages. WP is a directory of packet-radio users and the PBBSs they call "home," but with an important difference. Usually, such directories are large files that are copied onto every PBBS and are then downloaded by users when they want to look up someone. They have to be updated and redistributed on a regular basis; and this becomes increasingly difficult as more users are added. WP is different in that it is a directory that exists only in one place: the WD6CMU PBBS.

Of course, this would be of little help if there were no way for people to access the information in the directory without connecting to WD6CMU, so WP can also be accessed by sending mail to it from your local PBBS. A program at the WD6CMU PBBS will automatically pick up, read and answer mail addressed to WP @ WD6CMU. This program appears like a live operator answering mail, except that it does so four-times-an-hour, 24-hours-a-day.

The messages addressed to WD6CMU must be in a specific format, otherwise, the PBBS will ignore them. A request for information from WP is called a "query." A request to add information to WP is called an "update." You can have as many updates or queries in a single message to WP as you want, but each one must be on a separate line of the message. The format of a query line is this:

WA1LOU QTH?

where WA1LOU is the call sign of the station whose home PBBS you wish to find.

The format of an update line is:

WA1LOU QTH W1AW

where WA1LOU is the station's call sign and W1AW is the PBBS at which WA1LOU receives mail.

WP is designed as an aid in addressing your mail. SYSOPs can use it to find the proper address for a "dead letter" and newcomers can use it to locate a familiar call sign. The goal is to keep the information centralized so it is always up to date, and to keep the amount of information that has to be sent over the PBBS network small.

Conclusion

The applications of packet radio are so varied that nearly every ham radio operator can satisfy his or her niche. If not, hams, more than anyone else, have the ability to construct their own packet-radio niches. Witness the scratch-built niches described in this chapter.

As the first decade of amateur packet radio closes and a new decade begins, you can still experience the growth and evolution of telecommunications without a telephone. Today, packet-radio networks are being developed, improved and, ultimately, perfected. New packet-radio applications are being born and nurtured. Packet-radio software is being written, rewritten and rewritten again. Packet-radio hardware is being designed, massaged and tested. Packet radio is alive!

And though this is the end of the book, it can be the beginning of your packet-radio experience!

APPENDIX A

TNC-1 and TNC-2 Command Sets

The following tables list the command sets of the TAPR TNC 1 (Table 1) and TNC 2 (Table 2). The tables include the name of each command, the default setting of the command, the command's optional parameters and a description of the command's function. If default and selectable parameters are not included, then the command is an *immediate* command, otherwise, it is a *configuration* command. Each table is subdivided into the various command categories: character, identification, link, monitor, reinitialization, serial port and timing commands.

Table 1
TNC-1 Command Set

Character Commands

Command	Default	Parameters	Description
BKondel x	ON	ON/Off	selects how deletions are displayed by DTE
CANline n	$18 <CTRL-X>	0 - $7F	selects cancel line input control character
CANPac n	$19 <CTRL-Y>	0 - $7F	selects cancel packet input control character
COMmand n	$03 <CTRL-C>	0 - $7F	selects Command Mode entry control character
DEbug n	$05 <CTRL-E>	0 - $7F	selects debug program entry character
DELete x	ON	ON/Off	selects delete input editing control character ($7F or $08)
PASs n	$16 <CTRL-V>	0 - $7F	selects "pass" input editing command control character
REDispla n	$12 <CTRL-R>	0 - $7F	selects redisplay-line input editing control character
SEndpac n	$0D <CR>	0 - $7F	selects Converse Mode control character that forces packet transmissions
STart n	$11 <CTRL-Q>	0 - $7F	selects restart control character for TNC output to terminal
STOp n	$13 <CTRL-S>	0 - $7F	selects stop control character for TNC output to terminal
XOff n	$13 <CTRL-S>	0 - $7F	selects the stop control character for terminal output to TNC
XON n	$11 <CTRL-Q>	0 - $7F	selects restart control character for terminal output to TNC

Identification Commands

Command	Default	Parameters	Description
Beacon x	Every 0	Every/After 0 - 255 (x 10 sec)	enables/disables beacon transmissions
BText n	none	0 - 128 ASCII characters	enters contents of beacon
CWid x	ON	ON/Off	enables/disables automatic station identification
Id	—	—	transmits station identification in CW
IDText x	none	0 - 128 ASCII characters	enters contents of station identification
MYcall x	none	call sign [and optionally SSID (0-15)]	enters call sign (and optionally SSID)

Command	Default	Parameters	Description
MYVadr n	31	0 - 31	selects address byte for VADCG protocol operation
Unproto x	CQ	call sign (Via call sign1,... call sign8)	selects unprotocol mode packet destination (optionally, via call sign1,... call sign8)

Link Commands

Command	Default	Parameters	Description
AX25 x	ON	ON/Off	on: selects AX.25; off: selects VADCG protocol
CAlibra	—	—	transfers to modem Calibration Mode
CONMode x	COnvers	COnvers/TRans	selects automatic entry into Converse or Transparent Mode after connection
Connect x	—	call sign (Via call sign1,... call sign8)	initiates connection to call sign (optionally, via call sign1,... call sign8)
CONOk x	ON	ON/Off	accepts/rejects connect requests
CONVers	—	—	transfers from Command Mode to Converse Mode
CR x	ON	ON/Off	enables/disables adding send-packet character to Converse Mode packets
DIGipeat x	ON	ON/Off	enables/disables AX.25 repeater function
Disconne	—	—	initiates disconnection from connected station
FULldup x	Off	ON/Off	enables/disables full duplex mode
Hbaud n	1200	50 - 4800 (bauds)	selects radio port data rate
LFadd x	Off	ON/Off	enables/disables adding <LF> after each <CR> in outgoing packets
MAXframe n	4	1 - 7 (packets)	selects maximum number of outstanding unacknowledged packets
Paclen n	128	1 - 256 (bytes)	selects number of bytes per packet that automatically force packet transmissions
PRogram	—	—	transfers to EPROM programmer routine

Command	Default	Parameters	Description
RETry n	10	0 - 15 (packets)	selects maximum number of times unacknowledged frames are retransmitted
TRACe n	$1000	a 16-bit value	sets protocol debugging functions
Trans	—	—	transfers from Command Mode to Transparent Mode
Vdigipea x	Off	ON/Off	enables/disables digital repeating of packets with appropriate VADCG address byte
VRpt x	Off	ON/Off	enables/disables translation of VADCG address byte for digital repeating
XMitok x	ON	ON/Off	enables/disables transmitting

Monitor Commands

Command	Default	Parameters	Description
DISPlay x	—	(optionally C, I, L, M, T, Tl)	displays status of TNC parameters
MAll x	Off	ON/Off	selects monitoring connected and unconnected or only unconnected packets
MCon x	Off	ON/Off	enables/disables monitoring while the TNC is connected
MFrom x	none	call sign1,... call sign10	selects station(s) whose originated packets will be monitored via Monitor command
Monitor x	ON	ON/Off	enables/disables packet monitoring
MTo x	none	call sign1,... call sign10	selects station(s) whose addressed packets will be monitored via Monitor command

Perm Command

Command	Default	Parameters	Description
PErm	—	—	permanently saves all parameter value changes in TNC permanent memory

Reinitialization Command

Command	Default	Parameters	Description
Reset	—	—	performs soft reset of TNC while retaining any changed parameter values

Serial Port Commands

Command	Default	Parameters	Description
Abaud n	—	50 - 19200 (bauds)	selects serial port data rate
ABIt n	1	1 - 2 (bits)	selects number of stops bits per word
AUtolf x	ON	ON/Off	enables/disables automatic <LF> sending after each <CR>
AWlen n	7	7 - 8 (bits)	selects number of data bits per word
Echo x	ON	ON/Off	enables/disables terminal character echo
ESCape x	Off	ON/Off	selects $ or <ESC> as escape character sent to terminal from TNC
Flow x	ON	ON/Off	enables/disables type-in flow control
Lcok x	ON	ON/Off	disables/enables translation of lowercase characters to uppercase
NUcr x	Off	ON/Off	enables/disables sending <NULL> characters to terminal after each <CR>
NULf x	ON	ON/Off	enables/disables sending <NULL> characters to terminal after each <LF>
NULLs n	0	0 - 30 (even no. of <NULL> characters)	selects even number of <NULL> characters to be sent via NUCR and NULF commands
PARity n	3	0,1,2,3,4 (= odd,even,mark, space,none)	selects terminal parity
Screenl n	80	0 - 255 (columns)	selects number of columns per line to be displayed by terminal
TXFlow x	Off	ON/Off	enables/disables TNC software flow control in Transparent Mode

Command	Default	Parameters	Description
Xflow x	ON	ON/Off	selects XON/XOFF or hardware (RTS) flow control

Timing Commands

Command	Default	Parameters	Description
AXDelay n	0	0 - 15 (x 120 ms)	selects delay between keying voice repeater and sending data
AXHang n	0	0 - 15 (x 120 ms)	selects voice repeater hang time
CMdtime n	1	0 - 15 (sec)	selects Transparent Mode timeout
CPactime x	Off	ON/Off	enables/disables periodic automatic packet transmission in Converse Mode
DWait n	2	0 - 15 (x 40 ms)	selects transmission delay (to avoid collisions)
FRack n	4	1 -16 (sec)	selects frame acknowledgment timeout
PACTime x	After 4	Every/After 0 - 15 (x 0.25 sec)	selects packet timeout
TXdelay n	4	0 - 16 (x 40 ms)	selects delay between keying transmitter and sending data

Table 2
TNC 2 Command Set

Character Commands

Command	Default	Parameters	Description
BKondel x	ON	ON/OFf	selects how deletions are displayed by terminal
CANline n	$18 <CTRL-X>	0 - $7F	selects cancel line input control character
CANPac n	$19 <CTRL-Y>	0 - $7F	selects cancel packet input control character
COMmand n	$03 <CTRL-C>	0 - $7F	selects Command Mode entry control character
DELete x	OFf	ON/OFf	selects delete input editing control character ($7F or $08)
PASs n	$16 <CTRL-V>	0 - $7F	selects "pass" input editing command control character
REDispla n	$12 <CTRL-R>	0 - $7F	selects redisplay-line input editing control character
SEndpac n	$0D <CR>	0 - $7F	selects Converse Mode control character that forces packet transmissions

STArt n	$11 <CTRL-Q>	0 - $7F	selects restart control character for TNC output to terminal
STOp n	$13 <CTRL-S>	0 - $7F	selects stop control character for TNC output to terminal
STReamsw n	$7C	0 - $FF	selects character that indicates new stream
XOff n	$13 <CTRL-S>	0 - $7F	selects stop control character for terminal output to TNC
XON n	$11 <CTRL-Q>	0 - $7F	selects restart control character for terminal output to TNC

Identification Commands

Command	Default	Parameters	Description
Beacon x	Every 0	Every/After 0 - 250 (x 10 sec)	enables/disables beacon transmissions
BText n	none	0 - 128 ASCII characters	enters contents of beacon
CMSg x	OFf	ON/OFf	enables/disables CTEXT message transmission after connection
CText n	none	0 -120 ASCII characters	enters contents of packet sent after a connection
Hld x	OFf	ON/OFf	enables/disables HDLC identification by digital repeater
Id	—	—	transmits special identification packet
MYAlias x	none	call sign [and optionally SSID (0-15)]	enters alternate call sign (and optionally SSID)
MYcall x	NOCALL-0	call sign [and optionally SSID (0-15)]	enters call sign (and optionally SSID)
Unproto x	CQ	call sign (Via call sign1,... call sign8)	selects unprotocol mode packet destination (optionally, via call sign1,... call sign8)

Link Commands

Command	Default	Parameters	Description
Ax25l2v2 x	ON	ON/OFf	selects Version 2.0 or 1.0 of AX.25 Level 2

Command	Default	Values/Range	Description
CALibra	—	—	transfers to modem Calibration Mode
CMSGDisc x	OFf	ON/OFf	enables/disables automatic disconnection after connection
CONMode x	Convers	Convers/Trans	selects automatic entry into Converse or Transparent Mode after connection
Connect x	—	call sign (Via call sign1,... call sign8)	initiates connection to call sign (optionally, via call sign1.... call sign8)
CONOk x	ON	ON/OFf	accepts/rejects connect requests
CONPerm x	OFf	ON/OFf	enables/disables maintenance of current connection
CONVers	—	—	transfers from Command Mode to Converse Mode
CR x	ON	ON/OFf	enables/disables adding send-packet character to Converse Mode packets
DIGipeat x	ON	ON/OFf	enables/disables TNC's repeater function
Disconne	—	—	initiates disconnection from connected station
FUlldup x	OFf	ON/OFf	enables/disables full duplex mode
LFadd x	OFf	ON/OFf	enables/disables adding <LF> after each <CR> in outgoing packets
MAXframe n	4	1 - 7 (packets)	selects maximum number of outstanding unacknowledged packets
NEwmode x	OFf	ON/OFf	enables/disables automatic transfer to Command Mode after disconnection
NOmode x	ON	ON/OFf	enables/disables manual-only mode transfers
Paclen n	128	0 - 255 (bytes) (0 = 256)	selects number of bytes per packet that automatically force packet transmissions
PASSAll x	OFf	ON/OFf	enables/disables accepting packets with invalid CRCs
RECOnnect x	—	call sign (Via call sign1,... call sign8)	initiates reconnection with currently connected station via different path
REtry n	10	0 - 15 (packets)	selects maximum number of times unacknowledged frames are retransmitted

TRACe x	OFf	enables/disables Trace Mode
Trans	—	transfers from Command Mode to Transparent Mode
USers n	0 - 10 (connections)	selects number of active requested connections that may be established

Monitor Commands

Command	Default	Parameters	Description
XMitok x	ON	ON/OFf	enables/disables transmitting
ASyrxovr	—	—	displays number of times software fails to service asynchronous receiver in time
BBfailed	—	—	displays number of times checksum of battery-backed RAM was in error
BBSmsgs x	OFf	ON/OFf	controls how certain messages are displayed in command and converse modes
BUdlist x	OFf	ON/OFf	ignores frames from stations listed/not listed by LCALLS command
CBell x	OFf	ON/OFf	enables/disables <BELL> when connection is established
CONStamp x	OFf	ON/OFf	enables/disables connect status message time stamping
CStatus	—	—	displays stream identifier and link state of the streams
DAytime n	none	yymmddhhmm (date and time)	displays or sets TNC clock
DAYUsa x	ON	ON/OFf	selects mm/dd/yy or dd-mm-yy format for display of dates
DIGISent	—	—	displays number of frames digitally repeated by TNC
DISPlay x	—	(optionally A, C, H, I, L, M, T)	displays status of TNC parameters
HEaderln x	OFf	ON/OFf	selects printing packets and headers on same line or on separate lines

Command	Default	Description
HEALled x	OFf	enables/disables random flashing of CON and STA front panel indicators
HOvrerr	—	displays number of times data is lost because HDLC receiver is not serviced in time
HUndrerr	—	displays number of aborted frames due to untimely servicing of HDLC transmitter
LCAlls x	none	enters call signs monitored or not monitored via BUDLIST command
MAll x	ON	selects monitoring connected and unconnected or only unconnected packets
MCOM x	OFf	enables/disables monitoring connect and disconnect frames via MONITOR command
MCon x	ON	enables/disables monitoring while the TNC is connected
MFilter	n1...n4 none	0 - $7F	select 1 to 4 ASCII characters to be stripped from monitored packets
MHClear	—	clears list of stations heard by the TNC
MHeard	—	displays list of stations heard by TNC since last time command was invoked
Monitor x	ON	enables/disables packet monitoring
MRpt x	ON	enables/disables display of digital repeater call signs for monitored packets
MStamp x	OFf	enables/disables monitored frame time-stamping
RCVDFrmr	—	displays number of frame reject frames received from connected station
RCVDIfra	—	displays number of I frames received from connected station
RCVDRej	—	displays number of reject frames received from connected station

Command	Default	Parameters	Description
RCVDSabm	—		displays number of received SABM frames addressed to the TNC
RXCount	—		displays number of received frames with good CRC
RXErrors	—		displays number of discarded frames due to length or bad CRC
SENTFrmr	—		displays number of transmitted frame reject frames
SENTIfra	—		displays number of transmitted I frames
SENTRej	—		displays number of transmitted reject frames
STREAMCa x OFf		ON/OFf	enables/disables displaying connected station's call sign after stream identifier
STREAMDbl x OFf		ON/OFf	enables/disables displaying two streamswitch characters for each one received
TRies n	none	0 - 15 (retries)	displays or enters the number of retries of currently selected stream
TXCount	—		displays number of correctly transmitted frames
TXQovflw n	0	0 - 9999	displays number of discarded frames due to small outgoing frame queue
TXTmo	0	0 - 9999	displays number of times TNC recovers from HDLC transmitter time-outs

Reinitialization Commands

Command	Default	Parameters	Description
RESET	—	—	reinitializes TNC and resets TNC parameters to default values
RESTART	—	—	reinitializes TNC using the TNC parameter values stored in RAM

Serial Port Commands

Command	Default	Parameters	Description
8bitconv x	OFf	ON/OFf	strips/passes eighth bit in Converse Mode
AUtolf x	ON	ON/OFf	enables/disables automatic <LF> sending after each <CR>
AWlen n	7	7 - 8 (bits)	selects number of data bits per word
Echo x	ON	ON/OFf	enables/disables terminal character echo
EScape x	OFf	ON/OFf	selects $ or <ESC> as escape character sent to terminal from TNC
Flow x	ON	ON/OFf	enables/disables type-in flow control
KIss	OFf	ON/OFf	enables/disables the Serial Line Interface Protocol (SLIP) between TNC and computer
LCok x	ON	ON/OFf	disables/enables translation of lowercase characters to uppercase
LCStream x	ON	ON/OFf	enables/disables uppercase conversion of character following streamswitch
LFIgnore x	OFf	ON/OFf	enables/disables TNC's lack of response to <LF> in Command and Converse Modes
NUcr x	OFf	ON/OFf	enables/disables sending <NULL> characters to terminal after each <CR>
NULf x	OFf	ON/OFf	enables/disables sending <NULL> characters to terminal after each <LF>
NULLs n	0	0 - 30 (<NULL> characters)	selects number of <NULL> characters to be sent via NUCR and NULF commands
PARity n	3	0,1,2,3 (= no,odd,even parity)	selects terminal parity
RXBlock x	OFf	ON/OFf	enables/disables sending data to terminal in RXBLOCK format
Screenln n	80	0 - 255 (columns)	selects number of columns per line to be displayed by terminal
TRFlow x	OFf	ON/OFf	enables/disables terminal software flow control in Transparent Mode

Command	Default	Parameters	Description
TXFlow x	OFf	ON/OFf	enables/disables TNC software flow control in Transparent Mode
Xflow x	ON	ON/OFf	selects XON/XOFF or hardware (RTS) flow control

Timing Commands

Command	Default	Parameters	Description
AXDelay n	0	0 - 180 (x 10 ms)	selects delay between keying voice repeater and sending data
AXHang n	0	0 - 20 (x 100 ms)	selects voice repeater hang time
CALSet n	2060	0 - 65535	selects count setting used for modem calibration
CHeck n	30	0 - 250 (x 10 sec)	selects connection inactivity timeout
CLKADJ n	0	0 - 65535	selects correction factor for TNC clock
CMdtime n	1	0 - 250 (sec)	selects Transparent Mode timeout
CPactime x	OFf	ON/OFf	enables/disables periodic automatic packet transmission in Converse Mode
DWait n	16	0 - 250 (x 10 ms)	selects transmission delay (to avoid collisions)
FRack n	3	1 - 15 (sec)	selects frame acknowledgment timeout
PACTime x	After 10	Every/After 0 - 250 (x 100 ms)	selects packet timeout
RESptime n	5	0 - 250 (x 100 ms)	selects minimum delay for acknowledgment packet transmissions
TXdelay n	30	0 - 120 (x 10 ms)	selects delay between keying transmitter and sending data

APPENDIX B

TNC-1 and TNC-2 Control Characters

ASCII	Hex	Dec	Command	Function
|	7C	124	STReamsw	indicates a new stream
<CR>	0D	13	SEndpac	sends a packet in the Converse Mode
<CTRL-C>	03	3	COMmand	transfers from Converse to Command Mode
<CTRL-E>	05	5	DEbug	transfers to TNC-1 debug program
<CTRL-H>	08	8	BKondel	display indication of a character deletion
<CTRL-H>	08	8	DELete	deletes a character
<CTRL-Q>	11	17	STArt	restart TNC output to terminal
<CTRL-Q>	11	17	XON	restart terminal output to TNC
<CTRL-R>	12	18	REDisplay	redisplays currently typed line
<CTRL-S>	13	19	STOp	stops TNC output to terminal
<CTRL-S>	13	19	XOff	stops terminal output to TNC
<CTRL-V>	16	22	PASs	includes following character in a packet
<CTRL-X>	18	24	CANline	cancels currently typed line
<CTRL-Y>	19	25	CANPac	cancels currently entered packet

APPENDIX C

TNC Messages

This appendix describes status messages that may be sent to a terminal by a TAPR TNC 1 or TAPR TNC 2 (or clone).

TNC 1

cmd:—Command mode command prompt; indicates that the TNC is waiting for a command

EH?—indicates that an entry could not be interpreted as a command by the TNC; a dollar sign ($) shows the problem area in the entry

HDLC can't init—indicates that the HDLC IC could not be commanded when the TNC was reset

High RAM size is n—indicates the size in *n* hexadecimal bytes of RAM installed at U8

Input ignored—indicates that a portion of an invoked command was ignored by the TNC; the beginning of the ignored portion is shown by a dollar sign ($)

Link state is: CONNECT in progress—indicates that the "Connect" command was invoked while the TNC was already attempting a connection

Link state is: CONNECTED to x (VIA x1, x2,... x8)—indicates that the "Connect" command was invoked while the TNC was already connected to station X [optionally, VIA digipeater(s) *x1* through *x8*]

Link state is: DISCONNECT in progress—indicates that the "Disconnect" command or the "Connect" command without options was invoked while the TNC was attempting a disconnection

Link state is: DISCONNECTED—indicates that the "Disconnect" command or the "Connect" command without options was invoked while the TNC was disconnected

Link state is: FRMR in progress—indicates that a protocol error occurred during a connection

Not while connected—indicates that you tried to change a parameter that could not be changed during a connection

PIA can't init—indicates that the PIA IC could not be commanded when the TNC was reset

RAM size is n—indicates that the TNC RAM was verified and that its size is *n* hexadecimal bytes

TAPR packet radio—displayed after a reset is performed by toggling switch 1 off; indicates that the TNC was initialized with parameter values stored in NOVRAM

too many packets pending—indicates that the Converse or Transparent command was invoked before a sufficient number of outstanding packets were acknowledged

Tucson Amateur Packet Radio Corporation

TAPR/AMSAT AX.25 level 2 version n.n—displayed after a reset is performed by toggling switch 1 on; indicates that the TNC was initialized with the default parameter values of version *n.n* of the TNC firmware

Value out of range—indicates that the value specified in a command was not an acceptable value; a dollar sign shows the problem area in the entered value

was—indicates the previous value of a parameter after a command is invoked to change that value

TNC 2

bbRAM loaded with defaults—indicates that RAM was loaded with default parameter values

cmd:—Command mode command prompt; indicates that the TNC is waiting for a command

FRMR sent: n—indicates that a protocol error occurred during a connection and a FRMR packet was transmitted to the remote TNC to synchronize frame numbers; the FRMR packet contains three bytes in its information frame represented in hexadecimal by *n*

FRMR rcvd:—indicates that a protocol error occurred during a connection and that a FRMR packet was received from the remote TNC

Link state is: CONNECT in progress—indicates that the ''Connect'' command was invoked while the TNC was already attempting a connection

Link state is: CONNECTED to x (VIA x1, x2,... x8)—indicates that the ''Connect'' command was invoked while the TNC was already connected to station *x* [optionally, VIA digipeater(s) *x1* through *x8*]

Link state is: DISCONNECT in progress—indicates that the ''Disconnect'' command or the ''Connect'' command without options was invoked while the TNC was attempting a disconnection

Link state is: DISCONNECTED—indicates that the ''Disconnect'' command or the ''Connect'' command without options was invoked while the TNC was disconnected

Link state is: FRMR in progress—indicates that a protocol error occurred during a connection

too many packets outstanding—indicates that the "Converse" or "Transparent" command was invoked before a sufficient number of the outstanding packets were acknowledged

was—indicates the previous value of a parameter after a command is invoked to change that value

*** *connect request:* x *(VIA* x1, x2,... x8*)*—indicates that the TNC has rejected a connect request from station *x* [optionally, VIA digipeater(s) *x1* through *x8*]

*** *CONNECTED to:* x *(VIA* x1, x2,... x8*)*—indicates that a connection occurred between the TNC and station *x* [optionally, VIA digipeater(s) *x1* through *x8*]

*** *DISCONNECTED*—indicates that a disconnection occurred

*** *LINK OUT OF ORDER, possible data loss*—indicates that a link failure has occurred with the Conperm parameter enabled

*** *retry count exceeded*

*** *DISCONNECTED*—indicates that a disconnection occurred because the allowed number of retries was exceeded

*** x *busy*

*** *DISCONNECTED*—indicates that a connect request from station *x* was rejected

?already connected to that station—in multiple connection operation, indicates that the "Connect" command was invoked to attempt a connection to a station that was already connected to the TNC

?bad—indicates that an entry could not be interpreted by the TNC as a parameter of the invoked command

?call—indicates that an entry could not be interpreted as a call sign by the TNC

?clock not set—After the "Daytime" command is invoked, indicates that the clock is not set.

?EH—indicates that an entry could not be interpreted as a command by the TNC

?not enough—indicates that an insufficient number of parameters were specified for the invoked command

?not while connected—indicates that an attempt was made to change the MYcall or AX25L2V2 parameter while connected or while attempting a connection.

?not while disconnected—indicates that an attempt was made to invoke a command that can only be used during a connection

?range—indicates that the value specified in a command was not an acceptable value

?too long—indicates that an invoked command contained too many characters

?too many—indicates that too many parameters were specified for the invoked command

?VIA—indicates that *VIA* was not used when invoking a command that specified digipeater call sign(s)

|A
Tucson Amateur Packet Radio
TNC 2 AX.25 Level 2
Version 2.0 Release x.x.x
*Checksum $*x
cmd:—displayed after you turn on or Reset the TNC; *x.x.x* indicates the revision level of the TNC firmware and *x* indicates the TNC firmware checksum

APPENDIX D

ASCII Character Set

The following table lists the ASCII character set, including each character's decimal, hexadecimal and binary value and each control-character's name.

Character	Decimal	Hex	Binary	Name
NUL	0	00	00000000	null
CTRL-A (SOH)	1	01	00000001	start of heading
CTRL-B (STX)	2	02	00000010	start of text
CTRL-C (ETX)	3	03	00000011	end of text
CTRL-D (EOT)	4	04	00000100	end of transmission
CTRL-E (ENQ)	5	05	00000101	enquiry
CTRL-F (ACK)	6	06	00000110	acknowledge
CTRL-G (BEL)	7	07	00000111	bell
CTRL-H (BS)	8	08	00001000	backspace
CTRL-I (HT)	9	09	00001001	horizontal tab
CTRL-J (LF)	10	0A	00001010	line feed
CTRL-K (VT)	11	0B	00001011	vertical tab
CTRL-L (FF)	12	0C	00001100	form feed
CTRL-M (CR)	13	0D	00001101	carriage return
CTRL-N (SO)	14	0E	00001110	shift out
CTRL-O (SI)	15	0F	00001111	shift in
CTRL-P (DLE)	16	10	00010000	data link escape
CTRL-Q (DC1/XON)	17	11	00010001	device control 1/X-on
CTRL-R (DC2)	18	12	00010010	device control 2
CTRL-S (DC3/XOFF)	19	13	00010011	device control 3/X-off
CTRL-T (DC4)	20	14	00010100	device control 4
CTRL-U (NAK)	21	15	00010101	negative acknowledge
CTRL-V (SYN)	22	16	00010110	synchronous idle
CTRL-W (ETB)	23	17	00010111	end of block
CTRL-X (CAN)	24	18	00011000	cancel
CTRL-Y (EM)	25	19	00011001	end of medium
CTRL-Z (SUB)	26	1A	00011010	substitute
ESC	27	1B	00011011	escape

Character	Decimal	Hex	Binary	Name
FS	28	1C	00011100	file separator
GS	29	1D	00011101	group separator
RS	30	1E	00011110	record separator
US	31	1F	00011111	unit separator
SP	32	20	00100000	space
!	33	21	00100001	
"	34	22	00100010	
#	35	23	00100011	
$	36	24	00100100	
%	37	25	00100101	
&	38	26	00100110	
'	39	27	00100111	apostrophe
(	40	28	00101000	
)	41	29	00101001	
*	42	2A	00101010	
+	43	2B	00101011	
,	44	2C	00101100	comma
−	45	2D	00101101	
.	46	2E	00101110	
/	47	2F	00101111	
0	48	30	00110000	
1	49	31	00110001	
2	50	32	00110010	
3	51	33	00110011	
4	52	34	00110100	
5	53	35	00110101	
6	54	36	00110110	
7	55	37	00110111	
8	56	38	00111000	
9	57	39	00111001	
:	58	3A	00111010	
;	59	3B	00111011	
<	60	3C	00111100	
=	61	3D	00111101	
>	62	3E	00111110	
?	63	3F	00111111	
@	64	40	01000000	
A	65	41	01000001	
B	66	42	01000010	
C	67	43	01000011	
D	68	44	01000100	
E	69	45	01000101	

Character	Decimal	Hex	Binary	Name
F	70	46	01000110	
G	71	47	01000111	
H	72	48	01001000	
I	73	49	01001001	
J	74	4A	01001010	
K	75	4B	01001011	
L	76	4C	01001100	
M	77	4D	01001101	
N	78	4E	01001110	
O	79	4F	01001111	
P	80	50	01010000	
Q	81	51	01010001	
R	82	52	01010010	
S	83	53	01010011	
T	84	54	01010100	
U	85	55	01010101	
V	86	56	01010110	
W	87	57	01010111	
X	88	58	01011000	
Y	89	59	01011001	
\	90	5A	01011010	
[	91	5B	01011011	
	92	5C	01011100	
]	93	5D	01011101	
^	94	5E	01011110	
—	95	5F	01011111	
'	96	60	01100000	
a	97	61	01100001	
b	98	62	01100010	
c	99	63	01100011	
d	100	64	01100100	
e	101	65	01100101	
f	102	66	01100110	
g	103	67	01100111	
h	104	68	01101000	
i	105	69	01101001	
j	106	6A	01101010	
k	107	6B	01101011	
l	108	6C	01101100	
m	109	6D	01101101	
n	110	6E	01101110	
o	111	6F	01101111	

Character	Decimal	Hex	Binary	Name
p	112	70	01110000	
q	113	71	01110001	
r	114	72	01110010	
s	115	73	01110011	
t	116	74	01110100	
u	117	75	01110101	
v	118	76	01110110	
w	119	77	01110111	
x	120	78	01111000	
y	121	79	01111001	
z	122	7A	01111010	
{	123	7B	01111011	
|	124	7C	01111100	
}	125	7D	01111101	
~	126	7E	01111110	
DEL	127	7F	01111111	delete
	128	80	10000000	
	129	81	10000001	
	130	82	10000010	
	131	83	10000011	
	132	84	10000100	
	133	85	10000101	
	134	86	10000110	
	135	87	10000111	
	136	88	10001000	
	137	89	10001001	
	138	8A	10001010	
	139	8B	10001011	
	140	8C	10001100	
	141	8D	10001101	
	142	8E	10001110	
	143	8F	10001111	
	144	90	10010000	
	145	91	10010001	
	146	92	10010010	
	147	93	10010011	
	148	94	10010100	
	149	95	10010101	
	150	96	10010110	
	151	97	10010111	
	152	98	10011000	
	153	99	10011001	

Character	Decimal	Hex	Binary	Name
	154	9A	10011010	
	155	9B	10011011	
	156	9C	10011100	
	157	9D	10011101	
	158	9E	10011110	
	159	9F	10011111	
	160	AO	10100000	
	161	A1	10100001	
	162	A2	10100010	
	163	A3	10100011	
	164	A4	10100100	
	165	A5	10100101	
	166	A6	10100110	
	167	A7	10100111	
	168	A8	10101000	
	169	A9	10101001	
	170	AA	10101010	
	171	AB	10101011	
	172	AC	10101100	
	173	AD	10101101	
	174	AE	10101110	
	175	AF	10101111	
	176	B0	10110000	
	177	B1	10110001	
	178	B2	10110010	
	179	B3	10110011	
	180	B4	10110100	
	181	B5	10110101	
	182	B6	10110110	
	183	B7	10110111	
	184	B8	10111000	
	185	B9	10111001	
	186	BA	10111010	
	187	BB	10111011	
	188	BC	10111100	
	189	BD	10111101	
	190	BE	10111110	
	191	BF	10111111	
	192	C0	11000000	
	193	C1	11000001	
	194	C2	11000010	
	195	C3	11000011	

Character	Decimal	Hex	Binary	Name
	196	C4	11000100	
	197	C5	11000101	
	198	C6	11000110	
	199	C7	11000111	
	200	C8	11001000	
	201	C9	11001001	
	202	CA	11001010	
	203	CB	11001011	
	204	CC	11001100	
	205	CD	11001101	
	206	CE	11001110	
	207	CF	11001111	
	208	D0	11010000	
	209	D1	11010001	
	210	D2	11010010	
	211	D3	11010011	
	212	D4	11010100	
	213	D5	11010101	
	214	D6	11010110	
	215	D7	11010111	
	216	D8	11011000	
	217	D9	11011001	
	218	DA	11011010	
	219	DB	11011011	
	220	DC	11011100	
	221	DD	11011101	
	222	DE	11011110	
	223	DF	11011111	
	224	E0	11100000	
	225	E1	11100001	
	226	E2	11100010	
	227	E3	11100011	
	228	E4	11100100	
	229	E5	11100101	
	230	E6	11100110	
	231	E7	11100111	
	232	E8	11101000	
	233	E9	11101001	
	234	EA	11101010	
	235	EB	11101011	
	236	EC	11101100	
	237	ED	11101101	

Character	Decimal	Hex	Binary	Name
	238	EE	11101110	
	239	EF	11101111	
	240	F0	11110000	
	241	F1	11110001	
	242	F2	11110010	
	243	F3	11110011	
	244	F4	11110100	
	245	F5	11110101	
	246	F6	11110110	
	247	F7	11110111	
	248	F8	11111000	
	249	F9	11111001	
	250	FA	11111010	
	251	FB	11111011	
	252	FC	11111100	
	253	FD	11111101	
	254	FE	11111110	
	255	FF	11111111	

APPENDIX E

Sources

The following listings represent sources of packet-radio products (hardware and software, commercial and noncommercial) and information (books, periodicals, articles and organizations).

Hardware and Software Suppliers

The parentheses after each listing contain the type of hardware and/or software offered by the supplier, according to the following legend:

1—digipeater hardware
2—hardware accessories
3—modem hardware
4—networking hardware
5—networking software
6—PBBS software
7—RF modem hardware
8—terminal emulation software
9—TNC hardware
10—TNC software

A & A Engineering, 2521 W LaPalma, #K, Anaheim, CA 92801, tel 714-952-2114 (10)

Advanced Electronic Applications, Inc (AEA), PO Box C-2160, Lynnwood, WA 98036, tel 206-775-7373 (3, 7, 9)

Amatech International, 6026 N Greenwood, Clovis, CA 93612 (5)

Amateur Packet Alaska, AX.25 Communications Trail, Ester, AK 99725 (2)

Thor Andersen, LA2DAA, Riddersporen 6, N-3032 Drammen, Norway (6)

Bill Ashby & Son, Box 332, Pluckemin, NJ 07978 (9)

Ashton, PO Box 1067, Vestal, NY 13851, tel 607-748-9028 (8)

Australian Amateur Packet Radio (AAPRA), 59 Westbrook Ave, Wahroonga, NSW 2076, Australia (3, 10)

John Bennett, N4XI, 5805 Whitethorne Dr, Evansville, IN 47710 (6)

Tom Bray, WB8COX, 3373 E Fairfax Rd, Cleveland, OH 44118 (8)

Brincomm Technology, 3155 Resin St, Marietta, GA 30066 (8)

Bob Bruninga, WB4APR, 59 Southgate Ave, Annapolis, MD 21401 (6)

California Packet Concepts, PO Box 4469, Visalia, CA 93278, tel 800-233-0301 or 209-625-8429 (9)

Brian Carling, AF4K, 208 Bristol Downs Drive, Gaithersburg, MD 20877 (8)

CompuServe, 5000 Arlington Centre Blvd, Columbus, OH 43220 (5, 6, 8, 10)

Mike Curtis, WD6EHR, 7921 Wilkinson Ave, North Hollywood, CA 91605 (6)

Greg Day, KC8JN, 109 Meadow Rd, Wintersville, OH 43952 (6)

Dan Diehlman, AE6G, 5478 N Bond, Fresno, CA 93710 (8)

Digital Radio Systems, Inc. (DRSI), 2065 Range Rd, Clearwater, FL 34625, tel 800-999-0204 (3, 5, 9, 10)

Larry East, W1HUE, 119-7 Buckland St, Plantsville, CT 06479 (8)

Electron Processing Inc, PO Box 708, Medford, NY 11763, tel 516-764-9798 (2)

Electrosoft, 1656 S California St, Loveland, CO 80537 (8)

Roy Engehausen, AA4RE, 780 Lisa Ct, Gilroy, CA 95020 (6)

Engineering Consulting, 583 Candlewood St, Brea, CA 92621, tel 714-671-2009 (2, 6, 8)

ESC Products Co, PO Box 92, Redmond, WA 98052, tel 206-881-0709 (3)

S. Fine Software, PO Box 6037, State College, PA 16801 (8)

Bdale Garbee, N3EUA, 4390 Darr Cir, Colorado Springs, CO 80909 (5)

Georgia Radio Amateur Packet Enthusiast Society (GRAPES), PO Box 871, Alpharetta, GA 30239-0871 (3)

GLB Electronics, Inc, 151 Commerce Pkwy, Buffalo, NY 14224, tel 716-675-6740 (3, 7, 8, 9)

Steve Goode, K9NG, 140 W Wood, Apt 314, Palatine, IL 60067 (3)

HAL Communications Corp, PO Box 365, Urbana, IL 61801, tel 217-367-7373 (9)

Monty Haley, WJ5W, Rt 1, Box 150-A, Evening Shade, AR 72532, tel 501-266-3614 (6, 8)

Hamilton and Area Packet Network (HAPN), Box 4466, Station D, Hamilton, ON L8V 4S7, Canada (8, 9, 10)

Hamtronics, Inc, 65-H Moul Rd, Hilton, NY 14468-9535, tel 716-392-9430 (7)

Heath Co, Benton Harbor, MI 49022, tel 800-444-3284 (3, 8, 9)

Kalt & Associates, 2440 E Tudor Rd, Anchorage, AK 99507, tel 907-248-0133 (8)

Kantronics, 1202 E 23rd St, Lawrence, KS 66046, tel 913-842-7745 (1, 3, 4, 8, 9)

Joe Kasser, G3ZCZ, PO Box 3419, Silver Spring, MD 20901, tel 301-593-6136 (8)

Barry Kutner, W2UP, 614-B Palmer Ln, Yardley, PA 19067 (10)

Lloyd Computer Services, VE3BKB, 7 Westrose Ave, Toronto, ON M8X 1Z9, Canada (8)

MFJ Enterprises Inc, PO Box 494, Mississippi State, MS 39762, tel 800-647-1800 or 601-323-5869 (2, 3, 8, 9)

William Moerner, WN6I, 1003 Belder Dr, San Jose, CA 95120 (6)

N3EFN, RD 2, Box 40-31, Guys Mills, PA 16327 (10)

N4PY Software, Route 3, Box 260, Franklinton, NC 27525 (8 RTP + IBM)

Newsome Electronics, 16975 Allen Rd, Trenton, MI 48183, tel 313-479-2100 (9)

Stuart Olson, 6625 W Coolidge St, Phoenix, AZ 85033 (8)

PacComm Packet Radio Systems Inc, 3652 West Cypress St, Tampa, FL 33609, tel 800-223-3511 or 813-874-2980 (1, 2, 3, 7, 8, 9)

Packet Radio User's Group (PRUG), PO Box 66, Tamagawa, Setagaya, Tokyo 158, Japan (3)

Packeterm, Box 835, Amherst, NH 03031 (9)

Pavillion Software, PO Box 803, Amherst, NH 03031 (6)

Craig Rader, N4PLK, 922 Baltimore Dr, Orlando, FL 32810 (3, 10)

Radio Amateur Telecommunications Society (RATS), 206 North Vivyen St, Bergenfield, NJ 07621 (5)

Ramsey Electronics, Inc, 2575 Baird Rd, Penfield, NY 14526, tel 716-586-4754 (8)

David A. Rice, KC2HO, 144 N Putt Corners Rd, New Paltz, NY 12561 (8)

Richcraft Engineering Ltd, No 1 Wahmeda Industrial Park, Chautauqua, NY 14722 (10)

Dick Roux, N1AED, 25 Greenfield Dr, Merrimack, NH 03054 (6)

Southern Software Systems, Route #1, Box 1030, Hahira, GA 31632, tel 912-896-2640 (8)

Mike Staines, WA1PTC, 10 Sorrento Rd, Wallingford, CT 06492 (6)

Summit Concepts, Suite 102-190, 1840 41st Ave, Capitola, CA 95010 (8)

Lynn Taylor, WB6UUT, 463 Myrtle St, Laguna Beach, CA 92651 (8)

Texas Packet Radio Society, PO Box 50238, Denton, TX 76206-0238 (4, 5, 8)

Tono Corp, 98 Motosoja-Machi, Maebashi-Shi, 371, Japan (9)

Trans Com, Inc, 703-13 Annoreno Dr, Addison, IL 60101, tel 312-543-9055 (2)

Tucson Amateur Packet Radio Corporation (TAPR), PO Box 12925, Tucson, AZ 85732, tel 602-323-1710 (3, 5, 9, 10)

Vancouver Amateur Digital Communications Group (VADCG), 9531 Odlin Rd, Richmond, BC V6X 1E1, Canada (3, 9, 10)

W1EO, 39 Longridge Rd, Carlisle, MA 01741 (8)

Wake Digital Communications Group (WDCG), c/o Randy Ray, WA5SZL, 9401 Taurus Ct, Raleigh, NC 27612 (6)

Watt Engineering, PO Box 1848, Goleta, CA 93116, tel 805-964-0099 (2)

Kathy Wehr, WB3KRN, RD #1, Box 193, Watsontown, PA 17777 (6)

Zeltwanger Electronics, PO Box 4995, Natick, MA 01760 (8)

Information

The following listing of packet-radio information sources consists of a bibliography and more.

Electronic Industries Association, EIA Standard, Interface Between Data Terminal Equipment And Data Circuit-Terminating Equipment Employing Serial Binary Data Interchange, EIA-232-D, Electronic Industries Association, 1987

Electronic Industries Association, EIA Standard, Interface Between Data Terminal Equipment And Data Communication Equipment Employing Serial Binary Data Interchange, RS-232-C, Electronic Industries Association, 1969

International Standards Organization, Reference Model of Open Systems Architecture, ISO, 1979

Abrams, C., "From TUs to Communications Processors," *QST*, April 1988

Anderson, R., "Modifying the VADCG TNC to Use 2716 EPROMs," *QEX*, January 1983

ARRL, *First ARRL Amateur Radio Computer Networking Conference,* Volumes 1 and 2, ARRL, 1981

ARRL, *Second ARRL Amateur Radio Computer Networking Conference,* ARRL, 1983

ARRL, *Third ARRL Amateur Radio Computer Networking Conference,* ARRL, 1984

ARRL, *Fourth ARRL Amateur Radio Computer Networking Conference,* ARRL, 1985

ARRL, *Fifth ARRL Amateur Radio Computer Networking Conference,* ARRL, 1986

ARRL, *Sixth ARRL Amateur Radio Computer Networking Conference,* ARRL, 1987

ARRL, *Seventh ARRL Amateur Radio Computer Networking Conference,* ARRL, 1988

ARRL, *Eighth ARRL Amateur Radio Computer Networking Conference,* ARRL, 1989

Arvo, T, *Digital Digest,* bimonthly, Arvo & Associates, Inc

Aschenbrenner, T. and T. McDermott, "The TEXNET Packet-Switching Network, Parts 1-3," *Ham Radio,* March, April and June 1987

Bailey, M., "The Packeteer Addictive Syndrome" *QST*, November 1988

Ball, R., "TAPR TNC Modification for 12 V Use," *QEX*, June 1985

Ball, S., "*QST* Profile: Douglas Lockhart, VE7APU, Packet Radio Pioneer," *QST*, March 1989

Biolcati, M., "A Tuning Aid for Packet Radio, RTTY and SSTV," *QEX*, September 1988

Bloom, J., "Digital Radio Systems PC*Packet Adapter," *QST*, February 1989

Borden, D. and P. Rinaldo, "The Making of an Amateur Packet-Radio Network," *QST*, October 1981

Borden, D., "Data Communications," *QEX*, December 1981, February, April, June, July, September 1982 and January 1983

Borden, D., "Data Communications: Applications of Packet Radio," *QEX*, January 1984

Borden, D., "Data Communications: HF Networking," *QEX*, October and November 1982

Borden, D., "Data Communications: STD Packet Radio," *QEX*, July 1983

Borden, D., "Data Communications: The Synchronous Line Analyzer," *QEX*, April-May 1983

Botner, J., "A Packet Radio Adapter for the IBM PC," *QEX*, January 1985

Brenndorfer, K., "RUDAK—A Status Report," *QEX*, January 1987

Brooker, J., "The Michigan Packet Radio Frequency Plan," *QEX*, March 1986

Carpenter, R., "Routine Packet-Radio Meteor Burst Contacts on Six Meters," *QEX*, October 1984

Connors, D. and T. Clark, "PACSAT—A New AMSAT Satellite Project," *QEX*, November 1982

Connors, D., "Bibliography on Minimum-Shift Keying," *QEX*, March 1983

Cupp, F., "A 220-MHz 9600-Baud Data Radio System for Packet," *Ham Radio*, February 1989

Davidoff, M., *The Satellite Experimenter's Handbook*, ARRL, 1984

Deasington, R., *X.25 Explained: Protocols For Packet Switching Networks*, Second Edition, Ellis Horwood Ltd, 1986

Dorr, J., "Single-Op Plus Packet," *The National Contest Journal*, September/October 1988

Everitt, D., *The NODE*, monthly, Doug Everitt, N5DUB

Feeny, T., "FM/RPT: Digipeater," *QST*, March 1983

Ferry, R., "Public Service: The 1986 Pittsburgh Marathon," *QST*, October 1986

Forsyth, M., "The Inside Story of the PK-232," *QST*, May 1988

Fox, T., *AX.25 Amateur Packet-Radio Link-Layer Protocol, Version 2, October 1984*, ARRL, 1984

Friend, G., J. Fike, H. Baker and J. Bellamy, *Understanding Data Communications*, Texas Instruments Inc, 1984

Fuller, B., *DIGICOM/64 Technical Operations Manual*, N3EFN, 1989

Goode, S., "BER Performance of TAPR TNC Modem," *QEX*, August 1983

Goodman, R., "Packet Radio: Worked All States and Beyond," *QST*, June 1989

Gregory, J., "No-Modification HF Packet With the TAPR TNC-1 or Heath HD-4040," *QEX*, April 1986

Grubbs, J., *Digital Communications with Amateur Radio*, Master Publishing, Inc., 1988

Grubbs, J., *Get ***Connected To Packet Radio*, QSKY Publishing, 1986

Grubbs, J., *The Digital Novice*, QSKY Publishing, 1987

Hale, B., "Product Review: AEA PK-232 Multi-Mode Digital Communications Terminal," *QST*, January 1988

Hale, B., "Product Review: MFJ Enterprises MFJ-1270 Terminal Node Controller," *QST*, September 1986

Hall, J., "Product Review: Kantronics KPC-2400 Packet Communicator," *QST*, November 1987

Hart, T., "RAM Drive for Packet Radio," *Ham Radio*, December 1987

Hart, T., "Using Macros with Packet," *Ham Radio*, October 1988

Healy, J. and J. Kilgore, "Product Review: MFJ-1278 Multi-Mode Data Controller Revisited," *QST*, September 1989

Horzepa, S., *Gateway: The ARRL Packet-Radio Newsletter*, biweekly, ARRL

Horzepa, S., *Your Gateway to Packet Radio*, ARRL, 1987

Horzepa, S., "FM/RPT: ASCII/RPT," *QST*, February 1980

Horzepa, S., "FM/RPT: Digital Repeater Coordination," *QST*, June 1984

Horzepa, S., "FM/RPT: New England Novice Packet Frequency," *QST*, June 1988

Horzepa, S., "FM/RPT: Packeting in Detroit and St Louis," *QST*, May 1983

Horzepa, S., "FM/RPT: The Packet Racket," *QST*, March 1987

Horzepa, S., "FM/RPT: Why ASCII?," *QST*, April 1980

Horzepa, S., "On Line" column, eight times per year, *QST*

Horzepa, S., "On Line: Can Packet Radio Be Saved?" *QST*, August 1989

Horzepa, S., "On Line: Enter the Golden Age of Amateur Radio Software," *QST*, August 1988

Horzepa, S., "On Line: FBD & SASDM," *QST*, January 1989

Horzepa, S., "On Line: Heathkit HV-200 YAPPS About Packet Radio," *QST*, November 1988

Horzepa, S., "On Line: More Ham Software Here!," *QST*, July 1989

Horzepa, S., "On Line: More Packet Radio POPCORN," *QST*, October 1986

Horzepa, S., "On Line: Netiquette: Using the Packet-Radio Network of 1989," *QST*, February 1989

Horzepa, S., "On Line: No Contest: the Computer Advantage," *QST*, February 1988

Horzepa, S., "On Line: Packet Radio—A Novice's Reflections," *QST*, August 1984

Horzepa, S., "On Line: Packet Radio—The Software Approach," *QST*, February 1984

Horzepa, S. "On Line: Packet Radio—What's the Difference?" *QST*, February 1985

Horzepa, S., "On Line: Packet Radio for the Commodore," *QST*, February 1986

Horzepa, S., "On Line: Packet Radio for the Rest of Us," *QST*, October 1985

Horzepa, S., "On Line: Packet Radio In Liberia," *QST*, August 1987

Horzepa, S., "On Line: Packet Radio POPCORN," *QST*, August 1986

Horzepa, S., "On Line: Packet Radio Primer," *QST*, July 1986

Horzepa, S., "On Line: Packet Update," *QST*, May 1985

Horzepa, S., "On Line: Packet-Radio Bits," *QST*, November 1987

Horzepa, S., "On Line: Packet-Radio Networking Leaps Forward," *QST*, May 1987

Horzepa, S., "On Line: Putting Packet Radio on Taiwan," *QST*, May 1989

Horzepa, S., "On Line: RS-232-C: The Amateur Radio Connection," *QST*, April 1984

Horzepa, S., "On Line: Survey Results," *QST*, October 1988

Horzepa, S., "On Line: The Latest Computer Wares for You," *QST*, August 1987

Horzepa, S., "On Line: The Packet Radio Service," *QST*, August 1985

Horzepa, S., "On Line: TRS-80 Model 100: Packet Radio Auto-Answer Mailbox," *QST*, April 1986

Horzepa, S., "On Line: VK Commodore Packet-Radio Package," *QST*, February 1987

Horzepa, S., "On Line: VK-Packet News," *QST*, November 1986

Horzepa, S., "Packet Radio" chapter of *The ARRL Operating Manual*, Third Edition, ARRL, 1987

Horzepa, S., "The Shopper's Guide To Packet Radio TNCs," *QST*, March 1987

Hutchinson, C., "Product Review: Heathkit HK-232 Packkit Multi-Mode Digital Communications Terminal," *QST*, January 1988

Ingram, D., *Mastering Packet Radio*, Howard W. Sams & Co, 1988

Jahnke, B., *The ARRL Repeater Directory, 1989-1990 Edition*, ARRL, 1989

Johnson, L., "Join the Packet-Radio Revolution," *73*, November 1983—January 1984

Johnson, L., "The TAPR PSK Modem," *QEX*, September 1987

Kelly, K., *Signal: Communication Tools for the Information Age*, Harmony Books, 1988

Kesteloot, A. and D. Borden, "Xerox 820-1 Compendium," *QEX*, June 1986—January 1987

Kilgore, J., "Product Review: MFJ Enterprises MFJ-1278 Multi-Mode Data Controller," *QST*, July 1989

Kleinschmidt, K., *The 1990 ARRL Handbook For The Radio Amateur*, ARRL, 1989

Kuhlen, H., "RUDAK Lives," *QEX*, November 1985

Latta, G., "HF Packet: Comments and Tips," *QEX*, December 1986

Leinweber, G., M. Pizzolato, J. Vanden Berg and J. Botner, "4800 Baud Modem for VHF/UHF Packet Radio," *Ham Radio*, August 1988

Loftesness, S., "HamNet," CompuServe, electronic information service special-interest group

Loughmiller, D. and B. McGwier, "Microsat: The Next Generation of OSCAR Satellites Parts 1 and 2," *QST*, May and June 1989

Magnuski, H., "National Standards for Amateur Packet Radio Networks," *Conference Proceedings of the Eighth West Coast Computer Faire*, 1983

Mayo, J., *The Packet Radio Handbook, 2nd Edition*, Tab Books, Inc, 1989

Mayo, J., "Amateur Packet Radio Networking and Protocols, Parts 1-3," *Ham Radio*, February, March and April 1988

McLanahan, D., "A Packet Radio Primer," *Ham Radio*, December 1985

McLanahan, D., "The Practical Packet for the Holidays," *QST*, December 1987

McLarnon, B., "A 1200-Bit/s Manchester/PSK Encoder Circuit for TAPR TNC Units," *QEX*, November 1987

McLarnon, B., "New Directions in HF Data Transmission Systems Parts 1 and 2," *QEX*, December 1987 and January 1988

McMullen, T., "Elmer's Notebook: Packet Radio for the First Timer," *Ham Radio*, March 1989

McMullen, T., "Elmer's Notebook: Packet Radio," *Ham Radio*, October 1987

Meagher, J., "C-64 and GLB PK-1 Interface Circuit," *Ham Radio*, March 1987

Meagher, J., "C-64 and GLB PK-1 Interface Circuit," *Ham Radio*, April 1988

Meagher, J., "Packetimer for the PK-1," *Ham Radio*, March 1987

Meijer, A. and P. Peeters, *Computer Network Architecture*, Computer Science Press, 1982

Meinzer, K., "Packet Radio and Radio Communication Requirements," *QEX*, March 1983

Miller, J., "A Packet Radio PSK Modem for JAS-1/FO-12," *Ham Radio*, February 1987

Miller, J., "Decoding OSCAR Telemetry, Parts I and II," *73*, May and June 1989

Miller, T., "A Cheap n' Easy Modem," *QST*, June 1988

Miller, T., and E. Hare, "A Simple Tuning Indicator," *QST*, July 1988

Moore, J., "'Packet' Meteor Scatter Communications," *QEX*, December 1983

Morrison, M., D. Morrison and L. Johnson, "Amateur Packet Radio: Parts 1 and 2," *Ham Radio*, July and August 1983

Nelson, R., "The Omni-Shift Tuner—A Comprehensive Tuning System for HF Packet/AMTOR/RTTY," *QST*, March 1987

Newkirk, D., "Novice Enhancement Goes Digital," *QST*, July 1987

Palm, R. and D. McGrath, "Product Review: AEA PAKRATT™ Model PK-64," *QST*, June 1986

Pechura, M., "Exploring Packet Radio with KISS," *Ham Radio*, October 1988

Pechura, M., "Formatted Display of Packets Using KISS," *Ham Radio*, December 1988

Pratt, C., and V. Yarbrough, "Pictures by Packet" *QST*, May 1988

Price, H., "Packet Radio—A Closer Look," *QST*, August 1985

Price, H., "What's All This Racket About Packet?," *QST*, July 1985

Richardson, R., *Synchronous Packet Radio Using The Software Approach, Volume I*, Richcraft Engineering Ltd, 1983

Richardson, R., *Synchronous Packet Radio Using The Software Approach, Volume II*, Richcraft Engineering Ltd, 1984

Riley, M., *Emergency Coordinator's Manual*, ARRL, 1984

Rinaldo, P., *Operating an Amateur Radio Station*, ARRL, 1989

Rinaldo, P., ed., *QEX*, ARRL Experimenters' Exchange, monthly, ARRL

Rinaldo, P., "A Digital Weekend," *QEX*, January 1989

Rinaldo, P., "Agreement on Packet Radio Standards," *QEX*, November 1982

Rinaldo, P., "Amateur Radio Technical Conferences," *QEX*, November 1988

Rinaldo, P., "Amateur Satellites on the Horizon," *QEX*, January 1988

Rinaldo, P., "AMSAT Announces PACSAT Project," *QEX*, September 1988

Rinaldo, P., "AO-13 and Beyond," *QEX*, August 1988

Rinaldo, P., "ARRL Board Approves AX.25 Packet-Radio Link-Layer Protocol," *QST*, December 1984

Rinaldo, P., "HF Packet Initiative," *QEX*, July 1989

Rinaldo, P., "OSCAR 10 Packet-Radio Teleport Experiments," *QEX*, April 1984

Rinaldo, P., "Packet Radio Gathers Force," *QEX*, June 1984

Rinaldo, P., "Packet-Radio Repeaters," *QEX*, March 1984

Rinaldo, P., "PPRS 'Golden Packet' Award," *QEX*, April 1985

Rinaldo, P., "STA Extension for SKIPNET Autoforwarding Network," *QEX*, February 1989

Rinaldo, P., "Standard Alternatives for HF Packet Modems," *QEX*, June 1987

Rinaldo, P., "Technical Excellence," *QEX*, April 1988

Rinaldo, P., "The Great 1989 HF Packet Design Quest," *QST*, May 1989

Rinaldo, P., "Two Worlds Meet: NTS and Packet," *QEX*, July 1987

Rogers, G., *Packet User's Notebook*, CQ Communications, Inc, 1988

Rouleau, R. and I. Hodgson, *Packet Radio*, Tab Books, Inc, 1981

Sager, P., "Happenings: ARRL Requests Packet STA," *QST*, August 1987

Sanford, J., "Decoding Data Signals," *Ham Radio*, December 1988

Schetgen, B., "Product Review: Pac-Comm TNC-200 Terminal Node Controller," *QST*, June 1987

Schetgen, M., "At the Foundation: SAREX: The Next Generation," *QST*, February 1989

Schreiber, W., "The Weekender: Going Digital," *Ham Radio*, January 1989

Stallings, W., *Tutorial: COMPUTER COMMUNICATIONS: Architectures, Protocols, and Standards*, IEEE Computer Society, 1985

Stuntz, S., "A Packet Terminal for Atari Computers," *QST*, November 1987

Sumner, D., "It Seems To Us...: Good News For Packeteers," *QST*, May 1986

Sumner, D., "It Seems To Us...: Packet Fever," *QST*, April 1986

Tanenbaum, A., *Computer Networks*, Prentice-Hall, Inc., 1981

Thompson, M., "The Birth of a New Bird," *QEX*, June 1986

Titus, J., "New Books: Packet Radio," *QST*, January 1983

Vitello, R., *The New England TCPer*, bimonthly, Rich Vitello, WA1EQU

Wade, B., "Packet Radio Conference Bridge," *Ham Radio*, April 1987

Ward, J. and M. Wilson, "Product Review: TAPR, Heathkit and AEA Terminal-Node Controllers," *QST*, November 1985.

Williams, P., "Packet Radio Frequency Recommendations of the Committee on Amateur Radio Digital Communication," *QST*, March 1988

Winter, P., "Packet Radio in Emergency Communications," *QST*, September 1986

Wolfgang, L., "Product Review: Kantronics All-Mode Communicator," *QST*, June 1989

Yamada, M. and T. Kushida, "NET98.EXE: A Japanese Version of the KA9Q Internet (TCP/IP) Package," *QEX*, July 1989

Yamashita, F., "A PSK Demodulator for the JAS-1 Satellite,"*QEX*, August 1986

Organizations

Organizational periodicals, if any, follow the organization's address.

Amateur Packet Alaska (APA), AX.25 Communications Trail, Ester, AK 99725

Amateur Radio and Computer Club (AMRAC), 9 Hollydene Villas, Southampton Rd, Hythe, Southampton, S04 5HU, Great Britain

Amateur Radio Research and Development Corp (AMRAD), PO Drawer 6148, McLean, VA 22106-6148, *AMRAD Newsletter*

American Radio Relay League (ARRL), 225 Main St, Newington, CT 06111, *Gateway: The ARRL Packet-Radio Newsletter, QEX, QST*

Arizona Packet Radio Association, 8402 E Angus Dr, Scottsdale, AZ 85251

Bavarian Amateur Packet Radio Group (BAPR), c/o Thomas Kieselbach, DL2MDE, Narzissenweg 10, 8031 Wessling, Federal Republic of Germany

British Amateur Radio Teleprinter Group (BARTG), Pat and John Beedie, GW6MOJ and GW6MOK, Ffynnonlas, Salem, Llandeilo, Dyfed, SA19 7NP, Wales, *Datacom*

Central Illinois Packet Radio User Society (CIPRUS), c/o Larry Keeran, K9ORP, RR 1, Box 99B, Downs, IL 61736-9717

Central Iowa Technical Society (CITS), c/o Ralph Wallio, WØRPK, 1250 Hwy G24, Indianapolis, IA 50125

Cherryville Repeater Association, Box 308, Quakertown, NJ 08868

Chicago Amateur Packet Radio Association (CAPRA), PO Box 8251, Rolling Meadows, IL 60008, *The CAPRA Beacon*

Cincinnati Amateur Packet Radio Experimenters Society (CAPRES), c/o John Schroer IV, KA8GRH, 948 Halesworth Dr, Forest Park, OH 45240

Connecticut Digital Radio Association (CONNECT), c/o Tom Hogerty, KC1J, 83 Harold Rd, Farmington, CT 06032

Eastern Packet Radio of Michigan (EPROM), c/o Jay Nugent, WB8TKL, 3081 Braeburn Cir, Ann Arbor, MI 48104

Florida Amateur Digital Communications Association (FADCA), 812 Childers Loop, Brandon, FL 33511, *FADCA>Beacon*

Georgia Radio Amateur Packet Enthusiast Society (GRAPES), PO Box 871, Alpharetta, GA 30239-0871, *Grapevine*

Haifa Amateur Group For Digital Communications, PO Box 7238, Haifa 31071, Israel

Hamilton and Area Packet Network (HAPN), Box 4466, Station D, Hamilton, ON L8V 4S7, Canada

HEX 9 Group, PO Box 151, Orilla, ON L3V 6J3, Canada

Los Angeles Area Packet Group (LAPG), PO Box 6026, Mission Hills, CA 91345

Melbourne Packet Radio Group (MPRG), c/o David Furst, VK3YDF, 11 Church St, Hawthorn, Vic 3122, Australia

Mid-Atlantic Packet Radio Club, c/o Tom Clark, W3IWI, 6388 Guilford Rd, Clarksville, MD 21029

Midlands AX.25 Packet Radio Users Group (Maxpak), c/o David Bentley, G4RVK, 10 Churnet Grove, Perton, Wolverhampton, UK, *Digicom*

Mississippi Amateur Radio Digital Association (MARDA), c/o Patrick J. Fagan, WA5DYV, 2412 E Birch Dr, Gulfport, MS 39503

Mt Ascutney Amateur Packet Radio Association, c/o Carl Breuning, N1CB, 54 Myrtle St, Newport, NH 03773

Mt Beacon Amateur Radio Club, PO Box 841, Wappingers Falls, NY 12590

New England Packet Radio Association (NEPRA), PO Box 208, East Kingston, NH 03827, *NEPRA PacketEar*

NORD > < LINK, c/o Hans Georg Giese, DF2AU, Hinter dem Berge 5, D-3300 Braunschweig, Federal Republic of Germany

Northern California Packet Association (NCPA), 6608B Alhambra Ave, Suite 111, Martinez, CA 94553, *NCPA Download*

Northwest Amateur Packet Radio Association (NAPRA), c/o John Gates, N7BTI, 750 Northstream Ln, Edmonds, WA 98020, *Zero Retries*

Ohio Packet Enthusiasts Club (OPAC), c/o Bob Ball, WB8WGA, 830 Riva Ridge Blvd, Gahanna, OH 43230

Oimo Club, c/o PRUG, PO Box 66, Tamagawa, Setagaya, Tokyo 158, Japan

Oregon Digital Network Coordination Council (ODNCC), 7860 SW 69th Ave, Portland, OR 97223

Pacific Packet Radio Society (PPRS), PO Box 51562, Palo Alto, CA 94303

Packet Radio Organization of Montana (PROM), c/o Glenda Allen, KE7TB, 165 Conifer Rd, Libby, MT 59923

Packet Radio User's Group (PRUG), PO Box 66, Tamagawa, Setagaya, Tokyo 158, Japan

Packeteers of Long Island (POLI), c/o Alex Mendelsohn, AI2Q, 92 Hathaway Ave, Elmont, NY 11003, *The POLI Parrot*

Pennsylvania Packet Association (PaPA), c/o Bryan Simanic, WA3UFN, 9 Wild Cherry Dr, DuBois, PA 15801

Radio Amateur Satellite Corp (AMSAT), PO Box 27, Washington, DC 20044

Radio Amateur Telecommunications Society (RATS), c/o J. Gordon Beattie, Jr, N2DSY, 206 North Vivyen St, Bergenfield, NJ 07621

Radio Society of Great Britain (RSGB), Lambda House, Cranborne Road, Potters Bar, Herts EN6 3JE, *Radio Communication*, *Connect International*

Rochester Packet Group, c/o Fred Cupp, W2DUC, 27 Crescent Rd, Fairport, NY 14450

Rocky Mountain Packet Radio Association (RMPRA), c/o Bill Flynn, AI0C, 286 S Nome St, Aurora, CO 80012-1212, *RMPRA>Packet*

San Diego Packet Group (SDPG), c/o Mike Brock, WB6HHV, 10230 Mayer Cir, San Diego, CA 92126

San Diego Packet Radio Association (SANDPAC), c/o Barry Gershenfeld, 5085 Arroyo Lindo Ave, San Diego, CA 92117, *San Diego Packet Radio Association Newsletter*

South Carolina Amateur Radio Digital Society (SCARDS), PO Box 1281, Columbia, SC 29202, *SCARDS Newsletter*

Southern Amateur Packet Society (SAPS), c/o Wayne Harrell, WD4LYV, Rte 1, Box 368, Sycamore, GA 31790

Southern California Digital Communications Council (SCDCC), PO Box 4357, Chatsworth, CA 91313, *The I-Frame*

St Louis Area Packet Radio (SLAPR), 9926 Lewis & Clark, St Louis, MO 63136

Sydney Amateur Digital Communications Group (SADCG), PO Box 231, French's Forest, NSW 2086, Australia, *The Australian Packeteer*

Texas Packet Radio Society (TPRS), PO Box 50238, Denton, TX 76206-0238, *The TPRS Quarterly Report*

Tucson Amateur Packet Radio Corporation (TAPR), PO Box 12925, Tucson, AZ 85732, *Packet Status Register*

TwinsLAN Amateur Radio Club, c/o Kermit Kramer, W0RFD, 1121 Xerxes Ave S, Minneapolis, MN 55405, *The TwinsLAN Beacon*

Utah Packet Radio Association (UPRA), c/o Bart Van Allen, KA7ZFD, 11883 S Kinney Cir, Riverton, UT 84065, *RMPRA>Packet*

Vancouver Amateur Digital Communications Group (VADCG), 9531 Odlin Rd, Richmond, BC V6X 1E1, Canada, *The Packet*

Wake Digital Communications Group (WDCG), c/o Randy Ray, WA5SZL, 9401 Taurus Ct, Raleigh, NC 27612

Western Michigan Packet Radio Association (WMPRA), PO Box 4612, Muskegon, MI 49444

Wisconsin Amateur Packet Radio Association (WAPRA), PO Box 1215, Fond Du Lac, WI 54935, *Badger State Smoke Signals*

APPENDIX F

Glossary Of Packet-Radio Terms

<CR>—abbreviation for carriage return

acknowledgment timer—the AX.25 timer that causes the TNC to interrogate the linked TNC when a packet is not acknowledged before the timer expires; also called the T1 timer

address—the identification of a packet source or destination

address field—the field in an AX.25 frame containing the call signs of the source and destination of the frame and, optionally, the call signs of one to eight digipeaters

AFSK—abbreviation for audio-frequency-shift keying

ALOHA—the packet-radio protocol that was used by the University of Hawaii's ALOHANET, in which stations transmitted randomly without checking to see if the channel is busy

ALOHANET—the University of Hawaii's packet-based radio system that provided communications between its central computer and the university community that was dispersed throughout the Hawaiian Islands

Amateur Radio Research and Development Corporation (AMRAD)—a Northern Virginia-based Amateur Radio organization that was instrumental in early United States packet-radio developments, including the adoption of the AX.25 protocol

amateur X.25 (AX.25)—the link-layer packet-radio protocol based on the CCITT X.25 packet-switching protocol

American National Standard Code for Information Interchange (ASCII)—a seven-bit digital code used in computer and radioteleprinter applications

AMPRNET—ARPANET's name assignment for the amateur packet-radio TCP/IP network

AMRAD—abbreviation for Amateur Radio Research and Development Corporation

AMSAT—abbreviation for The Radio Amateur Satellite Corporation

Application layer—Level 7 of OSI-RM that provides an interface between the other OSI-RM layers and the user application

ARPANET—an early long-distance packet-switching hard-wired network that was developed under the Defense Advanced Projects Research Agency (DARPA, formerly ARPA)

The ARRL Repeater Directory—an annual ARRL publication that lists repeaters, including dedicated packet-radio digipeaters, by state or province

ASCII—abbreviation for American National Standard Code for Information Interchange

asynchronous—a data transmission timing technique that adds extra bits of information to indicate the beginning and end of each transmitted character

audio-frequency-shift keying (AFSK)—a method of transmitting digital information by switching between two audio tones fed into the transmitter microphone input

autobaud—the ability of a communications device to automatically adapt to whatever data rate is used by the terminal connected to it

automatic line feed—a DTE or DCE function that causes a line feed control character to be sent whenever a carriage return control character is sent

AX.25—the link-layer packet-radio protocol based on the CCITT X.25 packet-switching protocol

backbone—a packet-radio network that transfers mail automatically; access to this network is limited to PBBSs

backbone frequency—the operating frequency of the backbone network

backspace—a DTE key or a control character that deletes previously typed characters

Balanced Link Access Procedure (LAPB)—the CCITT X.25 link-layer protocol that was the model for AX.25

battery-backed RAM (bbRAM)—RAM that is powered by a battery to enable it to store data while its host device is turned off

baud—a unit of signaling speed equal to one pulse (event or symbol) per second in a single-channel transmission

baud rate—the speed at which information is transferred, usually expressed in bauds or bits per second; also called bit rate and data rate

bbRAM—abbreviation for battery-backed RAM

BBS—abbreviation for bulletin-board system

Bdale's Mailer (BM)—an application in the KA9Q Internet Protocol Package written by Bdale Garbee, N3EUA, that serves as a front end to the Simple Mail Transfer Protocol (SMTP)

beacon—a TNC function that permits a station to automatically send unconnected packets at regular intervals

Bell 103—the designation for the telephone company standard for modems that transfer data at 300 bauds using 200-Hz frequency-shift-keyed tones at 2025 and 2225 Hz; commonly used for HF packet applications

Bell 202—the designation for the telephone company standard for modems that transfer data at 1200 bauds using frequency-shift-keyed tones at 1200 and 2200 Hz; commonly used for VHF packet applications

binary—the base-two number system that uses the numerals 0 and 1 *birdie*—radio interference that occurs at a single radio frequency

bit—binary digit, a signal that is either on/one or off/zero; bits are combined to represent alphanumeric and control characters for data communications

bit rate—the speed at which information is transferred, usually expressed in bauds or bits per second; also called baud rate and data rate

bit stuffing—a process that prevents AX.25 fields from having the same unique contents of the flag field; also called zero bit insertion

bit/s—abbreviation for bits per second

bits per character—the number of bits that are combined to represent alphanumeric and control characters for data communications

bits per second (bit/s)—a measure of the speed at which information is transferred

BM—abbreviation for Bdale's Mailer

buffer—a portion of computer memory that is set aside to temporarily store data that is being received or transmitted

bulletin-board system (BBS)—a computer system where messages and files can be stored for other users

byte—a group of bits, usually eight in number

calling frequency—an operating frequency that is used only for establishing communications. Once communications have been established on the calling frequency, the operators switch to a less-used frequency.

carriage return (<CR>)—a DTE key or a control character that is used to indicate the end of a line of typed information; it causes the DTE display to begin printing at the left-hand margin

carrier—an electromagnetic wave that may be varied in order to transmit information

Carrier Detect (CD)—common name for Received Line Signal Detector

cathode ray tube (CRT)—a vacuum tube with a phosphor coating on the inside of the face. CRTs are used in oscilloscopes, as the "picture tube" in television sets and in computer monitors and video-display terminals.

CCITT—abbreviation for International Telegraph and Telephone Consultative Committee

CD—abbreviation for Carrier Detect

character bits—the bits that represent an alphanumeric or control character

checksum—check summation; the sum (in hexadecimal) of the bits in the TNC software in ROM, it should be equal to the checksum published in the TNC manual

Clear To Send (CTS)—an RS-232-C/EIA-232-D serial interface signal. CTS informs the DTE that the DCE is able to transmit data.

clone—a device that duplicates another device

collision—a condition that occurs when two or more packet-radio transmissions occur at the same time. When a collision occurs, neither packet reaches its destination.

command mode—the TNC operating mode where the TNC is waiting for command input from the user

command mode character—a control character that causes the TNC to enter the command mode

configuration command—a TNC command that selects a parameter that is used by the TNC when it performs a task

connect—to establish a communications link (a connection) between two packet-radio stations

connection protocol—a Network-layer protocol that sets up and maintains a clearly defined path for the transfer of packets between the source and destination during a single data communications session; also called virtual circuit protocol

connectionless protocol—a Network-layer protocol that transfers each packet independently along the best available route; also called datagram protocol

control field—the field in an AX.25 frame that indicates the frame type

CRT—abbreviation for cathode ray tube

CSMA—abbreviation for Carrier Sense Multiple Access; a channel-access arbitration scheme in which packet-radio stations listen for the presence of a carrier on a channel before transmitting

CTS—abbreviation for Clear To Send

Data Carrier Detect (DCD)—common name for Received Line Signal detector

data circuit-terminating equipment, data communications equipment (DCE)—the device that provides communications between a DTE and radio equipment or telephone lines

data communications software—a computer program that causes a computer to function as a DTE for the purpose of transferring data over a communications medium

data rate—the speed at which information is transferred, usually expressed in bauds or bits per second; also called baud rate and bit rate

data terminal equipment (DTE)—a device that is used to interface between a human and a computer to allow the human to exchange information with the computer

datagram protocol—a Network-layer protocol that transfers each packet independently along the best available route; also called connectionless protocol

DCD—abbreviation for data carrier detect

DCE—abbreviation for data circuit-terminating equipment, data communications equipment, or Digital Communications Experiment

DCE Ready—EIA-232-D serial-interface signal, formerly called Data Set Ready, that informs the DTE that the DCE is prepared for data communications

default—the state of a TNC parameter after the TNC is initially turned on or reset

demodulation—the process of retrieving information from a modulated carrier

destination—the intended recipient of a packet frame

dibit—a group of two bits. Dibit modulation is a technique for transferring two bits of information during one time period (two bits per baud)

digipeater—digital repeater, a device that receives, temporarily stores and then retransmits (repeats) packet-radio transmissions that are specifically addressed for routing through the digipeater

Digital Communications Experiment (DCE)—a test performed using UoSAT-OSCAR 11 to prove that satellites could be used to store and forward packet-radio messages

DISC—abbreviation for Disconnect frame

Disconnect frame (DISC)—an AX.25 unnumbered frame that terminates a connection

Disconnected Mode frame (DM)—an AX.25 unnumbered frame that indicates the rejection of a Set Asynchronous Balanced Mode frame

DM—abbreviation for Disconnected Mode frame

download—to receive files from a PBBS or other packet-radio station

DTE—abbreviation for data terminal equipment

DTE Ready—an EIA-232-D serial-interface signal that informs the DCE that the DTE is prepared for data communications. This signal was called Data Terminal Ready under RS-232-C.

dumb terminal—a simple DTE that provides only basic input and output functions

duplex—a mode of communications where you transmit on one frequency and receive on another

Earth-to-moon-to-Earth (EME)—mode of communications in which VHF and UHF signals are reflected off the moon; also called moonbounce

EASTNET—the packet-radio network linking the northeastern US

echo—a DTE and DCE (TNC) function that prints each character typed at the DTE keyboard on the display

EIA—abbreviation for Electronics Industries Association

EIA-232-D—the current EIA standard for DTE-to-DCE interfacing that specifies the interface signals and their electrical characteristics; it replaces EIA RS-232-C

Electronic Industries Association (EIA)—an organization composed of representatives of the United States electronics industry. The EIA is involved in formulating data communication standards.

EME—abbreviation for Earth-to-moon-to-Earth

emulate—to mimic; often used to describe software that attempts to perform the function of hardware

end-to-end acknowledgment—the networking protocol in which only the destination station or node informs the originating station or node that it has received a packet correctly

ENTER—a key on a computer keyboard that causes the computer to accept the information previously typed at its keyboard

enter—to use a key (the ENTER or RETURN key) on a computer keyboard to cause the computer to accept the information previously typed at its keyboard

EPROM—abbreviation for erasable programmable ROM

erasable programmable ROM—read-only memory whose contents can be deleted (by ultraviolet light) and replaced

escape, escape code, escape characters—a sequence of alphanumeric characters that are typed at a DTE keyboard to cause the DCE to exit the current operating mode and return to the previous operating mode

FCS—abbreviation for frame check sequence field

field—a subdivision of an AX.25 frame

File Transport Protocol (FTP)—a protocol in the KA9Q Internet Protocol Package that allows the user to transfer files to or from the computer at another node

flag field—the field in an AX.25 frame that indicates the beginning and end of a frame

flow control—the stopping and restarting of the transfer of characters between the DTE and a DCE (TNC)

FO-12—abbreviation for Fuji-OSCAR 12

Frame Reject frame (FRMR)—an AX.25 unnumbered frame that indicates that the source station is unable to process a frame and that the error is such that resending the frame will not correct the problem

frame—a group of AX.25 fields consisting of an opening flag, address, control, information, frame-check-sequence and ending flag fields

frame check sequence field (FCS)—the field in an AX.25 frame that is used for frame error checking

frequency-shift keying (FSK)—a method of transmitting digital information by switching an RF carrier between two separate frequencies

FRMR—abbreviation for Frame Reject frame

FSK—abbreviation for frequency-shift keying

FTP—abbreviation for File Transport Protocol

Fuji-OSCAR 12 (FO-12)—amateur satellite launched in 1986 by Japan AMSAT; aboard the satellite is a digital transponder for packet-radio applications

full-duplex—a communications mode where it is possible to transmit and receive simultaneously

Gateway—a packet-radio newsletter published biweekly by the ARRL

gateway—a device or PBBS function that allows packet-radio stations on different operating frequencies to communicate with each other.

H bit—a bit in the SSID of each digipeater address that causes packets to be repeated in the correct digipeater sequence

half-duplex—a communications mode where you alternately transmit and receive

hang time—the transmission of an unmodulated carrier by a voice repeater after each transmission to indicate that the repeater is functioning; also called squelch tail

hardware flow control—flow control that is controlled by DCE-(TNC) and DTE-originated signals on the serial interface between the two devices

HDLC—abbreviation for High-level Data Link Control

header—the non-data portion of a packet frame. The header precedes the data portion of the frame.

hexadecimal—the base-16 numbering system that uses the numerals 0 through 9 and the letters A through F

hidden transmitter—a packet-radio station that can be heard by only one of two other stations that are connected; in such a situation, the two stations that cannot hear each other may transmit simultaneously, which results in the reception of interference or a packet collision by the third station

High-level Data Link Control (HDLC)—an ISO standard defined for the Link layer of OSI-RM

host mode—a TNC function that allows it to communicate with the host computer in a language that is more efficient than the English language used by the TNC to communicate with a user

I frame—abbreviation for Information frame

immediate command—a command that causes the TNC to perform a task immediately

Information frame (I frame)—an AX.25 frame that contains user data

information field—the field in an AX.25 frame that contains the user data

input frequency—the operating frequency of a full-duplex repeater's receiver and a user's transmitter

intelligent terminal—a DTE that provides numerous support functions as well as basic input and output functions

International Standards Organization (ISO)—an international organization responsible for formulating computer communication standards

International Telegraph and Telephone Consultative Committee (CCITT)—an International Telecommunication Union agency involved in formulating international data communication standards

Internet Protocol (IP)—a Level 3 or Network-layer protocol included in the KA9Q Internet Protocol Package

IP—abbreviation for Internet Protocol

IP address—a 32-bit binary number that is assigned to each computer at each packet-radio station in the TCP/IP network as that computer's identification for the routing of packets by the Internet Protocol

ISO—abbreviation for International Standards Organization

KA-Node—Kantronics' implementation of a node-to-node acknowledgment network protocol

KISS—an acronym for "Keep It Simple, Stupid," a Link-layer nonprotocol for serial input and output that supports Serial Line Interface Protocol (SLIP), written by Mike Chepponis, K3MC

LAPB—abbreviation for Balanced Link Access Procedure

layer—one level of the seven-level hierarchy of the OSI-RM

Level 1—the Physical layer of OSI-RM

Level 2—the Link layer of OSI-RM

Level 3—the Network layer of OSI-RM

Level 4—the Transport layer of OSI-RM

Level 5—the Session layer of OSI-RM

Level 6—the Presentation layer of OSI-RM

Level 7—the Applications layer of OSI-RM

line feed—a control signal that causes a DTE display to begin printing on the next line

Link layer—Level 2 of OSI-RM that arranges data bits into frames and provides for the errorless transfer of the frames over a communications link

log off—to inform a PBBS that you are finished using the system

log on—to inform a PBBS that you wish to begin using the system

mail-forwarding—a PBBS function that allows its users to send mail to the users of other PBBSs

mailbox—a packet-radio message receiving and sending system at an individual station

mark—one of the two elements in a binary code; it often represents the on state or 1

message header—the non-data portion of a packet-radio message that contains the message number, type, status, intended recipient and other routing information

meteor scatter—mode of communications that uses the ionized trails of expired meteors to reflect VHF and UHF signals *minimum-shift keying (MSK)*—frequency-shift keying where the shift in hertz is equal to half the signaling rate in bauds

modem—modulator-demodulator; an electronic device that permits digital equipment to use analog communications media for data communications

modulation—the process of varying a carrier to represent information

moonbounce—mode of communications where VHF and UHF signals are reflected off the moon; also called Earth-to-moon-to-Earth

MSK—abbreviation for minimum-shift keying

multiple connections—the ability to establish and maintain connections with more than one station simultaneously

multiport controller—a packet-radio device, such as a TNC or network node, that provides connections for more than one set of radio equipment

multiport digipeater—a device that may receive and transmit on different operating frequencies with different parameters on each frequency

NET.EXE—a TCP/IP implementation for the IBM PC written by Phil Karn, KA9Q

NET/ROM—a network and transport layer implementation for the TNC 2 written by Ron Raikes, WA8DED, and Mike Busch, W6IXU; it features node-to-node acknowledgment

Network layer—Level 3 of OSI-RM that routes frames through a network of links

network—a system of interconnected packet-radio stations designed for the efficient transfer of packets over long distances

network node controller (NNC)—a device that acts as an interchange for the transfer of packets through a network

NNC—abbreviation for network node controller

node—a junction point within a network

node-to-node acknowledgment—the networking protocol in which each node in the path of a packet informs the previous node in the path of a packet that it has received the packet correctly

non-return to zero, inverted (NRZI)—a baseband encoding technique where a data zero causes a change in signal level at the start of a bit interval, while a data one causes no change

nonvolatile RAM (NOVRAM, NVRAM, NV-RAM)—memory that stores data while its host device is turned off

NOVRAM—abbreviation for nonvolatile RAM

NRZI—abbreviation for non-return to zero, inverted

null—a non-printing control character that is used to insert additional time in a data string in order to compensate for slower electronic or mechanical equipment

NVRAM, NV-RAM—abbreviation for nonvolatile RAM

octet—a unit of measurement that is the equivalent of a byte or eight bits

Open Systems Interconnection Reference Model (OSI-RM)—a model formulated by the International Standards Organization that permits different computer systems to communicate with each other as long as the communication protocols used by the computer systems adhere to the model

OSI-RM—abbreviation for Open Systems Interconnection Reference Model

output frequency—the operating frequency of a full-duplex repeater's transmitter and a user's receiver

overhead—the non-data portion of a packet; each packet's header and trailer

Packet Communications Experiment (PCE)—UoSAT-D's packet-radio digital store-and-forward communications transponder

packet assembler/disassembler (PAD)—a device that accepts data from a DTE and formats it into packet frames for transmission via a communications medium. The PAD also accepts packet frames received via a communications medium, extracts data from the packet frame and transfers the data to a DTE.

packet-radio bulletin-board system (PBBS)—a BBS that is accessed via packet radio

PACSAT—a proposed AMSAT packet-radio satellite

PAD—abbreviation for packet assembler/disassembler

parallel interface, parallel port—an interconnection that transfers bit-encoded information character-by-character or byte-by-byte in parallel

parity—a method of checking the accuracy of a received character by adding an extra bit in order that the character will have an even or odd number of one bits depending on the type of parity used (even or odd)

path—the route between two connected packet-radio stations consisting of digipeaters and other packet stations

PBBS—abbreviation for packet-radio bulletin-board system

PCE—abbreviation for Packet Communications Experiment

phase-shift keying (PSK)—a method of transmitting digital information by varying the phase of a carrier between two values

Physical layer—the lowest level (Level 1) of OSI-RM. The physical layer involves the mechanical and electrical transfer of data bits from one device to another.

PID field—abbreviation for protocol identifier field

point-to-point—communications between two radio stations without assistance from an intermediary radio station

polling protocol—a communication protocol where each station is checked regularly and in an orderly manner to see if it is ready to send data; if a polled station has data to send, it transmits its data after being polled, and the controller then checks the next station in the system

port—a circuit that allows a device to communicate with external devices

Presentation layer—Level 6 of OSI-RM that provides for the translation or interpretation of transferred data *protocol*—a set of recognized procedures

protocol identifier field (PID)—the field in an AX.25 frame that indicates the type of Network-layer protocol that is in use

PSK—abbreviation for phase-shift keying

the quick brown fox message—a test message that is commonly used in RTTY, AMTOR and packet-radio communications because it contains each numeral and letter of the alphabet; the complete message is THE QUICK BROWN FOX JUMPS OVER THE LAZY DOG 0123456789

radio port—the TNC port that is connected to a radio transceiver (or transmitter and receiver)

The Radio Amateur Satellite Corporation (AMSAT)—an Amateur Radio organization that was instrumental in early United States packet-radio developments; also responsible for United States amateur satellite developments

The Radio Amateur Telecommunications Society (RATS)—an Amateur Radio organization that was responsible for the development of the RATS Open System Environment X.25 Packet Switch protocol

RAM—abbreviation for random-access memory

random-access memory (RAM)—a data storage device that can be written to and read from

RATS—abbreviation for The Radio Amateur Telecommunications Society

RATS Open Systems Environment (ROSE)—a networking protocol based on the virtual circuit or connection protocol; it uses node-to-node acknowledgment and network node addressing based on the CCITT X.121 numbering scheme

RD—abbreviation for Received Data

read-only memory (ROM)—a data storage device that can only be read

Receive Not Ready (RNR)—an AX.25 supervisory frame that indicates that the destination station is not able to accept any more information frames

Receive Ready (RR)—an AX.25 supervisory frame that indicates that the destination station is able to receive more information frames, acknowledges properly received information frames, and clears a busy condition that has been previously set by an RNR

receive state variable—a number assigned in sequence to a received packet; it is compared with the send sequence number to make sure that packets have been received in the correct order

Received Data (RD)—an RS-232-C/EIA-232-D serial-interface signal that consists of data from the DCE that was received over the communication medium and demodulated by the DCE

Received Line Signal Detector—an RS-232-C/EIA-232-D serial interface signal, commonly called Carrier Detect, that informs the DTE that the DCE is receiving a "suitable" carrier over the communications medium

REJ—abbreviation for Reject frame

Reject (REJ)—an AX.25 supervisory frame that is transmitted by the destination station to request that the source station retransmit a frame

Request To Send (RTS)—an RS-232-C/EIA-232-D serial-interface signal that informs the DCE that the DTE has data for transmission

RF modem—a device that consists of a modem and a radio transmitter and receiver

RNR—abbreviation for Receive Not Ready frame

ROM—abbreviation for read-only memory

ROSE—abbreviation for RATS Open Systems Environment

ROSE X.25 Packet Switch—the network node controller of the RATS Open System Environment

round table—a conversation between more than two stations

RR—abbreviation for Receive Ready frame

RS-232-C—the former Electronics Industries Association standard for DTE-to-DCE interfacing that specifies the interface signals and their electrical characteristics; it has been replaced by EIA-232-D

RTS—abbreviation for Request To Send

RTTY—abbreviation for radioteletype

RUDAK—acronym for Regenerativer Umsetzer für Digitale Amateurfunk Kommunikation, a digipeater designed and built by AMSAT-DL for use on board Amateur Radio satellites

S frame—abbreviation for Supervisory frame

SABM—abbreviation for Set Asynchronous Balanced Mode frame

SD—abbreviation for Send Data

SDLC—abbreviation for Synchronous Data Link Control

secondary station identifier (SSID)—a number that follows a packet-radio station's call sign to differentiate between two or more packet-radio stations operating under the same call sign

Send Data (SD)—an RS-232-C/EIA-232-D serial interface signal that consists of data from a DTE that is intended for transmission by the DCE over the communication medium; also called Transmitted Data

send sequence number—a number assigned in sequence to a transmitted packet; it is compared with the receive state variable to check that packets are received in the correct order

Serial Line Interface Protocol (SLIP)—a Level 2 or Link-layer protocol included in the KA9Q Internet Protocol Package that provides a simple serial-data transfer between the Network-layer protocols and the EIA-232 interface of the Physical layer

serial—the transfer of bit-encoded information bit-by-bit

serial interface, serial port—an interconnection that transfers bit-encoded information bit-by-bit (serially); the TNC connection for a terminal or computer

Session layer—Level 5 of OSI-RM; manages data-communication activity and the interaction of that activity

Set Asynchronous Balanced Mode (SABM)—an AX.25 unnumbered frame that initiates a connection between two packet stations

Signal Ground—an RS-232-C/EIA-232-D serial-interface signal that provides a common ground reference for all the other interface signals except Shield (pin 1)

Simple Mail Transfer Protocol (SMTP)—a protocol included in the KA9Q Internet Protocol Package that provides an automatic message-forwarding function

simplex—a communications mode where you transmit and receive on the same frequency

sliding window protocol—a Transport-layer protocol that provides end-to-end error control to counteract lost, duplicate or out-of-sequence packet frames

SLIP—abbreviation for Serial Line Interface Protocol

SMTP—abbreviation for Simple Mail Transfer Protocol

software approach—the emulation of TNC hardware functions in software

software flow control—flow control that is managed by control characters typed at the DTE or sent from the DCE (TNC)

source—the station that originates a packet frame

SOUTHNET—the packet-radio network linking the southeastern United States

space—one of the two elements in a binary code; it often represents the off state or 0

squelch tail—the transmission of an unmodulated carrier by a voice repeater after each transmission to indicate that the repeater is functioning; also called hang time

SSID—abbreviation for secondary station identifier

start bit—an extra bit that precedes a character to indicate its beginning in asynchronous communications

start character—a non-printing control character that is used to restart the flow of data

stop bit—one or more extra bits that follow a character to indicate its end in asynchronous data communications

stop character—a non-printing control character that is used to stop the flow of data

store and forward—the process of receiving and holding data from one radio station for the purposes of relaying that data to another station at a later time

stream—one connection between two stations in a multiple-connection application *streamswitch*—a character that indicates a change in the stream being addressed in multiple-connection packet-radio applications

Supervisory frame (S frame)—an AX.25 frame that controls the communications link

Synchronous Data Link Control (SDLC)—an IBM standard defined for the Link layer of OSI-RM

synchronous—a means of data transmission timing that uses a modem's internal clock to synchronize data

system operator (SYSOP)—an individual who runs and maintains a bulletin-board system

T1 timer—the AX.25 timer that causes the TNC to interrogate the linked TNC when a packet is not acknowledged before the timer expires; also called the acknowledgment timer

TAPR—abbreviation for Tucson Amateur Packet Radio Corporation

TAPR alpha board—the initial, short-lived TNC offering from TAPR that was based on the 6502 microprocessor

TAPR beta board—the second TNC offering from TAPR; based on the 6809 microprocessor, it was the forerunner of the TAPR TNC 1

TAPR board—a TAPR TNC

TCP—abbreviation for Transmission Control Protocol

TCP/IP—abbreviation for Transmission Control Protocol/Internet Protocol; the Defense Advanced Research Projects Agency protocols that are used as Network- and Transport-layer amateur packet-radio protocols by Phil Karn, KA9Q, in his Internet Protocol Package

TD—abbreviation for Transmitted Data

Telnet—a terminal-emulation protocol included in the KA9Q Internet Protocol Package that provides communications with the live operator of another node

terminal—short for data terminal equipment or a computer emulating data terminal equipment

terminal emulation software—a computer program that causes a computer to function as a DTE for the purpose of transferring data over a communications medium

terminal node controller—an Amateur Radio packet assembler/disassembler; it may or may not include a modem

TexNet—a packet-radio network developed by the Texas Packet Radio Society. Composed of dual-port network control processors that provide AX.25-compatible user access on 2 meters and node-to-node linking at 9600 bit/s on 70 cm

time stamping—the process of noting the time and date of the occurrence of an event

TNC—abbreviation for terminal-node controller

TNC 1—the first TAPR TNC that was made available to the general public; it was based on the 6809 microprocessor

TNC 2—the second TAPR TNC that was made available to the general public; based on a Z80 microprocessor; its design was the most popular in amateur packet-radio history

trailer—the non-data portion of a frame at the end of the frame

Transmission Control Protocol (TCP)—a Level 4 or Transport layer protocol included in the KA9Q Internet Protocol Package that assures data integrity between the points of origination and destination

Transmitted Data (TD)—an RS-232-C/EIA-232-D serial-interface signal that consists of data from a DTE that is intended for transmission by the DCE over the communication medium; also called Send Data (SD)

transparent mode—the TNC mode that permits the transfer of data that is "invisible" to the TNC; it is used when it is necessary to transfer control characters that may be imbedded in data

Transport layer—Level 4 of OSI-RM that maintains a connection that is transparent to the source and destination

TTL interface—a digital interconnection based on transistor- transistor logic (TTL) voltages

Tucson Amateur Packet Radio Corporation (TAPR)—the Arizona-based Amateur Radio organization that was instrumental in packet-radio protocol and hardware developments in the United States

turnaround time—the time required to switch between the receive and transmit modes in a half-duplex application

type-in flow control—flow control that causes the TNC to stop sending characters to the DTE whenever a character is entered at the DTE keyboard; prevents displayed received characters from interfering with the display of keyed characters

U frame—abbreviation for unnumbered frame

UA—abbreviation for Unnumbered Acknowledge frame

UDP—abbreviation for User Datagram Protocol

UI—abbreviation for Unnumbered Information frame

unconnected packets—packets transmitted from a source station with no specific destination station being addressed; used for beacons, CQs, and round-table communications

Universal Asynchronous Receiver Transmitter (UART)—a circuit that converts parallel formatted data for transmission in serial format and also converts serial received data to parallel format

Unnumbered Acknowledge (UA)—an AX.25 unnumbered frame that acknowledges receipt and acceptance of an SABM or DISC

Unnumbered frame (U frame)—an AX.25 frame that controls the communications link and provides the capability to transmit frames containing information without a specified destination

Unnumbered Information (UI)—an AX.25 unnumbered frame that allows data to be transmitted from a source station with no specific destination station being addressed

UoSAT-OSCAR 11 (UO-11)—an amateur satellite that was used for the first successful packet-radio store-and-forward experiments, in 1985

upload—to send files to a PBBS or other packet-radio station

User Datagram Protocol (UDP)—a Level 4 protocol included in the KA9Q Internet Protocol Package that performs miscellaneous functions

user interface—the set of TNC commands and status messages that are available to the user

V-1 protocol—the first amateur packet-radio protocol developed by Doug Lockhart, VE7APU, and VADCG; also known as the VADCG or Vancouver protocol

VADCG—abbreviation for Vancouver Amateur Digital Communications Group

VADCG board—the VADCG TNC

VADCG protocol—the first amateur packet-radio protocol developed by Doug Lockhart, VE7APU, and VADCG; also known as the V-1 or Vancouver protocol

VADCG TNC—the first amateur packet-radio PAD; developed by Doug Lockhart, VE7APU, and VADCG

Vancouver Amateur Digital Communications Group (VADCG)—a Canada-based Amateur Radio organization that was responsible for the first popular packet-radio protocol and hardware developments in Amateur Radio

Vancouver protocol—the first amateur packet-radio protocol developed by Doug Lockhart, VE7APU, and VADCG; also known as the V-1 or VADCG protocol

VDT—abbreviation for video-display terminal

video-display terminal (VDT)—an input and output device that uses a cathode ray tube for output

virtual circuit—the appearance of a direct connection between the source and destination of a packet

virtual circuit protocol—a Network-layer protocol that sets up and maintains a clearly defined path for the transfer of packets between a source and destination during a single data communications session; also called connection protocol

WØRLI MailBox—public-domain PBBS software first written in Z80 assembler language, and then in C, by Hank Oredson, WØRLI

WA7MBL Packet Bulletin Board System—public-domain PBBS software written in Turbo Pascal by Jeff Jacobsen, WA7MBL

watchdog timer—a circuit that provides protection for the unattended operation of a device, such as a TNC

WESTNET—the packet-radio network linking the Western United States.

wormhole—a satellite-based packet-radio link

X.25—a packet-switching protocol formulated by the CCITT

Xerox 820-1—a surplus computer that used a Z80 microprocessor and ran the CP/M operating system; it was a popular computer for packet-radio applications, including the first PBBSs (using software written by Hank Oredson, WØRLI)

Xoff—transmitter off, a flow-control character used in ASCII file transfers. Xoff commands the transmitter to stop sending data.

Xon—transmitter on, a flow-control character used in ASCII file transfers. Xon commands the transmitter to continue sending data.

zero bit insertion—a process that prevents the other AX.25 fields from having the same unique contents of the flag field; also called bit stuffing

Index

YOUR GATEWAY
TO PACKET RADIO

PROOF OF
PURCHASE

Please use this form to give us your comments on this book. Tell us what you liked best about the book, and what improvements you would like to see us make in future editions.

Name

_____ Call sign _____

Daytime Phone (   ) _____ Age _____

Address _____

City, State, Zip _____

How long have you been licensed? _____

From ———————————————

———————————————

———————————————

Your Gateway to Packet Radio
Second Edition
American Radio Relay League
225 Main Street
Newington, CT USA 06111

•••••••••••••••••••••••••••••• please fold and tape ••••••••••••••••••••••••••••••••